THE DEATH OF THE LAW

Also by the author:
No One Will Lissen

THE
DEATH
OF THE LAW

Lois G. Forer

Judge, Court of Common Pleas
Philadelphia, Pennsylvania

DAVID McKAY COMPANY, INC.
New York

Library of Congress Cataloging in Publication Data

Forer, Lois G   1914-
   The death of the law.

      Includes bibliographical references and index.
      1. Justice, Administration of—United States.
2. Law—United States, I, Title.
KF384.F675   340'.0973   74-25722
ISBN 0-679-50523-7

The excerpt from *The Age of Anxiety*, by W. H. Auden, reprinted by permission of Random House, Inc.; copyright © 1947 by W. H. Auden. The excerpt from "Connoisseur of Chaos," by Wallace Stevens, reprinted by permission of Alfred A. Knopf, Inc.; copyright © 1942 by Wallace Stevens; copyright renewed 1970 by Holly Stevens. The excerpt from "America Was Promises," by Archibald MacLeish, reprinted by permission of Houghton Mifflin Company. The excerpt from "The Lawyers Know Too Much," by Carl Sandburg, reprinted by permission of Harcourt Brace Jovanovich, Inc., who published the poem in the collection *Smoke and Steel*. The portion of the lyrics of "Who Killed Davey Moore," by Bob Dylan, used by permission of Warner Bros. Music; © 1964 by M. Witmark & Sons; all rights reserved.

*For Morris, without whose constant encouragement
and help I would not have practiced law
for thirty-five years*

Acknowledgments

This book is the distillation of a lifetime devoted to the law—as a practicing private attorney, attorney for agencies of government, attorney in a poverty law office, law professor and judge.

I am grateful to many people who have made it possible for me to have this unusually large range of experiences. I can mention only a few: My husband, Morris L. Forer, Judge John Biggs, Jr., the late Justice Herbert B. Cohen, Governor Milton Shapp who appointed me to the bench, and the citizens of Philadelphia, Pennsylvania who elected me to a ten year term. The view from the other side of the bench provides a different perspective of the legal system from that seen by lawyers, litigants and the general public, one that is necessary to obtain a complete and accurate picture.

I owe an enormous debt to my colleagues of the bench and bar, my professors, my students, my former clients and the litigants and lawyers who appear in court before me. From all of them I have learned about law and problems of legal administration, human behavior and the extraordinary, intractable difficulties of living in our contemporary society.

Florence Owens and Greta Cherry have uncomplainingly typed and retyped the manuscript. Neal Goldstein, Robb Schatz and Franne McIntyre, performing the essential function of law clerks, have assisted me in the legal research.

My editor, Alan Tucker, has not only helped me, but his faith in the validity and importance of this subject which several years ago was not a question of widespread public interest encouraged me to persevere and complete the book.

Contents

Part Three

O woe is me to have seen what I have
seen, see what I see.
Hamlet, Act 3, Scene 1, Shakespeare

Introduction

"You don't write books to help people," Romain Gary explained. "You write books to get rid of them. To help yourself. I cannot resist human suffering: I fill my books with it and the books bring me a great deal of release, esteem and material comfort—and do nothing for the world, nothing in terms of solution, changes, help." [1]

I, too, have written this book to help myself, after days in court in which I find myself a participant in a mindless, archaic system which produces results that have little to do with justice. I see that law as a principle by which people conduct their lives is dead, that the entire legal system corrodes any sense of trust or truth. It is a juggernaut laying waste lives, businesses and social order. But I also have written in the belief that rational change is possible with effort, intelligence and a willingness to recognize reality.

This book was conceived and almost completed before the

revelation of lies and misconduct by government officials and employees and citizens embraced in the term "Watergate." The success or failure of Congress and the courts in exposing wrongdoing and prosecuting malefactors will not alter these premises and conclusions. The interrelated corruption of those who gave bribes and illegal campaign contributions and those who received them and gave illegal preferential treatment reveals not that a few individuals were morally myopic and faithless to their public trust but that conscious and willful disregard of the law is endemic in the United States. Knowledge of the sordid, seamy truth undoubtedly affects all of us, leaving some with a sense of repulsion and an unfortunate distaste for public service, others with envy that they were not recipients of illegal loot and favors. Many of the young and the poor are confirmed in their suspicions that the trappings of law—investigations, legislative hearings, court rulings on procedural issues that skirt fundamental questions, and the trials themselves—are but masks and costumes for a gigantic national entertainment, not unlike the bread and circuses of the old Roman Empire. Thoughtful citizens must ask themselves why and how the law has become a ritual process rather than a living principle animating the conduct of individuals and institutions. Why has law died and what were the causes of this fatal illness?

Those who point with pride to a few courageous individuals—judges, lawyers, legislators—should not delude themselves that the actions of these officials in utilizing legal process *after* exposure of wrongdoing by the mass media is evidence of the strength or vitality of the law. We hear relieved declarations at each hopeful turn of events in the national scene that the law really works and the system survives. But such joy is short lived and unfounded.

For example, a headline after the Supreme Court decision requiring President Nixon to turn over the tapes to special Watergate prosecutor Jaworski reads: "The Rule of Law Lives." This is a fatuously optimistic view. Had the Supreme Court decided the other way, would that one decision have killed the rule of law? Obviously, a law-abiding nation can survive bad court decisions. And the United States has survived many: for example, the Dred

Scott decision, the decision declaring the graduated income tax unconstitutional, and the ruling sanctioning the forcible removal of native Americans of Japanese descent from the West Coast. The contempt for law evidenced by "the president's men" and the Watergate conspirators is symptomatic of a lawless people who routinely lie and cheat and attempt to conceal these misdeeds. When an occasional individual is caught and prosecuted, he complains that since others do the same illegal acts it is unfair to prosecute him.

Similarly, after the resignation of President Nixon, Henry Steele Commager wrote, "Thus we have demonstrated to the world, and let us hope, to future generations that the Constitution is alive and well. . . ." One does not need to know history but only to recall recent newspaper reports to know that it was not the Constitution which brought about Mr. Nixon's downfall but a rare combination of fortuity, luck and stupidity. The fortuity is that the watchman in the night, Frank Wills, noticed the tape on the door and investigated. The luck is that counsel, by intuition, asked if there were any records of presidential conversations. The stupidity, which has not yet been explained, is that Mr. Nixon did not promptly destroy the tapes which led to his downfall. In the absence of any one of these three elements there would not have been any unmasking of the abuse of power and no so-called triumph of the system or revitalization of the Constitution.

No single court ruling or series of rulings can extirpate this attitude and restore the rule of law. Even if all the wrongdoers in high places were convicted, the system would not be vindicated. The bargains made with confessed criminals such as Dean, Liddy, Hunt and former Vice-President Agnew have further robbed the law of its tattered remnants of credibility and justice. Every judge in the nation must ask himself this question for the foreseeable future: How can I sentence an ordinary thief to jail when he and I know that Agnew is a free man?

Watergate did not cause these problems. The corrosive failure of law as a principle of conduct in American life long preceded Watergate. To ignore the evident failures of the law and the legal system prior to 1973 and concentrate on wrongdoing in high places is easy and dramatic. But it is misleading. Lawlessness is not the exclusive prerogative of the powerful. The thesis of this book is that America is a nation of scofflaws, regardless of each individual's wealth, education and social status. The growing numbers of street crimes committed by poor, violent and disaffected people and the crimes committed by the powerful may be shocking and excessive, but both the powerless and the powerful have habitually violated the law. In other times and other nations, rulers abused their trust and acted arrogantly and corruptly. At the other extreme, street criminals, like the poor, have been a part of almost every society. Historian J. H. Plumb suggests that violent crimes by poor young men are the natural vengeance of youth against the aged. In seventeenth- and eighteenth-century Europe it was a common occurrence for the wealthy middle-aged and elderly to be held up and robbed on the street by poor, hostile and envious youths.

What is unusual and significant today is the fact that average, decent citizens of all ages and both sexes have little regard for law. Few Americans believe that law binds them in their conduct or protects them from the misdeeds of others. The restrictions imposed by law are treated as inconveniences to be avoided, circumvented or ignored. It is common knowledge that the law will not prevent crimes nor provide civil redress for wrongs suffered. Neither the indigent nor the working poor look to the police, lawyers or the elaborate structure of courts to secure their rights. People of moderate income are discouraged by exorbitant costs and long delays. The motto "Equal Justice Under Law," engraved on the marble portico of the United States Supreme Court building, is a cruel lie to all Americans who are poor, or nonwhite, or young, or old, or female, or who differ from the common consensus in their beliefs and life-styles.

The decade of the sixties saw global turbulence. Students rioted in many lands. Many people fought and many others refused to bear arms. Some governments fell. Others became more repressive. Belief in the efficacy of law for solving the economic, social and political injustices suffered by many people in many nations was one of the unmourned casualties of this era. The death of law occurred slowly, by attrition, and still has not been noticed by most Americans. But the effects of the death of law are more acute in the United States than in other countries because we have been educated to believe that the legal system is the means for resolving all of our problems peacefully and fairly, that through law we can obtain social justice and personal liberty.

Awareness of the invalidity of an idea comes first to those who are in a position to see the failure of its operations. Priests who are disillusioned by the functioning of a theocracy are often the first to become apostates while the public continues to worship dead gods. It is perhaps fitting, then, that one who was an attorney in private practice, a government lawyer, a lawyer for a poverty agency, and who is now a judge should be aware of the death of law before it is recognized by the general public.

All of us feel lost and lonely on this shrinking, polluted planet which whirls seemingly without purpose in ever-expanding space. One wakes in the night alarmed by the creaking of the wall as it shifts with the wind. Is it an intruder? The Chief Justice of the United States Supreme Court opens his own front door armed with a gun. The frightened citizen rises and tests the locks on his door. He is terrified on the streets. He is uneasy at home. He fears the present and dreads the future. No wonder he wants the certainty and comfort of his childhood faith in the law.

"To know things as they are is better than to believe things as they seem," Tom Wicker, syndicated columnist, has declared. I too believe that knowledge of reality, even though painful and disquieting, is preferable to false illusions. The disparity between belief in assumptions as to equal justice and the reality of injustice in the administration of law in the United States is enormous. It is a fact that the legal establishment prefers to ignore, although countless Americans who have had the misfortune to get caught up in the legal system either by being accused of crime or by seeking civil redress in the courts know the reality. Most of us prefer not to examine our assumptions in the light of actual circumstances and facts, however.

From observing and listening to hundreds of prospective jurors being questioned, I find that Americans profess a firm belief in the rule of law. It is a ritualistic, hieratic faith. But obedience to law is foreign to their daily experience, and crime is an omnipresent fact of life.

A jury panel represents a fascinating microcosm of American society. Prospective jurors are randomly selected from the entire community. An average panel contains forty to sixty men and women of all social, economic and ethnic groups. The age range is from eighteen to perhaps eighty. The jurors file into the courtroom wearing their big jury buttons a little self-consciously. They are serious and concerned about the unusual tasks they may be chosen to perform: to decide the guilt or innocence of a fellow citizen accused of a serious crime or to deny or award monetary damages to a member of the community. Simply, directly and without apparent reservation, the prospective jurors answer the questions put to them.

Most Americans have been questioned by opinion polls for their views on candidates and cosmetics and for their preferences in politicians and products. Such questions are narrow and the range of responses is limited. Except on voir dire (questioning of prospective jurors) few people not engaged in the legal system have ever been asked their beliefs about law and justice, the duty of the citizen and the responsibility of the state. Searching questions are put to prospective jurors. Their answers reveal an extraordinary consensus. Almost every prospective juror unhesitatingly states that he believes it is his duty to follow the law and that he will do so regardless of his private opinions, that he will not be swayed by prejudice or sympathy, that he will convict the guilty and acquit those not proved beyond a reasonable doubt to be guilty, regardless of the heinous nature of the crime charged. From these responses given with certainty and conviction, one might be led to conclude that the United States is composed of law-abiding citizens unanimously dedicated to the rule of law.

Further questioning, however, reveals that almost half of these citizens, or their close friends and members of their immediate families, have been the victims of crime. Their verdicts often show a similar disregard for law. I have seen persons who have killed friends or acquaintances in an argument over a dollar. And I have seen juries acquit them. Apparently the violent taking of life is justified in the minds of many people as an appropriate response to small injuries or insults. I have seen a father who beat his small son to death. He claimed that he was chastising a disobedient child and accidentally killed him. He, too, was acquitted. But a man who stood outside a pawnshop while his friend climbed in a window and stole a broken radio was convicted of burglary and larceny. Real societal values are shockingly revealed in these cases. Similarly, in civil cases, I have seen a jury award a nice middle-aged, middle-class white woman $127,000 damages for a minor injury that healed within six months. The next week a jury drawn from the same community awarded $10,000 to a six-year-old black boy who suffered a permanent brain injury. These cases, while extreme, are not unusual. They illustrate the gap between belief in equal justice under law and the realities of law in operation.

Lawyers, social critics and the public at large ignore the realities because the principle of the rule of law has assumed a mythic role in American life. The nature of a myth is belief without proof or evidence. Indeed, a myth is a belief whose validity cannot be tested by the ordinary processes applied to other ideas. To an outsider not under the spell of the myth, it is illogical and irrational. Yet a myth has a tenacity and hold upon the believers that far exceeds that of fact or reason. The apothegm that in the marketplace of ideas truth will prevail is itself another myth, ancillary to the American myth of the rule of law. History teaches that the big lie often prevails over truth and that myths hold sway over masses of people for long periods of time in defiance of reality and reason. Eventually the myths lose their significance and are replaced by others. By then the fact situation has also changed and "truth" becomes a matter for antiquarians to debate.

Belief in demons flourished in the United States less than two centuries ago. Women believed to be witches were slain by the community. Significantly, the alleged witch was given a trial and under the rubric of due process and the rule of law was put to death. Belief in racial superiority flourished in Europe in our time. It survived despite the most obvious and clear evidence of its falsity. Again, the machinery of law was used to carry out mass killings on a scale unprecedented in history. Subsequently obedience to the rule of law was pleaded as a justification for torture, cruelty and slaying. Today in South Africa a similar belief, equally unsupported by reason or proof, prevails. It, too, is enforced by the machinery and processes of the law. Belief in the divine right of kings and emperors was enforced and implemented by law.

Law and the administration of the legal system are essential to the growth and survival of myth. The imprimatur of the established order and the weight of its power exercised under law promote the myth as official dogma. The administration of law is used to compel conformity by dissidents and unbelievers.

The legal system in any society exists for the purpose of conserving, maintaining and enforcing accepted norms of behavior. All societies, whether they be small tribal groups, empires, dictatorships or democratic governments, include some individuals who do not conform to the ideals and principles of the group. But the norms of behavior embody the prevailing beliefs of most of its members. The dissidents or outlaws are controlled by the legal system, whether it be a tribal council, a court of law or a dictator. Those whose behavior deviates too widely from the accepted standards are punished in accordance with well-understood procedures and subjected to equally well understood and accepted penalties.

No matter how unfair or brutal the penalties may seem to an outsider, if they are known and accepted by the members of the community, there is no problem of the viability of law. Thus, the stoning of an adulteress and the amputation of the right hand of a thief raise no problems in nations like Saudi Arabia. But in the United States imprisonment is not accepted by large numbers of people—both convicts and noncriminals—as a humane or civilized method of dealing with deviant, brutal and even dangerous individuals. Consequently, prison riots are commonplace. Research by lawyers and sociologists on the subject of prisons, prisoners' rights and the effect of imprisonment on the individual is fashionable. A number of courts have issued orders requiring that certain prisons be closed or drastically altered because they are "inhumane." Such orders are seldom enforced or enforceable. But they offer unmistakable evidence of the widespread dissatisfaction with the principal penalty established under American law.

When the number of nonconformists in any group becomes too large, the social order is disrupted. Such a quantitative change in the balance between those who accept the law, its doctrines and its penalties and those who reject them becomes a qualitative change. It is not merely that there is more crime and more disorder. There are also more policemen, more recourse to the courts, more and shriller demands for harsher penalties. A change in the quality of life occurs. Attitudes toward deviant behavior become more rigid and vindictive as the numbers swell. But the dogma of the rule of law is not overtly challenged or denied. When the dissatisfaction with widespread violation of law reaches a point that the public will not tolerate, the situation is ripe for a political coup, a revolution, conquest by a foreign enemy, or simply disintegration. The path of history is strewn with the shards of broken societies, powerless governments, vanquished and vanished peoples.

In past periods of upheaval or unrest, what Toynbee calls a "time of troubles," there was a general awareness that the old principles were no longer adequate. The leaders of change rallied the populace to a new religion, a new philosophy, or a new social order. They renounced the existing dogma and proclaimed a new faith. Christianity, Islam, and the Protestant Reformation arose out of a dissatisfaction not only with old gods but with the establishments that supported them. Similarly, the French, Russian and Chinese revolutions were explicitly dedicated to the destruction of the old order as well as the creation of a new order based on new beliefs. Such movements were iconoclastic, destroying old gods. They were also fanatically devout, enshrining new deities or dogmas. Whether the underlying causes leading to change were economic, ecological, demographic, religious or political or a combination of such factors, the appeal to the public was ideological. The leaders proclaimed a new set of principles by which individuals and governments were to be guided and they pronounced the obsequies of the old faith.

Mythic beliefs, supported by their respective legal systems, have not in other societies been based upon law. In the United States, the principle of the rule of law is extolled by the leaders of the establishment and by the various anti-establishment groups. Each group or faction denounces certain practices and certain types of behavior but none questions the viability and validity of law. There is little, if any, recognition that the rule of law is a myth. Thus even extreme philosophers and political figures who seek to change not only the American life-style but also the economic and political structure of society fail to recognize that the basic belief on which these institutions are founded has already crumbled.

In other societies after the death of the myth, the legal system survived relatively intact. This was true in Germany and Japan. Judges who administered the law under the Third Reich are now judges administering substantially the same civil and criminal law under a democratic government in West Germany and under a communist government in East Germany. Judges who served under the Emperor of Japan prior to World War II continued to administer Japanese law under the aegis of General MacArthur and later under the new Japanese constitutional government. The civil and criminal law applicable to the daily lives of the inhabitants of these countries and the administration of the legal system were not dependent upon the philosophy that dominated and sustained either the prior governments or the new governments.

American belief in the rule of law, however, cannot be separated from the functioning of the legal system. This symbiosis of the legal process and the national myth is peculiar to the United States. Law as a public symbol takes the place of a monarchy or a state religion as a unifying factor in society.

The "rule of law" as a principle governing the conduct of individuals and government is not an inherently malign concept like that of the superiority of one race and the inferiority and degradation of other races. Abstractly it does not strike the contemporary mind as unreasonable, like the belief in the divinity of a particular individual or the existence of witches or demons. Indeed, faith in the rule of law is a belief consonant with rationalistic eighteenth-century philosophy, with nineteenth-century human-ism, and with twentieth-century sociology and political science. It is a notion congenial to people educated in a liberal western tradition, imbued with ideas of individual liberty and dignity. It is compatible with a wide spectrum of economic and social theories. Neither the radicals of the "New Left" nor the extremists of the far right disavow a belief in the rule of law. Nor do the public officials accused of illegal conduct in the Watergate and related incidents. This protean quality of the rule of law may in some measure explain the widespread and continued acceptance of the faith long after its actual demise.

To date no American leader or effective group of dissenters has specifically renounced the rule of law or promulgated an alterna-tive philosophy that has gained acceptance. A few intellectuals who have challenged the conventional beliefs in individual liberty under the rule of law met with vehement denunciations. B. F. Skinner and Herbert Marcuse, for example, have been excoriated. Neither of them, however, has suggested that law as a conservator of the norms of behavior is dead. Their followings are largely confined to the well-educated young and have made little impact on public awareness. The most radical denunciation of the rule of law, by a philosophy professor who asserts in the Yale *Law Journal* [2] that before a law is entitled to obedience the government must affirmatively prove its validity, has not even caused a ripple in the placid, if not stagnant, pond of legal academia. The public is unaware of his heresy.

Intellectuals are torn by conflicting economic and political theories. The public is deeply divided by war and many social issues. Specific legal decisions such as school busing, school prayer, abortion and women's rights have polarized public opinion in many communities. But despite demands to impeach Earl Warren and Richard Nixon, there has been no movement to abolish the Constitution or the institutions of law and legal administration.

Under the rubric of the rule of law, the most divergent philosophies find a common meeting ground. Why, then, should one want to challenge a belief that is intellectually so appealing and apparently a unifying force in a nation subjected to extraordinary stresses and torn by opposing ideologies?

There are two compelling reasons to examine and expose the mythic nature of the rule of law. First, it is a false faith in the sense that it has ceased to exercise control over the actions of the professed believers. Second, continued nominal adherence to a belief in the rule of law as a fundamental principle of public and private conduct is destroying the legal system and with it the stability of society and government.

The government of the United States is uniquely based upon a functioning legal system. A monarchy, dictatorship, or junta can govern a nation irrespective of its legal system. Any such ruler will simply co-opt the machinery of the law to his service. But the nature of the constitutional structure of the United States makes its survival dependent upon a reasonably adequate functioning legal system embodying all of the components of government—the federal executive, including the enormous military and civilian agencies and employees, the Congress, the federal judiciary, the states and the local units of government. Our form of government requires the tacit consent of the great bulk of the population.

Force can compel unwilling obedience of the masses through fear of torture, death, disgrace or deprivation of property or liberty. Under our system of government obedience can be compelled, if at all, only through the enforcement of law. Americans have neither a tradition of monarchy, such as the British, nor the French notion of "La Gloire" to unite them in support of nation through scandals, debacles, and changes in government. In the United States, the concept of the rule of law is relied upon to sustain the nation through its crises and travails. Today vast numbers of Americans no longer voluntarily obey the law nor do they conduct their personal or business affairs in accordance with well-known and previously accepted legal principles. In an effort to obtain compliance with both the criminal and the civil law, the existing legal machinery has become overloaded and fails to function. When the legal system fails, as I see it failing daily and chronicle it in this book, then constitutional government is imperiled. Those values of individual liberty—religious, intellectual and personal—and those limitations on the power of the state over the citizen embodied in the Constitution may be lost. Justice Botein declared that there is a choice. "The balance finally struck between dignity and truth in our courts will be cast in the image of a society which has opted either for efficiency or freedom." [3] If Americans must make a choice between physical safety and individual liberty, safety will, I believe, prevail over liberty. The widespread popularity of the Nixon–Mitchell slogan—"Law and Order"—is indicative of a common desire for order, security and conformity. The fact is that although these exponents of hard-line law enforcement themselves violated the law and betrayed a promise that appealed to many, many Americans, clear-cut, simple notions of right and wrong, of the ownership of property, money in the bank, individual safety on the streets and personal financial security still have a strong hold on most Americans. In other generations, life was more difficult and insecure. People actually starved in affluent America in earlier generations. There was no welfare support, no social security, no medicare and no insured bank deposits. These facts are ignored in a wishful nostalgia for a simple, secure world that never existed, a world that can be found only in television shows like "The Waltons." If Americans are confronted with an either-or choice between apparent security— physical, social and financial—and individual liberty, with its difficult and delicate adjustments of the boundaries between one human being and another, one minority vis-à-vis the majority, then the impatient desire for simplistic immediate answers will lead to the sacrifice of liberty. The carefully and painstakingly developed legal concepts protecting the individual from the state, the powerless from ruthless dominance by the powerful, the inchoate interests of the community from reckless selfish uses of private property are all dependent upon a strong and viable legal system—which is now eroding.

So it is the contention of this book that the American faith in the rule of law is a myth and that reliance on this mythic belief is destroying the legal system. No mere patchwork, ameliorative tinkering with the laws, the courts and government agencies will suffice to save the structure of law. Nor can our system of values which the law is designed to protect and enforce long survive without fundamental change in the legal system. A reassessment of the role of law in contemporary American life is required. It is necessary to calculate reasonably and based upon factual evidence—not faith—what limits and controls law may be expected to exercise today. Those areas of conduct, public and private, that are not amenable to the existing legal system must be charted. Only then will it be possible to consider and make intelligent choices revising the function of law in our society and correlatively altering the machinery for enacting, administering and enforcing the law. At present, the myth prevents such an analysis. It compels us to cling to the law as it stands, and to worship it as a sacred institution. At the same time it serves as a scapegoat for all the failures of government, society and the individual.

It may be argued that lawlessness is endemic not merely to Americans but to the human species. Some ethologists claim that man is irretrievably violent and warlike. Other critics excoriate society for the shortcomings of the individual. It is not necessary to choose between the naked ape of Desmond Morris and the noble savage of Rousseau. These are hypotheses which biologists and social scientists may utilize for research and testing. They are of little aid to scholars and concerned citizens studying the legal system. It is obvious, though, that the dogma of the rule of law has permitted a society that is neither lawful nor orderly. There can be little doubt that whatever definition of justice one uses to measure the legal system, the system is found wanting.

In their daily behavior few people, regardless of socioeconomic status, restrain their conduct or curb their desires because of legal prohibitions. In choosing among available options, the question of legality is rarely a determinative factor. When the legal profession is consulted, all too frequently it is not to give advice as to what is permissible and what is impermissible but to devise means by which the client can avoid legal restrictions. The institutions of the law are utilized in this way to undermine the rule of law.

The members of the legal profession who should be most aware that the rule of law is a myth and not a fact appear to be unwilling to acknowledge this disquieting reality. On the contrary, they proclaim that domestic tranquility and world peace can be obtained through the rule of law. Charles S. Rhyne, former president of the American Bar Association, in a statement typical of many speeches by leaders of the legal profession, confidently declared: "A peaceful world can only be created out of law. I am certain this towering goal is now within the grasp of the people of the world."

Such optimistically irrational faith in law is popular. Proportionately more young people are studying law today than at any time in the past. Few have an awareness of the realities of the legal system. Many idealists, such as Ralph Nader, expect to "restructure society" through litigation. Priests and clergymen, social workers and psychologists in growing numbers abandon their callings and turn to the study of law with the kind of faith that led pilgrims of another age to seek Jerusalem.

At the same time, many other people are turning away from the Western tradition of government under law and reason and are seeking a solution to their problems in mysticism. Dwight J. Pentecost, professor of Bible exposition at Dallas Theological Seminary, noting the phenomenal popularity of books on evangelism and the imminence of the second coming of Christ, explains it as follows: "People see the problems of lawlessness, crime and anarchy and realize that no government can handle them. So they just instinctively cry out for help and turn to the supernatural." [4] Law Professor Charles Reich, abandoning the procedures and methodology of law, envisions a future of kindliness when human beings will have a heightened misty Consciousness III and when goodness and decency will prevail, apparently without policemen or a structured system of declaring rights and remedies and means of settling disputes through legal processes.[5]

Neither an uncritical faith in "the law" nor a flight from law to mysticism will provide an answer to the urgent problems of law and justice in the United States. The painful but necessary first step is a recognition of the death of the law.

In many disciplines the professionals are fully conscious of the limitations and obsolescence of their own expertise. They loudly proclaim the death of institutions and ideas. In recent years, we have been told by theologians that God is dead. Jacques Cousteau warns us of the imminent death of the oceans, and biologists foresee the death of nature. Psychiatrists proclaim the death of the family. Urban planners tell us that our cities are dying. Sociologists declare that sociology is futile and economists admit the inefficacy of economic science. Political scientists recognize the limitations of power. Philosophers plaintively ask whether ethics is dead. A general writes a "Premortem on the Death of the Army." Strident criticisms of other disciplines have been effective in compelling re-examinations of principles and methods. In a very practical way, society has begun to protect its natural resources, to revise its views of urban problems and solutions. The dismantling of the huge Igoe Pruitt low-cost housing project in St. Louis is a triumph of reason and fact over sociological dogma.

Similar questioning of fundamental tenets of the law is lacking. Many lawyers do point out the flaws and shortcomings of the courts, the police and correctional institutions. Some critics do suggest that there are limits to the criminal sanction. The selection of the judiciary is hotly debated. Congress is accused of being "sapless."[6] The Supreme Court is charged, more in sorrow than in anger, with inflicting a deep if not mortal wound upon itself.[7] More strident opponents of particular court decisions do denounce and urge defiance of these rulings. But few, if any, politicians or legal scholars acknowledge the death of the rule of law itself. While conceding some faults and flaws, lawyers tell themselves the American legal system is the greatest one ever devised by man.

This attitude of urbane self-criticism and self-congratulation was recently crystallized in a little volume of essays entitled, "Is Law Dead?" [8] The Association of the Bar of New York City, to celebrate its centennial, commissioned a number of scholars to write a book addressed to this question. The authors, eminent law professors, philosophers, lawyers and students of government, treated it as a rhetorical question. With rare exception they found the answer to their questions in Plato. They looked to the past and closed their eyes to the realities of today, ignoring the problems of tomorrow. Few others even ask the question. Perhaps they fear the answer.

The death of law is visible to those who will look at the shambles of our legal system, the ever-mounting crime rate, and the contempt with which the legal process is treated by millions of Americans—rich and poor, officials, outcasts, and ordinary citizens. The mind, however, dismisses the message of the senses. Our consciousness rejects an alien thought as our bodies reject a foreign substance. We do not like to be confronted with the loss of an old concept. We fear and hate the notion that a familiar belief is no longer valid. Misology, or hatred of ideas, is nothing new. A hypothesis that compels us to re-examine the received wisdom of the past is rejected. It is this fear of the new idea which prevents the development of new concepts and viable institutions which will permit a just and orderly conduct of daily life.

An idea that is believed to be central to the conduct of human affairs acquires a sanctity that protects it from attack when other concepts can more freely be subjected to critical analyses. The heretic is often treated more harshly than the common criminal because heresy threatens the status quo and disturbs the complacency of everyone. All of us feel threatened by a collapse of faith, whereas we can discount the crimes of individuals. The criminal has placed himself outside the system. His wrongdoings can be explained by his sinful nature, the inequities of society, or perhaps even a genetic mistake. He may threaten society but he does not disturb our faith in the norms of individual behavior or the stability of institutions.

An attack on the basic principles of social organization is entirely different. Old beliefs die hard and slowly. It is more painful to give up a concept than to face the rational alternative of an analytical appraisal of its viability. The more the evidence accumulates as to its death, the more frantically we cling to the false comfort of the old faith. We fear that human society will disintegrate once we admit that our beliefs are shattered.

It is well to remember that mankind has survived the death of other ideas. History is replete with bloody martyrdoms of those who proclaimed the end of false gods, but the severity of the repressions could not revitalize dead beliefs. Mankind has learned to live without idols, without panoplies of gods and goddesses, to adjust to his displacement from the center of the universe, and so forth.

The individual man and woman was no more or no less brutal in his personal behavior after the death of the Ptolemaic theory than he was before. Acceptance of the invalidity of the concept, how-ever, enabled scientists to evaluate empirical evidence and to learn much about the physical world. Recognition of the death of law will not change individual human behavior. It will not abolish crime and delinquency or restore honesty and fair dealing in government and business. It may, however, remove an underlying cause of frustration and an obstacle to a more accurate appraisal of the difficulties of maintaining both individual liberty and an ordered society.

Individual liberty and an ordered society: I am not ready to abandon *either* of these goals. Anarchy has, in the past, led to repression rather than freedom. Emphasis on social stability at the expense of individual liberty, at the other extreme, has likewise ultimately led to violence and disorder, since the human spirit has not yet been programmed to docility.

William James observed that ". . . the way it works on the whole is the final test of a belief." [9] In this book I shall, like a modern Vergil, guide the reader through the circles of the legal system, revealing how it works on a day-by-day basis. Along the way, of course, certain practical improvements will occur to the visitor. Such changes, if adopted, would probably alleviate some injustices and should not be ignored. But the significant and inescapable conclusion of those who examine the actual functioning of the administration of justice in the United States must be the need for a drastic reformulation of the role of law in American life.

This book does not proclaim a new faith. It hoists no banner for unthinking pilgrims to follow seeking a promised land of instant fairness, justice and equality for all. By examining the actual operations of the legal system and the present use of law, unclouded by myth, this book suggests that if Americans recognize these realities they can make meaningful, fundamental changes leading to a viable society which will protect and conserve individual liberties and also meet the extraordinarily complex demands of a distraught and disillusioned people. It urges the public and especially the members of the legal profession to search for new governmental and social structures through which the ideals of equality and justice can feasibly be realized.

This book is divided into three parts. Part I sets forth the evidence of the death of the law and explores the implications of national lawlessness to the continued viability of our constitutional form of government. The etiology of this epidemic of illegal behavior is examined. The peculiar role of law in American life and government and the extraordinary and unrealized expectations of the American people are shown to have contributed to the death of the law.

Part II contains a detailed narrative description of the American legal system in operation and its component parts. Each segment of the legal structure and each of the classes of persons required to operate the system are shown as they actually function, not as the conventional wisdom and textbooks have taught us to view them. The problems and operations of the legislatures, trial courts, appellate courts, policemen, lawyers and judges are revealed with illustrations of their routine, day-to-day activities. The failure and frustrations of those who are part of the legal system and the effects upon the people who are caught up in the system as criminal defendants, civil litigants and ordinary citizens are also described.

The evident failure of each segment to function adequately, promptly and effectively is shown to be a contributing factor in the death of the law.

Part III discusses the philosophical and practical problems of the citizen who attempts to reconcile the dictates of conscience with the duty to obey the law. The old but timeless question of what is justice is examined in the context of American law and the expectations of our society. Finally, the book concludes with a recognition of the limitations of law both theoretically and as an institution to restructure society, the family and the individual to conform to the ideals and promises of the American dream. It suggests the recognition of these limitations and the creation of supplemental and alternative means to achieve both individual liberty and a stable and adequate social order.

PART I

I protest everything
Including my existence
And especially yours.

Graffito

Kill a man, kill a man. It is good
to kill a man.
One who has not killed a man moves
around sleepily.

Amharic poem, quoted
by Murphy, *In Ethiopia*
With a Mule

1: The Banality of Lawlessness

The banality of lawlessness permits average, ordinary citizens to ignore the crimes committed by other average, ordinary citizens. Brutal murders, skyjacking, wiretapping, lying and stealing by high public officials capture the headlines, but the endemic disregard of law by those who consider themselves "good citizens" constitutes a much greater danger to the social order. Misbehaving public officials can be convicted of crime and removed from office; the illegal conduct of the majority of the people cannot be dealt with on an individual case-by-case basis. The lawlessness of the great masses of respectable people is perilous because it is deemed acceptable behavior. Criminologists are concerned with "deviant" behavior. I am concerned with a norm that is essentially lawless in a society based upon a rule of law.

In this chapter, any number of unnoticed, unremarked actions

3

by average good citizens are described not because they are significant in themselves but because they reveal a public attitude of acceptance of illegal conduct. Such small incidents, I believe, foreshadow a disastrous weakening of the structure of society. It is my purpose by calling attention to these events to raise the alarm of the larger peril.

A people who habitually disobey the law and who feel no sense of wrongdoing or criminality in such conduct have in effect overthrown their government. That such an attitude has developed spontaneously and unconsciously makes the danger more insidious. A frontal attack on national institutions would doubtless be resisted. A dramatic and public flouting of legal convention raises an alarm. The firing of Archibald Cox as special prosecutor and the resignation of Attorney General Elliot Richardson affronted the public sensibility. These acts constituted a public desecration of the mythic gods of law and justice. A military coup may provoke resistance and a passionate defense of the system which has been overthrown. Recognition of danger is necessary in order for the public to defend those values and institutions that are threatened with destruction. But the daily countless small violations of law by average citizens occur without notice or comment. This death of law by attrition can be as fatal and final as death by violence.

A decade ago few city dwellers were aware of the dwindling number of birds. Even those who did notice dismissed it as a temporary or unimportant phenomenon. However, Rachel Carson dramatically focused public concern on a threatened danger by describing a future silent spring in which no birds would sing. She pointed out the need for drastic changes in the common use of pesticides. While the experts ridiculed her, the public read, considered and demanded action.

In this book, I do not depict some future imaginary community. Nor am I extrapolating from present data. Every act of lawlessness described has already occurred, not once but many times. These acts are not confined to any city or any section of the country. Similar lawlessness has taken place and is continuing in cities, towns and rural areas throughout the nation. Because these acts have increased so insidiously since the 1950s and are now a fact of daily life, we accept them as we did the dwindling of the bird population, ignoring the significance and the danger.

Since children subconsciously mirror the tacit values of the society in which they live, let us begin by observing some acts of average American children.

On April 29, 1971, six-year-old children in Philadelphia refused to attend school and picketed the school because the Board of Education had increased the school day by twenty minutes. The press carried pictures of little tots carrying their signs, marching up and down in front of the school. Their parents did not reprimand them. No city official criticized either the children who were illegally absent from school or their parents who permitted them to play truant. Nor did their teachers reprimand the children. Perhaps the teachers were aware of the hypocrisy of appealing to the children to obey the school attendance law when they had been out on an illegal strike the preceding week. A half million other children throughout the nation were also out of school because of teacher strikes and other disputes. Many of the children who were nominally attending school were in fact cutting classes, vandalizing the school buildings, "shaking down" fellow students, mugging the teachers, and committing countless illegal acts both trivial and serious. At least 30 percent of all high school pupils in metropolitan public schools are truant every day. The crime rate among thirteen- to fifteen-year-olds has increased more sharply than at any other age level. High school and college-age young people also violate the law in large numbers. Many smoke pot illegally. Others have raided draft boards, rifled the files of their university presidents, destroyed property, and prevented the holding of classes.

The action of the picketing six-year-olds did not provoke any comment from the City Council, which was itself in violation of a court order requiring it to appropriate funds so that the courts could continue to operate. The mayor was also defying a court order directing him to comply with "right to know laws" and reveal the sources of his campaign funds. The Board of Education was in violation of an order of the Human Relations Commission commanding the desegregation of the public schools.

The children had only to observe their parents—in all walks of life—to realize that their conduct was in the mainstream of American life. Countless citizens violate traffic laws and refuse to pay the fines imposed. In New York City alone, uncollected fines for parking violations amount to more than $4,000,000 a month. Transport workers and garbage collectors engage in illegal strikes, violating statutory law, injunctions imposed by the court, and the orders of their own union officials. A group of mothers halted the construction of a low-cost housing project by refusing to get off the property. They took their children, including those in baby carriages, and camped on a vacant lot. Other mothers formed a human chain around some large trees in the path of a new highway and prevented the felling of the trees and the construction of the road. Adult parishioners picketed a cardinal over the transfer of a popular teaching nun. In Forest Hills, Long Island, the residents refused to accede to the legal construction of low-cost housing. Their leader, Gerry Birbach, declared, "The battle of Forest Hills will be won in the streets."

Members of university faculties have participated in illegal research on welfare clients, subjecting them to pain, providing them with placebos instead of the birth control pills they had requested, and refusing them their legal allotments in order to establish scientific control groups. Other scientists have engaged in lethal experiments on prisoners, many of whom were incarcerated for far less immoral or illegal conduct. Most of these adults are parents. Children are aware of what their parents are doing. They know that the government is not prosecuting their parents for these illegal acts and that friends and neighbors express little, if any, disapproval. Lawless conduct in these cases is socially acceptable.

Although morality and legality are far from synonymous, law relies upon a moral consensus for its support. Law embodies either explicitly or implicitly the moral standards of the community. Occasionally a particular crime, such as the prohibitions on use of marijuana or alcohol, expresses an obsolete standard of behavior. In time, either by repeal of the statute or lessening of the penalties, the law and the public norm are brought into agreement. During the period of disagreement between law and public consensus, the law suffers from disobedience and futile and wasteful efforts to compel a form of behavior contrary to accepted standards. The United States has endured periods when widely approved conduct, such as drinking alcoholic beverages and union membership, was illegal. The nation also survived a long period when slavery was legal but considered immoral by at least half the nation. Until the present, however, we have never known a time when the norms of conduct were so contrary to the mandates of the law.

This disjunction between law and morals was sharply revealed to me in a routine murder case that I tried. It was so banal and ordinary a case that it was not even reported in the local press. Mrs. T, a black woman on relief, killed a black boy in the same slum neighborhood. The boy, it was alleged, had participated in a gang rape of Mrs. T's fifteen-year-old daughter. Although Mrs. T had made numerous complaints to the police, no investigation of the incident was made. The next time the boy came to Mrs. T's house looking for the girl, she invited him in and shot and killed him. At the trial, Mrs. T presented a parade of character witnesses. Relatives, friends, neighbors, school teachers, a nun and a priest testified to Mrs. T's good moral character and good reputation in the community. All of these witnesses knew that Mrs. T had nine illegitimate children by five different men, that she was living out of wedlock with her present paramour (politely called a common-law husband) and that she had always been on welfare. The elderly white priest explained: "Mrs. T is a good mother. She loves her children. In our community, that makes her a person of good moral character." The jurors, most of whom were legally married and employed or retired on pensions, by their decision agreed that Mrs. T was a "good woman."

In other social classes, the definition of a "good person" is equally elastic. The officials of General Electric who were convicted of violating antitrust laws and actually spent a few months in jail were leading citizens, respected in the business and financial world and members of elite "society." Several of them were elders of their churches and officials in large communal charities. The roster of their character witnesses resembled a local "Who's Who." The popular reaction to the charges against these men, their trial, conviction and sentencing was one of sympathy for them as unfortunates who had gotten caught. Moral condemnation for illegal conduct and for losses caused to stockholders and the public was conspicuously absent. Similarly, other leaders of the community—industrialists, lawyers, judges and professors—who have been arrested and convicted for sordid illegal acts of personal gain, unredeemed by any ideological or moral motivation, retain their social and financial positions as foremost citizens untainted by public censure or even disapproval.

A doctor prosecuted in federal court admitted to cheating the government of more than a half million dollars in medicare payments. He denied that he had done anything wrong. The judge who placed him on probation remarked, "Doctor, you are not really a criminal." The judge expressed the attitude of the community. Stealing from the taxpayers and defrauding poor, elderly sick people is simply not considered criminal conduct.

Moral myopia extends to all classes of society and many types of illegal conduct. Scientists who falsified the testing reports made to the government on defective airplane brakes also stated that they were not guilty of any wrongdoing. Their misconduct resulted not only in defrauding the government—and all the citizens—of millions but also in the deaths of many airplane personnel and passengers.

No one would wish to bring back the harsh and hypocritical moral standards described in Hawthorne's *The Scarlet Letter*. Recent historians have revealed the iniquitous behavior of "The Other Victorians," whose lives of sexual perversion flourished in the repressive and ostentatiously proper atmosphere of the late nineteenth century. The varieties of human experience—sexual, financial and social—cannot be wholly eliminated either by law or social pressures. However, a society that condones rather than condemns violations of law removes the threat of social stigma which usually operates on the middle and upper classes to inhibit illegal conduct. *The machinery of law enforcement then bears the entire burden of attempting to compel obedience to law.*

Institutions, like inanimate objects and human beings, have a breaking point. Each has a limited strength and a maximum burden which can safely be borne. The American legal system has its limits, though they have never been defined. It is almost a form of sacrilege to suggest that the law cannot cope with the problems of our society. Most people will readily admit deficiencies in many parts of the legal structure, but the inherent limitations of law itself is one of those unthinkable thoughts which must be not only acknowledged but also meditated upon and studied. Today the numbers of people who actually fear the retribution of a deity and punishment in a hereafter is drastically reduced. The fluidity of the social order and the mobility of Americans have all but eliminated the pressures of peer-group condemnation and neighborhood ostracism for many forms of illegal conduct. Family ties are weakened. Parental authority has been eroded by many influences. Often the earnings of the wife and/or the child exceed that of the husband-father. In a money-oriented society, power is an attribute of money. The American dream of upward mobility in which the child's economic, professional and social status is expected to be superior to that of his parents, as well as the demands for freedom by women, blacks, and young people, all contribute to the erosion of authority held for centuries by the older generation and particularly by the father or father substitute. Few of the religious, economic, social or familial constraints remain strong enough to inhibit individual conduct. The law, therefore, has become the primary if not the sole force to compel 200 million diverse and restless Americans to behave in ways that are ethical, honest, humane and with due regard for the rights of others. This is a burden too great for one nebulous belief known as "the rule of law" and one institution, the legal system.

Unthinking belief in law and lip service to obedience to law are prevalent. Those who denounce violence and crime in the streets while condoning white collar crime are unaware of their inconsistency. But street criminals themselves see little difference between their behavior—most of which stems from clumsy, stupid and unsuccessful attempts to steal—and that of the more polite, successful, and financially profitable embezzlements, fraud, and cheating committed by the wealthy and powerful. In such a society, where there is no concerted and impartial disapproval of all violations of law, formal legal sanctions are clearly inadequate to deter, apprehend or punish crime.

A few statistics bear out this conclusion. In the first nine months of 1971, according to the FBI, 4,426,000 major crimes were reported. In 1970, eleven serious crimes were committed every sixty seconds. Of course, the number of less serious crimes is much larger. And the number of unreported crimes is impossible to estimate with any certainty. Doctors believe that fewer than one in ten rapes is reported.

The number of undetected crimes must be astronomical. Ninety percent of college students queried in a poll admitted that they had committed at least one act for which they could have been arrested. Obviously a large percentage of these violations of law which are not reported or prosecuted are committed by "good citizens."

Child abuse, the most common cause of death in children under the age of two, illustrates the double standard of law enforcement and public attitudes with respect to the middle class and the indigent. Child abuse, as any pediatrician knows, is widespread among the well-to-do. But it is rarely reported by private physicians. Hospitals and clinics that treat the indigent do report the more serious cases of battered babies. Accordingly, only the poor are arrested and prosecuted for child beatings and other cruelties. Similarly, shoplifting by the wealthy in specialty shops and department stores is commonplace. These cases are almost always "adjusted." The poor who steal less expensive items from supermarkets are routinely arrested, prosecuted and punished.

Although almost 90 percent of all criminal defendants are indigent, crime is by no means the exclusive prerogative of the poor and the urban slum dweller. Crime has spread to the affluent suburbs and even the rural hinterlands. In 1973, one in three city dwellers was the victim of crime and one in five suburban residents. The gap is closing. Reported crime in 1972 rose more sharply in the suburbs than in the inner cities. Even these official statistics grossly under-report crime. White-collar crime is rarely included. Much crime in the slums is not reported because of a sense of futility. A person living in a low-income housing project knows that his stolen TV set will never be returned, nor will the carefully hoarded money seized by a purse snatcher. Therefore, why waste the time, effort and carfare to go to the police station?

Despite statistics and sociological studies which indicate that crime per capita today is no greater than in other times and other societies, everyone knows that neither his person nor his property is safe. As crime spreads, so does fear. Fear leads to weapons for self-protection. The number of people who own firearms—legally and illegally—cannot even be estimated. The Dallas International Bank, which is six blocks from the Texas School Bank Depository where Lee Harvey Oswald shot President Kennedy, gave a Browning shotgun to every depositor who placed $1,000 in a savings account. Business at the bank boomed.

It is not surprising to learn that more Americans have been killed by guns fired by their fellow citizens in civilian life than in all of our wars. As the carnage on the street continues, fear grows and more and more people arm themselves. Little is done by the Congress, the state legislatures or city councils to prohibit the private ownership of firearms. The government and the citizens recognize that official law enforcement agencies, despite their growing personnel, increasing budgets and sophisticated weaponry, are ineffective. There are more private police and security guards than government policemen. Many of these private agents are armed. The government itself is helping citizens to arm themselves. The Law Enforcement Assistance Administration has given financial support to citizens' groups which seek to provide their own self-protection. It is appalling that more than a century after Sir Robert Peel established a police force for the City of London, replacing the common practice of hiring private body-guards, the United States government is encouraging the citizenry to rely on their own force and use of weapons to repel crime. Little concern is expressed that such programs may constitute a regressive movement to the vigilantism of the frontier, of citizens' posses, and ultimately of citizen punishment through mob beatings and lynchings.

The citizen groups who apply for and receive funding for these local peoples' police do not consider themselves lawless. They act out of desperation, having seen again and again the inability of government to protect them from vicious, violent and unprovoked attacks on the street, in their homes and businesses. But these same citizens have often refused help to others who were in distress and being attacked.

Most bystanders turn away from crimes committed in their presence to avoid involvement. No one aids the victim, even though it is a little girl who is being beaten and raped. In Rochester, New York, at 5:30 in the afternoon of November 16, 1971, ten-year-old Carmen Colon appeared on the highway naked and tried to hail hundreds of passing cars. Two days later her body was found in a ditch. She had been raped and strangled. Countless people saw her but no one stopped to save the girl's life. Bystanders watching a crime have even helped the criminals to flee.

A witness in a murder case I was trying was testifying for the defense. He described the violent disposition and habits of his deceased friend. The witness, a young, healthy and husky man, stated that he had attended a party at which the deceased brutally beat another guest, a woman. "What did you do?" I asked him. "I sat and watched. It wasn't none of my business," he replied. A few weeks later he sat and watched another woman stab this same friend to death. That, too, was none of his business, he explained to the court.

The lawless conduct of government itself cannot be ignored in any assessment of the causes of the death of the law. Like our high school students, on the average 25 to 30 percent of the United States Senators are absent from legislative sessions, taking junkets abroad, courtesy of the taxpayers, and relaxing in resorts as the guests of special-interest groups. In Albany, New York, the state legislature met on December 29, 1971, and adjourned one minute later. In other state capitols lackluster assemblymen met without quorums, transacted little business of any consequence other than voting themselves raises.

Here are a few relatively unremarked examples of endemic lawlessness by government officials:

§The President's Domestic Council illegally awarded a contract without competitive bidding to H. Ross Perot, a Texas million-aire friend of President Nixon. The President entered into a so-called executive agreement for military bases in the Azores in violation of the Constitution. The Congress voted to purchase Rhodesian chrome in violation of a United Nations sanction which was supposed to be binding on the member states.

§The President illegally cut $3 billion in the taxes paid by business interests. The White House acknowledged that a contract was illegally awarded to a friend of the President by the President's Domestic Council.

§United States officials violated the National Environmental Pol-icy Act by constructing highways without complying with its mandatory provisions.

§The Internal Revenue Service, in direct violation of the law, allowed tax-exempt status to all-white schools established to circumvent the law. But Internal Revenue expressed shock at widespread corporate tax evasion.

§The Federal Communications Commission, which was created to insure the free flow of ideas, was found to be engaged in wiretapping. As were the CIA, the FBI, and countless state and local police agencies.

§A study by New York State Controller Arthur Levitt revealed that the state's intelligence agency illegally gives access to data on 4 million citizens, imperiling their rights.

§Policemen in many cities and counties have not only been "cooping" (sleeping on the job) but also making illegal arrests, beating innocent citizens and taking bribes.

§The New York police were accused by a State Commission of Investigation of "utter failure" to enforce antigambling laws.

§Even the Law Enforcement Assistance Administration awarded $600,000 in contracts, in Arkansas alone, in violation of the regulations governing the agency, to companies in which the officials of the agency had an interest.

§A House Judiciary Subcommittee issued a unanimous report finding that the Justice Department had not properly enforced the Federal Voting Rights Act in twenty-six Mississippi counties.

§The Fair Employment Commission was itself found guilty of discriminating against women. The United States Department of Justice illegally failed and refused to enforce the Federal Voting Rights Act, according to a unanimous report by a House Judiciary Subcommittee.

§The FBI violated its own antihijacking rules, resulting in the death of three people in Jacksonville, Florida, in October, 1971.

§Governor Rockefeller assured the public that ways would be found to "skirt" the United States Supreme Court ruling prohibiting public support of parochial schools. This is only a more urbane attitude than that of Governor Faubus of Arkansas, who defied federal marshals attempting to enforce the law requiring the end of public school segregation.

These are unusual acts of public defiance. Most violations of law by government officials are artfully concealed. When energetic reporters uncover misdeeds, prosecutions rarely follow. Therefore, former U.S. Attorney General Mitchell's tabulation of convictions of public officials assumes awesome proportions. He reported in 1972, before Watergate, that more than 170 current or former public office holders representing 21 cities, 12 counties and 25 states had been indicted and convicted in less than three years.

How much unprosecuted and undetected crime in high places

has occurred will never be known. But in each community, the people know which policemen can be bribed to ignore a traffic ticket, which officials can be paid not to report housing violations, sanitary regulations and a multitude of other laws designed to protect the public. Business people know the going price for changes in zoning ordinances, for liquor licenses and all types of government permits and laws. The price for various political offices—both elective and appointive—is also known in every city and town.

This deep, silent knowledge of "the way things are" is a kind of folk wisdom, permeating unconscious attitudes and influencing behavior. It creates a moral myopia conflicting sharply with the established rhetoric, the mythic faith in the rule of law. Torn between faith in law and the fact of lawlessness, the public appears to have developed a moral carapace or shell in order to cope with the intellectual and practical problems created by this discrepancy. The embezzling railroad president, the corrupt public official, and the knife-wielding street hoodlum are one in blindness to the wrongful nature of their own conduct.

Dennis M., on trial for murder, described his actions in a flat, monotonous tone. The horror of what he had done eluded him as evidently as the horror of the White House horrors eluded John Ehrlichman. Dennis is sixteen. His I.Q. is normal. While he is not a shining light at school, he reads fluently. He is good-looking and popular with the boys and girls. His girl friend was in court; stylishly dressed in flared pants and a body shirt. She had a modified Afro hairdo. She would not have looked out of place in an office, bank or department store. This is Dennis' story:

Q. "Tell us what you know concerning this incident."

A. "I remember the day that it happened. I had walked my girl home from school. She lives in the Project at Twenty-second and Diamond Streets and I walked her home like always. Taboo, Marvine and Pudgy and me, we was all together. Taboo, Marvine and Pudgy waited for me on the steps at Twenty-third and Dauphin and I walked my girl to her house. I walked back and met

Taboo, Marvine and Pudgy and then we had a free fall [a] with
Twenty-first and Norris Street. After the fight we walked down to
Twenty-second and Edgley, across the street from the State Store.
We sent a dude in to get some wine and was on the corner about
twenty minutes when Red walked up to all of us. Red walked up
next to me and said, Damn Solo,[b] I want to get a body. I said to Red,
it's about time that I get a body.[c] Then I said to Lil Red, do you want
to get one and he told me yes. I told Red if he could do the bit [d] for it
to go get the burner.[e] Lil Red walked down the street and went into
Lil Hot Rod's house. He walked in the door and came right out with
his hand in his coat pocket; he had this long brown coat on and he
had his hand in the pocket of the coat. As soon as he came up to me
on the pavement I started walkin' with Red and we didn't want to
let anybody know where we was goin. . . . We could see the corner
boys down at Twenty-first Street. They was really thick.[f] We was
hollerin' words back and forth to one another and Red came around
from the corner. One of the two boys that was on the same side of
the street as me bust at us with a shotgun and then Lil Red fired. Me
and Red was still on the block and the same dude fired the shotgun
again. The crowd had started to gather and I told Red to bust [g] at
the crowd and Red bust three times. Red walked up to me and he
said, Damn I didn't get nobody and I said to Red look back there
and I could see a boy lying in the street with red plaid pants on."

Q. "Why did you tell Red to wait till the boys came down?"

A. "I want to hurt somebody and if they was in a bunch we
could get one."

Q. "Why did Red want to get a body?"

A. "'Cause they was gang warin' and the Valley ain't had a body
since we kilt Bear awhile ago."

---

[a] Argot for rumble or gang fight.
[b] Solo is Dennis' nickname.
[c] "Get a body" means kill someone.
[d] Do the bit means serve one's sentence in jail.
[e] Burner means gun.
[f] Thick means crowded with people.
[g] Bust means shoot.

The boy with the red plaid pants was dead.

Neither Dennis nor his friends felt that Dennis' conduct was odd or reprehensible. They were with him in court. The family and friends of the dead boy were also in court. They treated his death with a passive acceptance of inevitability. The "why," which loomed so large in my mind, they did not ask. One does not waste energy on futilities.

The railroad president who used company funds to hire call girls, the city councilman who accepted money for legislation, the army officer who embezzled PX funds, and the cadets who cheated on their examinations all present the same bland, unemotional, factual accounts of their different violations of law. Their reasons have no more compelling logic than Dennis M.'s. These white-collar executives probably believe that they want more money, power and prestige. Many of them already have ample means and some have more money than the most profligate person could spend in a lifetime. Essentially their criminal conduct—kickbacks, embezzlement and fraud—is as irrational as that of the street criminal. Their bewilderment that they should be haled into court on charges is the same as his.

Gerald is a brilliant lawyer. In a dazzling series of maneuvers he pyramided corporations, sold stock, looted these companies, defrauding investors of over $5 million. He, too, described his financial legerdemain in a flat, matter-of-fact way. He argued that what he had done was entirely within the law. The impropriety or immorality of his transactions and the hardships inflicted on the unwary investors were of no concern to him.

I thought of Gerald's calm, egocentrism, his loyal and devoted friends and relatives as I listened to Rosa's testimony in my courtroom.

Rosa is a neatly dressed middle-aged woman who cares for her six children, sees that they go to school, feeds them and keeps house. There is nothing in her past history or in the court psychiatric examination to suggest that she is not normal. She testified in court that she saw her fourteen-year-old daughter having an argument with a neighbor. Rosa had previously told her child to stay on her own front steps, but the girl went across the street to the neighbor's doorway. Rosa walked over and plunged a knife in her neighbor's back.

"Where did you get the knife?" I asked her.

"It was in my pocket."

"What kind of a knife was it?"

"Oh, just a ordinary knife, the kind you carry with you," she replied.

Rosa, too, was accompanied by friends and neighbors who saw nothing remarkable or wrong in her behavior.

Gary is one of the few who gave a reason, faulty though it was, for what he did. Gary is twenty-one years old; he completed the eleventh grade in school. He is a Vietnam veteran and has a job. Here is his own account of a mortal stabbing:

"On Saturday, September 18, 1971, about eight thirty P.M. I was on Twenty-first Street between Sharswood and Jefferson Streets, sitting on the steps by myself, when Lorraine's brother, James, came and told me that some man had cussed at Lorraine and hit her. I went looking for him. James went with me. James pointed to the man later identified to me as Thomas Y———. He had just come out of the Pearl Theater. I caught up with him at the southeast corner of Ridge and Jefferson Streets. I asked him why he cussed at and hit Lorraine. He said he didn't do it and a lot of people said he did. I hit him in the mouth with my right hand. He staggered back. He kept saying, 'I didn't do it.' He turned around to Lorraine's brother and said, 'You know me, you know I didn't do it.' I then reached into my pocket and got my knife and stabbed him one time in the chest. He just stood there and looked at me. I turned away and folded the knife back up and took Lorraine home. I saw the police when they picked him up. I stood on the steps for about a half hour to an hour. I took Lorraine home first, then I came back and stood on the steps. I then walked to my aunt's house at 3002 North ——— Street. I turned on the radio to listen to see if he died or not, but it didn't come on the radio because if it did I was going to give myself up. I told my cousin, Bobby ———, 'I think I killed a man.' I then took a bath and went to bed. I stayed there until the police picked me up."

Q. "Gary, why did you stab Thomas?"

A. "Because he hit Lorraine and she is three months pregnant by me, and I figured that he was trying to make her lose the baby."

Q. "Gary, did you know Thomas?"

A. "I think his name is Thomas. That was the first time I saw him."

None of these people, either the street criminals or the white-collar criminals, acted out of mental derangement, intellectual incapacity or passion. It is often assumed that the lawbreaker has a calculus of risk-benefit, that he assesses the profit to be gained against the probabilities of detection, conviction and penalties to be imposed. The law's fictional reasonable man would operate in such a fashion. In fact, except for organized crime, which is conducted along businesslike methods, such a rational approach is most exceptional. The street criminal mugs and kills for a few dollars. Often the most vicious assaults net the assailant nothing. The risks are enormous, the harm likely to ensue from an armed robbery is incalculable and the profits usually meager. Nonetheless, such wanton and stupid acts take place daily.

The newspaper reader can only marvel at the stupidity of people in high places. David Halberstam has painstakingly revealed the perverse and continuous obtuseness of the leaders of the Kennedy and Johnson administrations in the conduct of foreign policy.[1] The actions of the White House plumbers and the Nixon inner circle reveal a total absence of this calculus of risk-benefit. The benefits of a few more votes, a few higher points on public opinion polls bear no relation to the risks and disasters that their conduct has brought about. One reads of a corporation president pleading guilty to having sexual relations with a minor *in the company offices!* The likelihood of detection, the loss of position, reputation and destruction of family ties could scarcely have been considered worth a few moments of pleasure. The obvious conclusion is that none of these people acted with reason. Putting aside the moral issues, the game simply wasn't worth the candle. But such an evaluation is seldom made before the act.

One cannot dismiss the moral or ethical implications of these actions. The street criminal who mugs or shoots, and the public official who lies or cheats are not, unfortunately, exceptional people. Their conduct does not differ widely from the public consensus. Cheating on one's income tax is common. The stratagems devised to help people avoid paying taxes, increase prices, take private expenditures as business expenses, and other forms of polite stealing occupy much of the time, energy and ingenuity of lawyers and accountants who seldom express a moral judgment on the actions of their clients.

Physical attacks by knife or gun by no means always provoke shock or outrage. Those individuals who act with violence, even causing death, in circumstances which logically seem to have little, if any, justification or provocation are also in the mainstream of America. The American Association for the Advancement of Science, in its studies of violence, points out that "the use of violence has widespread acceptance in the United States." According to surveys, 58 percent of Americans agreed that a man had a right to kill a person to defend his house even when no one's life is threatened.

The ubiquitous poll takers inform us that only 35 percent of the public consider a policeman shooting a looter to be an act of violence. Apparently, the public agrees with the orders of Chicago's Mayor Daley to shoot looters and Philadelphia's Mayor Rizzo's suggestion that the police "move on" student protestors. In the immortal words of George Wallace, the cure for rioting is "to knock some people in the head."

Lawyers, judges and psychiatrists can no longer dismiss the conduct of such a large proportion of Americans as aberrant. We cannot say that lawlessness is the work of the mentally ill or the socially and economically disadvantaged. These people, like Lieutenant Calley and Captain Medina, are acting in accordance with the norms they know. Nor can one dismiss the defendants —either brutal slayers or sophisticated embezzlers—as a different breed. Novelists entitle their fiction *Them* or *The Other*. What a judge painfully learns is that there is no clear demarcation between them and us.[2]

The standard that the law lays down for criminal responsibility no longer seems to be applicable. For almost five hundred years Anglo-American criminal law has been based upon the doctrine of "mens rea." To be guilty in law, one must have mental capacity and an understanding of right and wrong. Presumably one who knows what is evil has the free will to choose between good and evil. The test the law requires is mental capacity. Those who are insane, incompetents, infants or subject to delusions are deemed incapable of a guilty mind.

In 1581, William Lambard laid down this test of criminal responsibility: "If a mad man or a naturell foole, or a lunatike in the time of his lunacie, or a childe y apparently hath no knowledge of good nor evil do kill a man, this is no felonious acte, nor any thing forfeited by it. . . ."

In the intervening centuries much judicial time has been devoted to the question of the mental state of an accused person. With the advent of psychiatry as a distinct branch of medicine, the tests for criminal capacity are constantly under review and criticism. Every court that prides itself on being up to date has its own staff of psychiatrists and psychologists. Defendants are subjected to batteries of psychometric tests, interviews and analyses. Courtrooms are veritable battlegrounds of experts testifying as to the mental condition of the accused at the time he committed the act.

The law and the experts assume that the knowledge of good and evil and of right and wrong is a part of the natural endowment of every descendant of Adam and Eve who is not insane, an idiot, or an acute psychotic. But we lawyers and judges, who every day hear people openly admit that they have cheated, stolen, raped, robbed and killed, are ineluctibly forced to question this basic assumption.

A very few of the accused who admit their acts give some reason or justification. Rarely does it strike the observer as a rational excuse or that the crime is in any way proportional to the wrong or fancied wrong that the accused claims to have suffered.

The extraordinary defense of G. Gordon Liddy, who said that he planted wiretap equipment in Democratic Party Headquarters in the Watergate Apartments in Washington, D. C., to protect government leaders, is indistinguishable from that of many muggers and killers who claim they carry guns and knives for self-protection. Liddy, like most white-collar defendants, acted in secret and hoped to avoid detection. The justification, which seems to be a clever legal ploy, is probably sincerely believed.

Not all confessed criminals claim to have acted from good motives. Some do not even assert an excuse. Many steal to buy drugs. Others steal from boredom or merely the desire for money. I have rarely heard anyone even suggest that he was stealing from hunger or to provide necessities for his family.

Neither stabbings nor shootings are explained by an overwhelming passion—love, jealousy, vengeance. More often the precipitating catalyst was a quarrel over money. One man, whose slayer was on trial before me, was killed in a dispute over fifty cents. Is this the "hot blood," passion, rage or strong emotion that the law permits to reduce a killing from murder to manslaughter?

Lawyers, judges and court personnel who hear cases like these day after day are bewildered. The prosecutor urging a stiff sentence will argue that the defendant has not shown remorse or repentance, but what is even more disquieting is that so few law violators show any sense of wrongdoing. C. S. Lewis explains the difficulty which I, as a judge, have found in comprehending this attitude. Lewis noted that in his many discussions with ordinary British soldiers, "the greatest barrier [he felt in communicating with them] is the almost total absence from the minds of my audience of any sense of sin." [3] This absence from the minds of those who have violated the law of any sense of sin, shame or disgrace makes appeals to obedience to law futile. If one has no sense of wrongdoing in committing illegal and vicious acts, then the basis of law—free choice between right and wrong, between legal and illegal—no longer exists.

It must be recognized that the power of law has ceased to command the obedience or respect of a vast proportion of Americans. Many abhor street crime but condone white-collar crime.

Others have bitter scorn for the business criminal and compassion for the junkie, the slum dweller and the reliefer who violate the law. Such selective condonation and condemnation in itself defeats the viability of a rule of law. All of us are victims of white-collar crime, which raises taxes, the cost of goods, of government and of maintenance of the environment. At least one-fourth of us are the victims of burglary and street crime. At the same time all too many of us are also law violators.

To paraphrase Pogo, we have met the criminal and he is us. We are a nation of scofflaws.[4]

The implications of American endemic lawlessness are far-reaching. People ask in hushed tones: "What will happen if the President refuses to obey the United States Supreme Court?" It is a question which courts and Presidents have been wise enough to avoid for more than a century. Today we must ask ourselves another question which also has not arisen for more than a century: What will happen when 40 percent or 50 percent of the people refuse to obey the law? Obviously, constitutional government as we have known it will no longer exist.

A court can order the imprisonment of individual criminals and know that unless they flee the country or are pardoned they will be jailed. The order will be obeyed. But there are many situations in which a judge rightly fears an open defiance of law. A school system, for example, is ordered to give every child a hearing before he may be expelled. If the superintendent and school principals refuse to comply with the order and also refuse to appeal the order to a higher court, shouldn't they be imprisoned for contempt of court? A court orders a municipality to close an archaic, brutalizing prison. To replace the facility would cost a great deal of money. It is politically and economically unwise to raise taxes. Therefore, the court order is ignored. Should the mayor and his executives as well as the city council which refuses to enact new tax laws be jailed for contempt? One knows that the use of military force to compel government officials to obey a court order is a drastic remedy which must be used sparingly. One cannot call out the state or national guard except in the most exigent cases where clear moral issues are involved. Governor Faubus could not be permitted to defy the court and to outrage the sensibilities of all Americans to whom racial discrimination is not only illegal but also abhorrent. With hindsight one can say that if President Eisenhower had expressed strong support for the Court's decision, and if Congress had also expressed through resolutions and open comment strong condemnation, force might have been necessary.

Today one cannot rely upon public or political support for the enforcement of orders of a court duly entered after a due-process hearing in conformity with law simply because they are orders of a court. Nor does violation of a court order arouse public indignation. Many courts, therefore, ignore contemptuous conduct rather than risk confrontation. The judge and the public officials have job security. They run little personal risk by asserting power. But it is the viability of the law that is endangered by such an open rupture between courts and other government officials. It is the rule of law that is daily eroded and ultimately killed by such continued violations of law and orders of duly constituted courts.

America was promises—to whom?
° ° °

We do not ask for Truth now from John Adams
We do not ask for Tongues from Thomas Jefferson
We do not ask for Justice from Tom Paine
We ask for answers.
Archibald McLeish, "America Was Promises"

2: The Unredeemed Promise

Why are Americans more lawless than other people? The answer may vary depending upon one's profession. Some psychiatrists say that the lawless American is acting out his frustrations, like a misbehaving child. Psychologists, noting the extraordinarily high proportion of poor and nonwhites in our prisons, resort to theories of racial differences, genetic low intelligence and other claimed biological factors. Sociologists often attribute crime to the inability to adjust to a rapidly changing technological society that has no place for the unskilled. The female-headed family has been blamed for many ills, although in true matriarchal societies there is no more crime than in similar patriarchal societies.

Comparison of the habits of tribes in the far-off Pacific or Central Africa may provide useful insights to the scientist. But these analogies offer little guidance to those seeking answers to immediate problems. In more advanced Western nations, one also finds lawlessness but of a different quantity and quality than that in the United States. In France, it has for years been customary for the rich to evade taxes. While this fact causes economic strains, it has not destroyed or threatened the daily life of the citizens. England, like the United States, has had its government scandals, race riots, economic stringencies, an unpopular war in Northern Ireland, and profound social dislocations. Although crime has increased sharply, Britons do not live in fear of the omnipresent criminal nor are they profoundly disillusioned with their government. Both England and the United States are common-law countries with ostensibly similar guarantees of individual liberty, presumption of innocence and trial by jury. Although there has been some movement in England to "get tough" with criminals, there has not been an attack on the courts and the basic premises of the law.

Watching a steady procession of those accused of crime being prosecuted, jailed, released and indicted again and again, I find at least one of the underlying causes of lawlessness in the United States to be the law itself. I do not mean any particular doctrine, such as the presumption of innocence, or any congeries of judicial decisions implementing the rights of the accused. If the causes of endemic lawlessness were so superficial, the cure could easily be effected by changing these particular aspects of the law. This simplistic remedy has been tried and found useless. Preventive detention, no-knock laws, and "wall-to-wall police" in the District of Columbia have made little real change in the lawless nature of that community. Despite these laws and great expenditures of money, the residents of Washington, D. C., continue to behave like their fellow citizens in New York, Detroit, Chicago and all the other cities and towns in the United States.

A basic cause of American lawlessness is a situation unique to the United States: the promise of equal justice under law to be achieved by means of the legal system.

The concept of equal justice is not new. Almost eight centuries

ago, the British lords declared that the king was subject to the law
and the rule of law was pre-eminent. This bold doctrine subjected
the sovereign to the power of the Parliament. It was a struggle
not unlike that between the presidency under Nixon and the
Congress vying for supremacy. But in England, the doctrine had
little impact on the rights of the average Englishman in his political, financial and familial activities.

Two and a half millennia ago Pericles declared that the law
"secures equal justice to all alike in their private disputes." When
Pericles made his famous funeral oration, the brief golden age of
Athens was already ending. It had been a society in which slavery
was accepted without a moral qualm, where women had a legally
inferior status, and where infanticide was permissible. The state
was not restricted in its right to command the citizen. Courts
were not expected to resolve disputes between the citizen and his
government. Conscientious objectors to the war with Sparta, had
any dared to articulate such a position, would have been given
short shrift. Although the Athenians were fond of discussing the
law and the Republic, they did not consider that the individual
had rights which transcended those of the state.

Today the rights of the citizen, seen to be paramount to that of
the state, is a basic assumption of most Americans. Despite the
relentless pressure of the mass media—the talk shows on radio and
TV, the books analyzing every phase of human behavior, and the
popularity of dialogs—Americans do not discuss abstract concepts
like law and justice, the citizen and the state. We simply assume
as an article of faith that the state exists to serve and protect the
individual, that we are not the creatures of the state. During the
decades of the cold war, the totalitarian nations—China and the
Soviet Union and its satellites—were pictured as godless states in
which the individual was subservient, without religious, personal
or political liberty. This was, we were told, the fundamental
difference between democratic America and the communist or
totalitarian world. There is much truth in this oversimplified
dichotomy. A totalitarian government can, through brute force,
intimidation and economic coercion, compel obedience. A dem-

mocratic government is far more limited in the controls it can directly exercise over its citizens. A democratic society is more difficult to govern. It relies not upon the terrorized obedience of subject peoples but upon the willing cooperation of citizens.

I believe that a major reason for the failure of most citizens to cooperate with the government is dissatisfaction with the law itself. We have been promised equal justice under law and we do not have it. We have been promised that under law all conflicts can be resolved justly and fairly. We have ever more conflicts and fewer solutions.

The concept that the law exists to protect the rights of the individual vis-à-vis the state is very new in recorded history. It was not formulated until the eighteenth century. The rights of man, while a popular idea among many intellectuals in Europe, became part of the national ethos only in the United States. It was enshrined in the Constitution; it became part of the American dream, acquiring a sacred, mythic quality.

For two centuries this part of the American dream—equal justice for all under law—was believed to be an integral part of the promise of the American way of life. Even before independence, the refuse of Europe's prisons, its political and religious dissidents sought the fabled freedom of the new world. After the founding of the nation, dissatisfied and aspiring peoples of the Old World, drawn by this promise, struggled to reach these shores. Even after immigration was curtailed in the twentieth century, America continued to proclaim itself the land of promise, the land of equal opportunity. The immigrants found the streets were not paved with gold, but they still believed in the promise. Fulfillment was always just around the corner. Even the black slaves, brought here in chains and in human cargo boats, equated the United States with the promised land across the Jordan River where someday they would be free, free at last.

Equal justice under law, like liberty, was proclaimed throughout the land. But it never existed. The law itself, from colonial days up to the present time, was not structured to provide equal treatment to all people. The law of the United States was not created fresh and new in 1789 with the ratification of the Constitution. The colonists brought with them the law of England, with its age-encrusted practices and procedures and its substantive provisions. The law as it was introduced in the colonies and adopted by the new nation was not based upon the rights of man. It embodied many of the legal inequities developed over the centuries for the sharply stratified class society of England. The law of England as it was imported to the colonies and received by the new nation favored the property owner over the landless, the seller over the buyer, the employer over the employee, the male over the female, the adult over the child, the rich over the poor. The discrimination against nonwhites needs no documentation.

In two hundred years of efforts through legislation, litigation, peaceful protest, violent demonstration and civil war, unequal treatment of people by the law has not been extirpated. True, the poll tax was finally abolished in 1966.[1] The law still favors the landlord over the tenant, as anyone who reads a standard lease can see. Rent strikes are a recent phenomenon. In the '30s sharecroppers refused to be evicted and simply exercised so-called squatters' rights. These illegal acts have slightly moved the law but they have not succeeded in fully redressing the balance. Significantly, it has often been illegal or extralegal activities that have compelled changes in the law. Conduct has changed the law; the law has not changed human behavior. The Roman maxim, *caveat emptor*—let the buyer beware—still governs the law of sales. Neither the federal trade commission nor Ralph Nader has been able to substitute a requirement of full disclosure, warranties of fitness and durability and fair price for the old concept of arm's-length bargaining based upon the fiction of a willing buyer and a willing seller, equally intelligent, sophisticated and financially secure, operating in that mythical arena, the free marketplace.

Employees have through bitter and often violent and illegal struggles wrested from the law the right to organize, the right to strike, the right to speak freely when not on company property, the right to have a hearing before being fired. None of these rights is fully guaranteed by the law, and vast numbers of workers—

public employees, for example—are excluded from the right to strike and the right to engage in political action.

The much publicized women's liberation movement has theoretically provided women with the legal right to equal pay for equal work. Efforts at enforcement have often reduced the salary scale for men rather than raising it for women. The law has not succeeded in prohibiting economic discrimination against women in obtaining mortgages, all kinds of credit, insurance, free choice of employment and many other aspects of life. A woman must have the consent of her husband to have an operation in many states, but the reverse is not true. Under the impetus of the equal rights movement the law has not liberated women but has imposed upon them the burden of supporting their children and husbands, a burden many women in fact have carried for centuries.

Although children can no longer be bound out as apprentices for a term of years—a form of slavery—the law still denies them the right to trial by jury, the presumption of innocence, the right to lead an idle and dissolute life (which is not denied to adults), the right to medical care, treatment and often education suited to their individual capacities. The emotionally disturbed, the handicapped, the retarded and even the intellectually brilliant are in many communities forced to attend the same classes. Refusal to attend school is punishable by imprisonment (although under the fiction of the juvenile court law, the child is not punished, and the prison is called a "training school").

The divergence between the treatment of the rich and poor by the law has been documented again and again. But it is an undeniable fact that access to the machinery of the law requires the payment of fees. These can be waived for the indigent but not for the merely poor. The quality of legal services, despite notable exceptions, is still closely related to the ability to pay. And, of course, the interminable delays favor those who can afford to wait.

Briefly, this is the equal justice that the founding fathers and their descendants have bequeathed to us. It is important to note that not all of the inequities of English law were transported across the Atlantic. Those aspects of the law which had borne heavily upon the early immigrants were specifically eliminated by the Constitution. Georgia was settled largely by prisoners; Maryland and Pennsylvania were populated by Catholics and Quakers, respectively, who had been subjected to cruel religious persecution. Many settlers were impoverished younger sons. Consequently, the old laws of primogeniture, the rights of the landed gentry, the impressment (really servitude) of sailors and soldiers, the imprisonment of debtors, the infamous star chamber proceedings, and the establishment of an official church were specifically outlawed. But the law as it affected daily commercial transactions, prosecution and punishment of criminals, and familial rights and duties was imported with little change. It reflected and still reflects eighteenth-century England with its emphasis on a propertied, male-dominated society that gave little thought to the poor, the young or the old. It was a world in which nature was meant to be dominated by man, the lesser breeds exploited and transformed in the image of the English gentry, an intensely practical community where spiritual and intellectual matters were subservient to the interests of commerce and power. The law reflected this society and the interests of the upper classes and gentry who served as legislators, lawyers and judges.

The great documents of American history—the Declaration of Independence, the Constitution, the Gettysburg Address, Roosevelt's First Inaugural Address—have their genesis in another tradition, that of the eighteenth-century rationalists and reformers, the thinkers who gave the intellectual cachet to both the French Revolution and the American Revolution. The doctrine of the rights of man and the freedom of the individual formed the rhetoric and the promise of America. Historians cannot tell us how many Americans at the time of Independence were moved to act by such concepts. "Taxation without representation" was perhaps only a demagogic battle cry. The notion that each individual actually had unalienable rights which could not be divested by government, the will of the majority or even military might, may have been only a minor factor in the complex circumstances and events leading to national independence. But for later generations, and particularly the new immigrants who arrived in unprecedented numbers throughout the nineteenth century, the ideal of equal justice under law was more than rhetoric. It was more than a dream. It was a promise enshrined in the sacred document of the Constitution.

As the more enterprising members of each new group of immigrants struggled and clawed their way out of the slums and into the sunlight of the middle class, the belief in the American promise was strengthened. For if a "Honey Fitz," an Andrew Carnegie, and even a Hattie Carnegie, a Louis D. Brandeis, and a Ralph Bunche could make it into the mainstream of American life—wealthy, respected, secure—then the way was open to all the other members of minority groups. The French conscript was told that every private carried in his knapsack the baton of a marshal of France. And every American white male Protestant child was taught that he, too, could grow up to be President. Those who remained in the slums of poverty, ignorance and despair were considered simply stupid, lazy or worthless. The promise remained bright and shining. Only its redemption was postponed.

While poets may not be, in Shelley's romantic phrase, the unacknowledged legislators of the world, they often express most forcefully the beliefs and aspirations of their time. In the ages preceding political pollsters and sociological questionnaires, one must turn to the poets to find the common consensus. It is the poets who in each generation delineated the portrait of the ideal America and the self-image of the American.

Walt Whitman, the most American of our poets, celebrated himself—the "simple, separate person." He believed that he had the right, guaranteed by nature and government, to be a free individual, a man with a soul marching on to an assured perfectible future. He also celebrated his country. In the nineteenth century he sang of a confident world, aspiring and improving, a world that would fulfill the promises of the eighteenth century despite the bloodshed and horrors of war and the suffering and poverty that he saw and experienced. Yet in his eyes there was always the dream and, he declared, "It is wonderful."

This is the way he described "The United States to Old World Critics":

> Here first the duties of today, the lessons
>   of the concrete,
> Wealth, order, travel, shelter, products, plenty;
> As of the building of some varied, vast,
>   perpetual edifice,
> Whence to arise inevitable in time,
>   the towering roofs, the lamps,
> The solid-planted spires tall shooting to the stars.

How naïve and quaint he sounds, not the roaring individualist and advocate of free love, but a man bemused by the promise of wealth and order, plenty and growth. This myth of prosperity—a chicken in every pot, two cars in every garage, a color TV and a ranch house in Levittown for every American family—has tantalized and beguiled each generation of Americans until the present.

It was not until the post–World War II era that Americans of all colors, religions, ages and both sexes began seriously to demand that these promises be redeemed. For decades, many Americans had struggled to attain a better material life. They were aware of the injustices and privations that beset them. But these earlier rumblings of discontent had been treated as anomalies, unfortunate episodes provoked by malcontents whose inadequacies placed them outside the mainstream of aspiring Americans who were busily acquiring the products and plenty that Walt Whitman and all the other exponents of the American dream assured them were there and available to the strong and deserving.

History books read by school children gloss over the Whiskey Rebellion, the bloody clashes of coal miners and copper miners, the hardships of the mill workers in New England, the inhuman conditions in the sweatshops of New York City, and the march on

Washington by the unemployed in the early 1930s. All of these movements were put down with force, brutality and an exercise of power of dubious legality. In the aftermath of these struggles legislation was passed enabling workers to unionize, establishing a moratorium on mortgage foreclosures, granting relief to the unemployed, compensation to those injured in the carnage of railroad and factory operations, and limitations on hours of work in factories. The crises were often met with bullets. The promise was sometimes renewed with legislation. But the redemption of the promise was always postponed.

The promise of equal justice under law was also treated as a vague concept having little immediate application to the daily administration of law. Neither legislators nor judges tested the laws or the administration of justice against the constitutional standards of due process and equal protection. The robber barons in their ruthless exploitation of public lands and resources and their employees were not effectively restrained by the law. Just as the courts were used in England to sanction the closing of the commons, forcing the small farmers into the city slums to toil in the factories and mines, so were the courts in the United States used to protect the rich against the poor. Nor were the solid citizens who punished alleged thieves, cattle rustlers, runaway slaves and other malcontents without recourse to the formalities of formal accusation, indictment and trial punished by the law. The law was instead invoked to justify such conduct. The bloody work of vigilantes and lynch mobs is often treated as the illegal work of a few violent people, but the practice could not have persisted for so many years without great popular support. Like other practices which offend contemporary sensibilities, such as child labor, a fourteen-hour work day, slavery and flogging of prisoners, the law provided justification and respectability for them.

A typical example of judicial sanctification of such conduct is found in the writings of Judge Walter Clark. "The cause of lynching," he wrote, "is not a spirit of lawlessness. As a rule, the men who participate in it wish ardently to enforce justice. The truth is society feels that it must be protected against crime.

Whenever society has lost confidence in the promptness and certainty of punishment by the courts, then whenever an offense sufficiently flagrant is committed society will protect itself by a lynching." This was not written in the middle ages or by a judge of an emerging nation of Africa or Asia. It was written in 1894 by a judge of the North Carolina Supreme Court who had sworn to uphold and defend the Constitution of the United States.

Vigilantism and lynching are traditional American ways of expressing dissatisfaction with the law. There have been concerted campaigns to legalize whipping and to castrate convicts. In 1931, the Wickersham Report on "Lawlessness in Law Enforcement" detailed a horrifying picture of police brutality, coerced confessions and prison cruelty. The report on Attica in 1973 did not differ greatly.

The employment of small children in coal mines and factories was legally justified as late as the twentieth century.

Examples of legal justification of brutal and inhuman conduct can be found in every volume of judicial opinions from the English yearbooks dating from the Middle Ages to the present term of court.

Despite this long and accurately chronicled history of the law as the oppressor of the poor and the powerless, the belief in the American promise of equal justice under law persists. As recently as 1963, Martin Luther King poetically reaffirmed this American dream of justice and equality. A listening nation shared his dream because it was our dream, too. It was an inextricable part of the promise of America.

A perceptive foreigner, Gunnar Myrdal, points out that Americans have been deluded by the "rhetoric of moral overstrain." Myrdal recognized the American dilemma of a biracial nation a generation before the problem erupted into violence. The widespread recognition of moral overstrain is long overdue. The source of that overstrain is, I believe, the unrealistic, unrealizable promise of the law.

The turmoil of the sixties did not signify a recognition of this fact. On the contrary, it was an attempt by many dissatisfied segments of society to demand the redemption of the promise of equal justice under law. The chant of "Freedom Now," the upraised clenched fist, the marches on Washington, the demonstrations in the cities and on the college campuses were not the actions of people seeking to overthrow the government. They were instead, whether advisedly or not, attempting to demand what they believed were their Constitutional rights. They wanted the promise of equal justice under law redeemed at once. Equal justice, they believed, included the enforcement of social, economic and intellectual rights for many groups who had not been hitherto protected by the law.

Such groups, led by lawyers and encouraged by the leaders of the bar, judges and legislators turned to the courts in extraordinary numbers to seek resolution of their problems and to obtain legal declarations and implementation of rights involving an extraordinary range of problems and a wide range of people. The belief was fostered that the law and, in particular, the courts were the appropriate forum for the resolution of all these pressing and volatile social, economic, scientific and political issues. The great American dream of equal justice, in accordance with public pronouncements by responsible officials, was about to be fulfilled. Former Chief Justice Earl Warren, in a public address, urged that the legal fight, through litigation, "continue until every man, woman and child in this nation is accorded the human dignity and equality under the law which is the heritage of all of us." The old myth is continually repeated. This is the America that was promised to each of us.

Again and again the public is told that America promises every man, woman and child his day in court when his rights will be speedily protected and equally enforced. We are assured that America promises that the might of the mightiest government the world has known will be utilized to ensure that the decisions of a fair and impartial court are carried out. This is the dogma, the ritual words that are uttered on the Fourth of July, at the induction of new citizens, at graduation exercises, and on Law Day and at bar conferences.

The speakers are not conscious hypocrites. They, too, believe in the dream. Mr. Justice Warren has written opinions which do declare rights for the nonwhite, the poor and the unpopular. Lawyers can point with pride to laws prohibiting discrimination by reason of race, color, religion, national origin and sex. The law permits no restrictions on suffrage because of race, sex or property. The working person has the right to organize. Civil service employees are protected by tenure laws. A large proportion of Americans have the benefits of social security. The poor have welfare rights. All American children are entitled to free public schooling. Higher educational institutions are open to any who wish to attend regardless of background and ability. All persons accused of serious crime are entitled to be represented by counsel and at public expense if they are indigent. These are substantial rights guaranteed by law. No other government has implemented or even declared comparable rights for its citizens.

What the public sees, however, is not the words of judicial decisions and statutes. All of us see a world more sharply divided by race than before the decision of the United States Supreme Court in 1954 abolishing segregated schools. The jails are filled to overflowing with poor people, despite the decisions requiring free legal services for the indigent. The disparity in sentencing between middle-class whites and poor blacks and whites is a national scandal. Every day the press reports cases of leniency to wealthy whites and harshness to poor blacks. For example, on December 16, 1971, the *Philadelphia Bulletin* carried on page 16 this story: A fifty-five-year-old man with a record of fourteen convictions—three for sex offenses—was found guilty of raping a sixteen-year-old girl at knifepoint and placed on probation. On page 19 of the same paper on the same day, the readers learned that a sixteen-year-old boy was given ten to forty years for six rapes.

On January 19, 1972, the readers of the *Philadelphia Bulletin* again learned about equal justice under law. A fifty-seven-year-old successful white lawyer who pled guilty to a $1.5 million fraud was placed on probation, although he could have been sentenced to forty-eight years in prison and fined $85,000. The same day a black girl from a poverty-level family pled guilty to fraud of $105,000. Almost $25,000 was recovered from her. She was sentenced to two to five years in prison.

Similar stories of unequal treatment are to be found in the press of every community almost every day. The public sees that the product of the law is inequality and injustice. The public sees hundreds of thousands of Americans maimed and crippled in accidents awaiting four, five and even ten years for a court hearing to claim the damages due them. Despite laws establishing medicare and medicaid, 30 million ghetto residents do without adequate medical treatment. There is no right to medical services for children.

The gap between the necessities and amenities of life for the rich and the poor widens as the poor become poorer and the rich become richer. The interests of the urban resident are still underrepresented despite the one-man-one-vote judicial mandate; the census regularly fails to count large numbers of the urban poor. Children are still jailed for noncriminal acts. The mentally ill and the aged and the young are still legally committed to institutions as horrible as those described by Dickens. Solitary confinement of prisoners, outlawed in England at the turn of the century, continues in the United States. The environment deteriorates. Products are misbranded and unsafe. Political dissenters are spied on and excoriated. Americans see the failure of the law to resolve the important issues that divide the nation, destroy lives, and corrupt the processes of government.

It was the belief in the American promise of equal justice that welded a multiplicity of peoples into this extraordinary nation. That faith is dead. Anthony Lewis, while paying devout lip service to the efficacy of law, recognizes the problems that flow from the loss of faith. He writes: "A society without the cohesion of shared beliefs, with little deference to rank or tradition, can be an undisciplined society, selfish, even corrupt to judge by what we are learning about American law enforcement these days. Certainly it is a society difficult to govern."

The death of the law not only makes the task of government

exceedingly difficult, it directly affects the lives of millions of Americans. In the United States today law has assumed an extraordinary role in the affairs of the average person. Probably it is the first time in recorded history that law is perceived to be the sword and the shield of every man, woman and child. The rights of the individual have assumed an unprecedented importance which is neither widely understood nor widely accepted. The extension of rights both in a legal and a practical sense to the propertyless white male, the nonwhite male, the female and the child is very recent and still incomplete. But institutions which for centuries dealt with only a limited segment of the population and with only a limited range of subjects are now subjected to enormous strains and pressures by this extraordinary enlargement of the classes and numbers of persons who resort to the legal process and the new and unprecedented issues that the legal system is expected to resolve. The expectations of the entire citizenry are also changed. They demand that the law and all of the machinery of law enforcement provide protection, redress and equal justice for everyone at once. No legal system has ever attempted such an undertaking. Certainly none has remotely approached the realization of such a goal.

Americans, however, do not view the legal system in this broad perspective. We have been educated to believe in the rhetoric. We have been told that the law will correct the ills of society and provide just results for the individual. "There ought to be a law" is not merely a popular catch phrase; we do pass laws on almost every subject. We proceed under the spell of a simplistic faith that we can outlaw war, poverty and racism by legislative fiat. The most complex social problems involving production and distribution of goods, housing and services are expected to be solved not just by legislation but by the courts through litigation on a case-by-case basis. We expect courts and judges to decide these complicated and baffling questions and we further rely upon the public to obey all of the edicts of the courts. Equally naïve is our assumption that individual conduct—sex relations, intellectual development and social motivation—will yield to the force of law even when the law runs contrary to custom and desire.

We see prejudice and bigotry; we respond by making racial

discrimination illegal. There is corruption in the electoral process; we pass laws to control election campaigns. There is a drug problem; we make marijuana illegal. Children play hookey from school; we make truancy a crime. We pass laws regulating morals and private behavior. When the laws do not succeed in restructuring the individual, the family and society, we do not question the ability of law to effect these results. Instead, we blame law enforcement. Judges are accused of being "soft" on crime. The police are corrupt. Government is not "responsive."

Lawyers devise litigation to obtain court rulings and orders to effectuate what legislation has failed to accomplish. And thus we have "centers for responsive law." We cast these complex problems of behavior into the old molds of Constitutional issues, often obscuring the difficult economic, biological and social problems that intractably refuse to conform to the Procrustean bed of the Bill of Rights. We expect the courts to resolve the conflicts between the fiats of the legislatures and the claims of individuals. We expect the courts on the basis of discrete individual cases to establish rules for the operation of innumerable institutions. We ask the courts to decide every issue, from the proper length of a schoolboy's hair to the legality of the war in Vietnam, and to rule upon an incredible variety of social and scientific problems. Every question, from the quantum of care for patients in mental institutions to the ecological dangers posed by the underground explosion of nuclear devices, is litigated in the courts. We expect the courts to run the school systems and the railroads, to reapportion electoral districts, to curb the exercise of executive power, and compel action by the legislatures.

Neither the judges nor the majority of lawyers have been trained to deal with such problems. Professor Paul Freund of Harvard Law School points out that: "Judges frequently aren't equipped by training, staff or facilities to make these sorts of judgments—how to run a school or prison or hospital." Not only are judges ill equipped to handle these problems but also the rules, the forms and the methods of case-by-case litigation are inappropriate for ongoing regulation and management of complex institutions, each of which has its peculiar background, environment and problems. It is inevitable that a legal system which is expected to cope with such problems fails to function.

Judicial activism is criticized by many. The courts themselves, through the doctrine of judicial restraint or abstinence, have sought to avoid deciding many of these vexing questions. But when the legislatures fail to act or the multitude of executive officials and agencies act in ways that appear to be unjust, unreasonable or unauthorized, the citizen has only these options: protest, disobedience or litigation. Protest may give psychic satisfaction, but people are increasingly disillusioned by the futility of writing letters, conducting peaceful picketing, and engaging in demonstrations that may become violent and dangerous. Disobedience may lead to jail. The choice that is continually urged upon the public is resort to the law for redress.

In response to these pressures, the law is undergoing many changes. The Constitutional amendment giving suffrage to eighteen-year-olds is a dramatic example of public responsiveness to changed conditions. The United States Supreme Court decision striking down laws prohibiting abortion during the early months of pregnancy illustrates judicial responsiveness to a changing social climate. But the updating of the law in most areas is not accomplished by a single dramatic law or decision. It is a matter of slow and often inconsistent accretion, amendment and interpretation of existing law.

The notion that groups of individuals—unconnected by blood or property—may have common rights is also in a tentative and exploratory stage. The parameter of these rights is being pushed vigorously to encompass not only property and person but intangibles like aesthetic pleasures—silence, birdsong, visual and olfactory delights, cultural and intellectual satisfactions, and the protection of the physical environment and the social community. The social revolution is altering the legal status of the poor, the female, the black, the child and the old. Welfare is no longer considered a voluntary charity by the state but a legal entitlement. Women have the right to compel the government to take affirmative action to ensure their fair share of the good jobs and the advanced educational opportunities. The "color-blind" equality of the law is challenged and changed by color consciousness. The gray revolution of the elderly is also making inroads on the doctrine of equal treatment in public utilities and public facilities. Some have proclaimed that this is the "Century of the Child." His preferences as to parental custody, care, schooling and medical treatment are beginning to receive legal recognition. The relationships of the individuals in these classes to each other and to the dominant white middle-class male as well as to societal institutions have been radically and irreversibly changed.

All people now expect and demand not merely order, wealth and products—the desiderata and promise of Walt Whitman's America—but a desirable environment and greater options for different life-styles. Neither a guaranteed income nor a guaranteed job will suffice. There is a demand for the right to satisfaction and challenge in work, not just the right to subsistence. There is a demand for the right to choose whether or not to bear a child, whether or not to be bound to the middle-class standard of the nuclear family with the working father, the homebound wife, and the docile child in school. There is a demand for the right of the child to compel the school to adapt to his needs and desires rather than for him to conform to the standards of the school. The stability of family, neighborhood, schools, political institutions, industry and economy and government has been shaken by these cataclysmic changes in the shape of the American dream.

A society that provides for all and protects all in the exercise of these mutually conflicting individual and group desires is the new American dream. It is the new unrealized and unarticulated promise poured into the old bottles of eighteenth-century concepts and institutions. These symbiotic revolutions, social and legal, are having profound and disturbing effects, not only on the social order but also on the law and the administration of justice.

The mails are flooded with people writing to their legislators. Tens of thousands of citizens have peacefully marched to Washington, to their state capitols and to their city councils exercising their Constitutional rights "peacefully to assemble, and to petition the government for a redress of grievances." After decades of marching, meeting and petitioning, the citizenry has a sense of futility and powerlessness in coping with the problems that beset the nation. There is a temptation to look for scapegoats and panaceas, to seek an easy way out. As Rollo May points out, "Powerlessness corrupts."

Powerless people are abandoning the attempt to deal rationally with their problems. Nowhere is this more evident than in the law. Despite the emphasis on innovative ideas, experimental plans and pilot projects, there are few serious and comprehensive plans for changing the law—substantively or procedurally. Instead both scholars and the public naïvely rely upon the power of the law. They expect the overworked legal system, utilizing archaic and ineffective methods of litigation, to restructure society. Consequently, the courts have become the exhausted battlefield of a nation undergoing severe social, philosophical and economic dislocations. In this dimly understood struggle, the failures of the legal system are accentuated and have far-reaching effects upon the viability of the state. In other nations, the failures of the legal system are viewed simply as bureaucratic bungling, inefficiency or corruption. They do not also undermine the government or the social order.

The slow death of the law by attrition in the United States has inevitably followed from these profound changes in the expanded class of people who assert legal rights, and from the proliferation of these new rights without the alteration or reorganization of the methods of adjudicating these questions, framing decisions, and enforcing the orders of the courts; in a word, without changing the legal structure that is to implement and enforce the realization of this revised American dream.

This excessive and unrealistic expectation of institutions is a common American trait. A *New York Times* editorial comments: "The American people chronically expect too much of their schools. When society is in trouble, education is asked to furnish the cure, instantly and without much cost in money or reform.

These high hopes spring in part from an ingrained idealism: but they are also raised deliberately by those who want to avoid the hard questions involved in effective social, political and economic change." At least with respect to the school system there is a widespread awareness of its failings. Teachers, administrators, specialists, and the public are seeking answers. Many make radical suggestions to deschool America or to create alternative free schools. Such proposals may or may not have validity with respect to the educational system. The United States, however, can neither abolish the legal system nor establish alternative people's courts. Unless the American people abandon the concept of individual liberty within an ordered society, government must continue to provide some means for the peaceable resolution of private disputes, for the protection of the lives and property of all people, and for limitations on the power of the state.

While there is widespread dissatisfaction with the legal system, criticism has not been so pervasive and searching as that with respect to the educational system. Disparate shortcomings have been attacked without recognition of the wider problem. Often such studies have done more to obscure than enlighten. To accuse the Supreme Court of inflicting a perhaps mortal wound upon itself by an unpopular decision ignores the fact that there have been many bitterly hated and divisive decisions in the past. The causes of the death of the law are more complex and deep-rooted. There has been little serious study of the substantive laws that cause so much dissatisfaction or the procedures that are costly, time-consuming and result in intolerable delays, backlogs of untried cases, and prisons filled with poor people awaiting their day in court.

The failure to make these essential studies is not due to a lack of time or money devoted to legal research. In fact, the amount of so-called legal research is overwhelming. There are more than 364 law journals which publish monthly or quarterly studies on the most minute points of law. New journals are being launched with dismaying frequency. Former Dean Thomas M. Cooley II of the University of Pittsburgh Law School commented: "I have protested vigorously the perfect flood of bilge which emerges from our Law Reviews the country over." [2] But basic research into procedures and legal doctrines that are archaic and obstructive is sadly deficient.

The litigational process itself should be studied to determine if it can be made quicker, cheaper, less cumbersome and essentially fairer. Is it necessary that appellate courts limit their decisions to the specific facts of a particular case rather than deciding principles of broad application? Does the exclusion of certain evidence promote or conceal truth? We proceed on the assumption that the ineffable criterion of "due process of law" is met by holding a hearing in which the parties are represented by counsel. We do not question the qualifications of the tribunal or the counsel or the method by which counsel was selected or imposed upon the parties. We do not ask whether compliance with these formalities is conducive to the discovery of truth or whether the application of law results in fundamental fairness or justice. The requirement of adversary hearings imposes extraordinary burdens on the administration of institutions and on aggrieved individuals. Children are entitled to a due process hearing before suspension from school. Welfare recipients are entitled to a due process hearing before being cut off the relief rolls. The criteria for suspension and the criteria for relief may be grossly unfair, but if a hearing is held, due process is satisfied. Can the facts be adduced more easily and expeditiously by some other procedure? No one explores these problems.

Nor do we ask whether the enforcement of a court order entered in accordance with the required formalities will create more or less hardship and disorder, whether it will afford the affected people fairer treatment or merely lend an imprimatur of legality to arbitrary action. The numerous injunctions in labor disputes which have been deliberately flouted, often with the approval of vast numbers of citizens, and the court orders which have been flouted by school districts with the encouragement of the public have certainly weakened public respect for law.

In an attempt to cope with the overwhelming numbers of cases, courts have engrafted upon the ancient legal structure the methods of business (administrative officers), the concepts of sociology (compilation of statistics) and the hardware of technology (the ubiquitous computer). But the substance and procedures of the law remain relatively unchanged. What the substantive law should be, what questions the litigational process should be expected to solve, what changes are required in substance, procedure and personnel, what reasonable boundaries to the legal system should be delineated, and what alternative and viable methods should be provided for society to deal with those issues and conflicts which are beyond the ambit of the law are urgent problems besetting and weakening the structure of society and government.

These are basic and difficult questions. The answers will require a thorough revision of the legal system and the creation of new mechanisms to cope with problems that cannot be solved by courts and legislatures. Moreover, the input of physical and social scientists, economists and philosophers will be needed to determine the national aspirations and the ability of the environment, industry, technology and people to achieve an approximation of the new American dream. The purpose of asking and answering these questions is to make possible the realization of the promise of justice, of security, of freedom from want and curable illness, of a safe and aesthetically satisfying environment, of self-fulfillment through meaningful and satisfying work and leisure.

Obviously, no single book can provide answers to these questions. No single individual, even with extensive experience as defense counsel, prosecutor and judge, can adequately examine the many-faceted problems of the legal system and certainly not the broader social and economic implications. What one person can do is to provide a picture of the operations of the legal system in civil and criminal cases, and its effects on rich and poor litigants, on public and private issues.

One can point out the evident failure of the system in its entirety and in each of its parts to function so that a reasonably just result is obtained most of the time. One can demonstrate the need for fundamental and far-reaching changes and suggest the direction and thrust of those changes. No one can write a blueprint for a new legal structure and new laws and procedures. First, public awareness of the need for change is required. And then the careful thinking and analyses of experts in all fields of human behavior, physical and social sciences, economics and politics, and especially philosophy and ethics. Only through the cooperation and intelligent hard work of all these disciplines can a legal order be reconstituted that will redeem the promise of equal justice under law for everyone.

PART II

This section of the book provides a picture of the operations of each of the various parts of the legal structure and the roles and problems of the principal classes of functionaries. It does not present a statistical analysis. Accurate national figures are rarely available. Even when they are reasonably correct, they provide little understanding. In a computerized age, we are overwhelmed with numbers and lose sight of their significance. As it is easier to comprehend the death of one human being than the death of 6 million, so it is easier to understand injustice visited on one individual or one family than on hundreds of thousands. Therefore, this section presents a descriptive account of the day-to-day workings of our legal system. It shows how the legislature, the courts, the police, the lawyers and the judges are caught up in a system that fails to provide fair and just treatment for many of those on whom it operates. It also reveals the destruction of the law as a viable institution by the very process of law. The inevitable disillusionment and loss of faith by those caught up in the mazes of the legal system is revealed as the product of law in action.

> *Just because one case was right don't mean the system is right.*
>
> Cassius Clay
>
> *Something has happened to our system of responses. Troubled times have left a psychological mark on people.*
>
> Arthur Burns, Chairman of the Federal Reserve Board

3: The System

Anna Esposita called me in tears. "Judge, he beat me up again last night. My front tooth is broken. I'm so sore I can't get dressed. He just left the house or I couldn't phone you. Help me."

My impulse was to issue a bench warrant for Tony Esposita, have him picked up by the police and put in jail. A few nights behind bars would cool his hot temper and give Anna a chance to recuperate. But while I believed Anna, for both Anna and Tony had appeared before me in court only a few days before, there was no evidence properly adduced upon which I could legally act. A warrant for Tony's arrest must be sworn out before a magistrate. Then Tony will be brought to court. He will be entitled to bail that he can afford to pay. Then he will be free to return home until his case comes up for trial weeks later. Meanwhile he will let out his temper on Anna again. She will be lucky to escape this time with a broken tooth and a few bruises.

Anna is not the only person frustrated by the requirements of the law and denied protection and redress. Every day in countless courtrooms judges see situations which cry out for action which the law forbids. The mass media regularly report frustrations and injustices resulting from the deficiencies of the legal system: The following was reported in a monthly magazine:

Here's another lesson in how our legal system protects us. [Emphasis added.]

On January 29th, 1971, Pat Saffici came home to her Northeast Philadelphia apartment to discover that her husband Larry had skipped town with their two-year-old son Chris and $18,000 from their joint bank account. Not surprisingly, she tried to find them.

First she asked the cops. Larry was himself an ex-cop who retired in 1969. Because he had an injured index finger he had been collecting over $300 a month as a disability pension since he retired. The cops told Pat they didn't know where Larry was. But they did have one clue: his pension checks, which were being sent to the home of Larry's parents in Olney, were still being cashed even though Larry had disappeared.

Next Pat asked Larry's parents. They insisted they didn't know where Larry was.

Next Pat went to the District Attorney's office. They got a court order prohibiting Chris from being taken out of the U.S. without his mother's consent. But this order was impossible to enforce, because the State Department refused to revoke Larry's or Chris's passport. After all, Larry hadn't broken any law. All he had done was go somewhere with his own son and his own money.

Next Pat tried the courts. She filed suit against Larry on the theory that the son and the money belonged to her, too. The court issued four subpoenas ordering Larry to appear, but since nobody knew where he was, he never received them. But somehow he kept on receiving his police pension checks.

Finally, last December, the court ordered the city to hold

Larry's pension checks in escrow until he appears. But the City Solicitor's office kept right on sending him pension money until March. This time the money was sent to center city attorney Burton Satzburg, who represents Larry and his parents. Where was Satzburg forwarding the money? Satzburg refuses to say, and he insists he has no idea where Larry is hiding with Chris. "I don't want to know," he says.

Because he never answered his subpoenas, Larry is now legally a fugitive. He could have been arrested last month, when he was scheduled to appear in the police surgeon's office for a pension physical examination. He never showed up, but he wouldn't have been in any great danger if he had; the pension board neglected to tell the DA's office about Larry's examination.

After three years, Pat still hasn't seen or heard from her husband or her son, who would now be five.

Moral: Ours is a just and compassionate society that protects everybody, even someone who runs off with his wife's child and money.[1]

Lawyers and judges as well as magazine editors are aware of the urgent need to update the law so that the average citizen can receive prompt relief in the countless conflicts that arise in our complex society. But the enactment and repeal of laws is not within the jurisdiction of lawyers and judges. This is the responsibility of the legislatures—the Congress, the fifty state legislative bodies and the innumerable local councils.

Any discussion of the legal system should logically begin with the legislature.

The system, as I use the term, is the entire legal structure of the United States. It includes the laws and the agencies of government that enact, interpret and enforce the law. It is the organization of society under which all of us live and upon which we must rely for subsistence, protection and freedom.

This entire structure depends upon the lawmakers. It is their task to enact new laws to meet current problems, to repeal obsolete laws, and to modify unsatisfactory substantive and procedural laws. The Founding Fathers, who were eighteenth-century rationalists, conceived of government as a system of checks and balances, each part having a defined and limited function. The legislature was to enact the law, the judiciary to construe the law, and the executive to administer it. Although these neat distinctions have become blurred, essentially it is still the legislature that determines what the law shall be.

The legislatures decide what actions will be prohibited, what acts shall be crimes. They establish the penalties. Legislatures also decide what conduct shall be subject to civil restrictions and prohibitions, what conduct shall not be regulated, and what acts shall be entitled to protection as legal rights and the measure and mode of redress for infringement of those rights. Within the sketchy framework of the Constitution, legislatures establish the numbers of courts and judges, their salary and tenure, their jurisdiction and the procedures that must be followed. Although there are common-law crimes, common-law concepts of individual and property rights, and procedures which derive from centuries-old practice in the English courts of law and chancery, most of these matters have been modified or confirmed by statutes. With few exceptions, American law is the Constitution and the body of statutes enacted by the Congress and the state legislatures.

Congress is the most conspicuous legislative body in the United States. But every state has a legislature. Most municipalities, townships and counties have some form of lawmaking body. And hybrid governmental agencies such as water and sewer authorities, school boards, power commissions and redevelopment agencies have rule-making powers that often have the effect of creating law. Many departments and agencies, long considered to be part of the executive branch of government, such as the treasury and agriculture departments, through their rule-making power, have broad legislative jurisdiction.

The number of legislators in the nation is legion. The United States Congress is composed of 100 senators and 435 congressmen. In the fifty state legislative bodies there are a total of 7,345 members. New York State has 207 members. Only Nebraska has a unicameral body and it has 40 members. Most of these legislators are part-time public servants. Few state assemblymen and state senators are paid enough to enable them to give up their law practices or businesses and devote all of their time to their legislative duties. Moreover, they must spend a great deal of time and energy satisfying their constituents and seeing that they get re-elected. This is also true of congressmen who, in many districts, must campaign almost continuously. In the event of defeat, they must have a means of livelihood to which to return.

Even if the legislators were able to work uninterruptedly on legislation alone, this task would defy the most able, the best-educated and most diligent of people. In our highly complex, technological civilization no one person or group of people can understand the intricacies of banking, the problems of the farmers both big and small, the regulation of labor unions, the needs of the urban poor, mass transportation, the financing and setting of minimum standards for an educational system that must provide for the backward, the emotionally disturbed, the average, the talented and the disinterested and fit all of them to survive in a rapidly changing society. Even a relatively small question like the marketing of milk requires skilled, educated, expert advice and time for consideration. The problems of foreign policy and military and foreign aid with which the Congress must grapple are awesome. Congress does not have the time to devote to the drafting and consideration of a multitude of laws necessary for the domestic welfare. In a world of continuing foreign crises, fiscal turmoil, racial conflict, natural disasters and political friction, it is highly unlikely that Congress can or will in the near future devote sufficient attention to any of these pressing problems.

The enactment of most laws that affect the conduct of the individual citizen is, under the Constitution, entrusted to the state legislatures. These bodies have proved singularly inept. De Toqueville noted that state government was the weakest and most corrupt level of government, being distinctly inferior to the federal government and municipal governing bodies. But responsi-

bility for the basic law that affects the lives of most citizens—from
the water they drink, the air they breathe, the quality of merchandise they buy, and most of the crimes and penalties—is entrusted to the states. The legislatures of most states have failed to
enact appropriate legislation to protect the individual and the
community. Even so basic a matter as the criminal code has not
been substantially revised in the past ten years by most of the large
states. Herbert Spencer noted that law, being slow to change, is
often a government of the living by the dead. In our rapidly
changing social order, when the individual is subject to future
shock by the world about him, the mortality rate of law increases.

The difficult relationships between the core city and the satellite
suburbs have been almost totally ignored by the state legislatures.
Except for voluntary cooperative ventures in transportation and
other utilities and police protection, the suburbs resist contributing
to the costs of the cities' cultural institutions, their large low-income populations and, of course, their school problems. Daily
problems of installment sales, credit, warranties, landlord-tenant
relationships could be dealt with more effectively by up-to-date
comprehensive legislation than by rent strikes and the resulting
litigation, repossession of merchandise and litigation over alleged
defects and credit for payments already made. Compensation for
automobile accidents, development and payment for health-
delivery systems, as well as legal services for moderate-income
groups are problems now under consideration by many legislatures. They are not easy to solve. Legitimate competing interests
require recognition and appropriate adjustment.

No-fault insurance has received great notoriety as a panacea for
overcrowded court calendars, long delays between injury and
payment, high legal fees, and expensive insurance premiums. A
judge who hears numerous cases of rear-end collisions in which
liability of the striking vehicle is clear and the injuries undisputed
but in which the insurance company has refused to make any offer
of settlement for *ten* years until the case is called for trial, can only
wonder how no-fault will be enforced without litigation. Surely the
present system is unsatisfactory. But many of the remedies pro-

posed are equally defective. The almost insurmountable difficulties of devising and drafting necessary and appropriate laws by our legislatures as they now function must be recognized. Despite many strenuous and conscientious efforts, adequate legislative solutions have not yet been devised.

The legislative branch of government is often ignored in treatises on law, which place great emphasis on the courts and judicial decisions. But it must be remembered that the courts are bound to uphold and enforce the acts of the legislature, regardless of their wisdom or relevance, unless an act violates the Constitution. The responsibility of the legislature is twofold: to enact laws that are needed and to amend or repeal those that are obsolete. In a period of rapid social, economic and philosophic change, keeping the laws current is a difficult if not monumental task. Few legislative bodies have succeeded. Obsolete and unworkable notions of personal morals, family and social customs are perpetuated in the criminal laws of most states. Outmoded economic theories also underlie many regulatory statutes. These laws remain on the books. When they are enforced they breed hostility and resentment. When they are violated with impunity, the habit of lawless behavior is reinforced.

While essential and critical problems are ignored by the various legislatures, the quantity of new laws is overwhelming. The Ninety-first Congress alone during the Second Session enacted 335 public laws consisting of 1,384 pages. The number, length and obscurity of language of statutes, ordinances and regulations constitute a barrier between the citizen and his government.

State and local legislatures also pass new statutes at every session. Many create new prohibitions and regulations governing the ordinary conduct of Americans. They also provide penalties. The number of possible crimes proliferates at an alarming rate. The average citizen often may be unaware of many of the laws he violates. Frequently they are so long and so complex as to make compliance extremely difficult. A congressional staff study of welfare laws made public by United States Representative Martha W. Griffiths points out that the complexity of the laws makes compliance almost impossible. "Local welfare agencies are supposed to follow directions which may fill a bookshelf four feet wide," she observed. The extreme obscurity of the tax laws permits evasion by the clever and baffles the unsophisticated. Professor Boris I. Bittaker of Yale Law School pleaded with the House Ways and Means Committee for simplification of the tax laws, particularly those provisions that millions of ordinary individuals have to use. The tax laws have not been simplified. On the contrary, each new revenue law adds to the complexity and difficulty of compliance. For the poor and untutored there is little alternative to illegal conduct when compliance with the law is so difficult and so expensive. Complexity favors the wealthy and sophisticated who can afford to hire specialists who will find, if not devise, loopholes and special benefits.

The difficulties and expense for the average citizen in complying with the law inevitably promote lawlessness. Even a street-corner vendor, if he wishes to obey all the laws and ordinances governing such a small and simple enterprise, requires a lawyer. It has been observed many times that private individuals cannot secure justice without the aid of a professional to advise and represent them. Most people cannot afford such advice. Through ignorance and poverty they become law violators.

Since there are so many offenses that have no taint of immorality other than mere violation of a statute, breaking the law has almost ceased to be frowned upon. In a variant of Gresham's Law, the increase of crimes of no moral guilt has driven out the sense of moral guilt for all violations of law. The authority of law in the ordering of the social structure and in disputes between individuals and individual government has crumbled with serious consequences to the stability of society. In the field of criminal law, the widespread indifference to the force of law and the absence of a sense of sin is critical.

An equally serious factor contributing to the death of the law is the absence of legislation governing hundreds of difficult and continuing problems in American life. The law does not declare rights or remedies in innumerable situations. For example, who owns the information in a data bank—the person who provided the raw facts, the computer operator whom he employed, the company which owns or leases the computer? Who has a right to the enjoyment of a public park—the elderly people who sit on the benches, the children noisily playing ball, the young people singing and strumming guitars, the dog owners walking their pets, the vendors of homemade belts and jewelry? Who has a right to the use of beaches—local taxpayers, resident lessees, nonresidents, oil companies drilling under the continental shelf? Which interests should have priority? The legislature has not answered these questions.

The lack of clear, positive law governing the rights and duties of individuals, corporations and government causes unrest and encourages predatory activity. In the absence of a public policy stated by the legislature, people are guided by their own profit and convenience. Where there is no clearly applicable law, there is no standard of behavior. In these relatively new situations of conflict, there are no customs or habits providing an established and commonly agreed upon mode of behavior or set of priorities.

Most of our daily acts are governed by custom or usage. We rise in the morning, eat breakfast, go to work, return home at night. Middle-class adults and children live structured lives with time for work, for play, and a limited range of options. We do not decide a priori each day whether or not to go to work. We do not ask ourselves searching questions as to the value of labor or the greater good in playing golf on a nice day. If we see a car on the street with the key in the engine, we are conditioned not to consider seriously taking this beautiful and desirable object even though it is readily available.

If every act of daily life required a conscious weighing of values, a calculation of the risk of losing one's job by not going to work against the pleasure of a few extra hours sleep, a reassessment of whether returning home to the family would be more pleasurable than a night on the town, few people would be able to function at all. We would either be paralyzed by indecision or tergiversate wildly from one fancied delight to another. Especially in a sophisticated urban society, there must for survival be a consensus as to behavior. Can each individual decide for himself whether to drive on the left or the right side of the road or perhaps in the middle?

In a closed society with strong patterns of social conduct like Japan, the habits of courtesy, of recognition of status and mutuality of obligation, and observance of amenities make possible life in densely crowded conditions. Americans do not have this strong habit of behavior. Each generation of immigrants has discarded the old ties in favor of an open, mobile and strongly individualistic society. The ligament to bind these diverse peoples and interests into a viable community in the United States is obedience to law. Since we have become a nation of scofflaws we have no effective means to control selfishness, violence and destruction.

Obsolete and inappropriate laws can be ignored without too much risk to the individual. But a pattern of ignoring these relatively unimportant laws destroys the habit of obedience to law and promotes scofflawism. Even though individuals know that they are breaking the law, doing so with reluctance, they have no means of repealing old laws or creating new ones to govern changed, unprecedented conditions or to establish agreed upon principles to resolve new conflicts. When the legislatures fail to act, the public has only two choices: scofflawism or obedience to a foolish or archaic rule.

Members of an industry can adopt their own code and agree to be bound by the decisions of an arbitrator whom they select. Many industries and labor unions, frustrated by the failure of the law to provide prompt and adequate relief, have established these extralegal methods of creating their own rules and their own substitute courts. But such alternatives are not available to most people to solve their daily problems. Nor can government agencies change their jurisdiction, their budgets and their powers without legislative authorization. Consequently federal, state and local governments are often paralyzed by the failure of the appropriate legislative body to enact needed laws fairly and promptly. A dictator can act by fiat, but the President cannot do so except in extraordinary situations. Nor can a governor, a mayor or a county commissioner.

To take an obvious example, a city mayor or a state governor cannot order people to pay the taxes necessary to run the government unless there is a law imposing taxes. The legislature must enact a tax statute or ordinance or there is no obligation to pay. If the legislature fails to act, there are payless paydays, no welfare checks, and a drastic reduction of public services. The enactment of new laws and the repeal of old ones is an ongoing process in American government. But the legislatures during the past three decades have not kept up with the changing and expanding need for new laws. Some of the issues the legislatures must act upon are as old as mankind: crime and punishment, enforcement of promises, payment for goods, invasion of property. Others deal with new, uncharted questions involving cybernetics, outerspace, computers and nuclear energy.

Many state legislatures have recognized the public interest in the operations of government and have enacted "right to know" laws giving the citizens the right to attend meetings of government agencies, examine their minutes, and review their budgets. The United States Congress and a number of states have adopted laws preserving open space, wilderness areas and seashores, and providing economic incentives to discourage overbuilding and development of farm lands. Some states have abolished such "victimless crimes" as homosexuality between consenting adults. The right of retarded children and emotionally disturbed children to attend special public school classes has also been established by law in some states. Aesthetic and cultural needs have been recognized by Congress and also by states which appropriate monies for education, research, symphony orchestras, ballet companies and theaters. Several municipalities have enacted ordinances requiring a percentage of the cost of every building to be devoted to works of art. Medicare, imperfect though it may be, is an extraordinary and humanely motivated piece of legislation for a nation which only a generation ago considered social security to be a step toward socialism if not communism. But the needs and problems proliferate faster than the legislatures can act. The failure of Congress to act effectively on domestic problems is less conspicuous but no less dangerous than its failure in foreign affairs. In part, the legal profession is at fault. During the sixties, it was fashionable to rush to the courthouse for the answer to every problem. Lawyers sought to change the law through litigation and by means of landmark cases to restructure society. The legislative process was slighted if not altogether ignored.

The public and the press also have a tendency to overlook the legislative branch of government. The executive—the President, the governor or mayor—is a single individual. It is easier to praise or to blame a person with a name, a face and a public image than a large group of individuals with conflicting ideas, attitudes and policies. Similarly, a judge as a single individual or a court composed of nine easily identified people can be held responsible for specific decisions they have made. The Congress and the state legislatures are too large and too diverse easily to be held accountable for unwise action or inaction.

When the public cannot find a person on whom to pin the blame for the ills of society, it is fashionable to blame "the system." This word has become a popular catch-all phrase. It permits ventilation of anger, hostility or hopelessness without requiring identification of the parties responsible or the acts causing the trouble. It is a dangerously mindless excuse for irresponsibility and inaction.

Look at a few examples of the use of the "system" as a convenient scapegoat for errors and injustices. Sixty percent of the protesters at the 1971 May Day demonstration blamed the system not only for war but for repression, poverty and injustice. A Roper survey reports that nearly two-thirds of the people questioned felt that "things have gotten off on the wrong track." A Yankelovich opinion poll reveals that "six out of ten Americans believe that this society is democratic in name only." The pollsters and scholars are beginning to document what the man in the ghetto, the child in the juvenile detention center, and the newspaper reporter have known for a long time.

William J. Van den Heuvel, chairman of the New York City Board of Correction, when questioned about the suicide of a mentally disturbed prisoner declared: "This was the responsibility not of any individual, but of a system that doesn't work right." The system was also blamed for the plight of a fearless young doctor who fought the owner of the town's major company at the polls and won. But then the doctor was not only accused of rape but was also brutally beaten. His assailants were acquitted by a jury trial. Investigators Schuck and Wellford, reporting this sorry episode, entitled the story: "Democracy and the Good Life in a Company Town, St. Mary's, Georgia: Love it or leave it, *but don't try to mess around with the system.*" [2]

Former Attorney General John Mitchell, in speaking of treating alcoholics as criminals declared that, " 'this system' is a distortion of legal processes." He continued, ". . . we cannot blame the police or the courts for the system. . . ." In 1969, John P. Frank, a prominent lawyer and noted critic of American courts, wrote that civil justice "has broken down; the legal system fails to perform the tasks that may be expected of it . . . the collapse is now." As for criminal justice, the President's Crime Commission in 1967 said it "is overcrowded and overworked, undermanned, underfinanced, and very often misunderstood." In a satiric vision of Utopia, Nicholas von Hoffman sees "fractious middle-class children—reconciled to their parents as both generations agree that the system does work after all."

While the system is excoriated as the cause of all our problems, it is seldom defined or subjected to scrutiny. The democratic myth of law making assumes that all legislative bodies, federal, state and local, make conscious and informed decisions, duly reflecting the will of the people as to what rights shall receive legal protection and the manner and nature of that protection. The myth further assumes that such legislative decisions reflect a public consensus as to societal values, economic costs and administrative efficiency. Legal scholars base a vast congeries of jurisprudential theories on this illusory premise.

Professors Guido Calabrese and A. Douglas Melamed declared,[3]

". . . the law not only decides who is to own something and what price is to be paid for it if it is taken or destroyed, but also regulates its sale. . . ." They suggest, for example, that four legal rules govern the control of pollution, i.e., (1) nuisance with injunction, (2) nuisance with damages to the injured, (3) no nuisance but only purchase and sale in free market, and (4) injunction with compensation to the polluter. Using their example of a land-owning polluter, the theory that the law reflects a conscious choice of values and remedies is revealed as utterly fallacious. The professors argue that the law governs and controls a landowner whose use of his property is causing pollution. Take, for example, an apartment house owner whose furnace emits a great deal of sooty smoke. How does the law deal with this every day occurrence?

The professors' first rule is "nuisance with injunction." Without a statute defining the maximum allowable amount of smoke, a furnace is not likely to be considered a nuisance, especially one that has been in use over a period of years. To enjoin the owner from operating the furnace in winter would infringe the rights of the tenants to have heat. To compel the owner to put in a new furnace, at a cost which the rentals would not defray, would deprive the owner of his property. This rule is impractical and scarcely enforceable.

Rule 2—nuisance with damages to the injured. Assuming, for the moment, that the furnace could legally be considered a nuisance, to whom would damages be paid? The neighbors? If so, would it be the landowners or the tenants? Or users of the streets and parks in the vicinity, who are certainly damaged in their enjoyment of public property? A casual passerby? And how are damages to be assessed? Solution 2 creates more problems than it solves.

Rule 3 suggests purchase and sale in the free market. But the free market is a legal fiction. Land use is governed by innumerable haphazardly enacted and conflicting state statutes, local ordinances, and even federal laws governing parks, wilderness, highways, military installations and other federal interests. All of these enactments are subject to individual claims of violation of constitutional rights. Zoning laws may prohibit a factory in a particular location, or a multiple dwelling unit. The owner of property can sell his land only for uses permitted by law. Regulation by the marketplace—willing seller and willing purchaser agreeing upon a price—is subject not only to land-use restrictions but also to all the vagaries of the market, changes in taste or fashion, economic factors such as the availability of financing and the size of this particular market. In no way does the availability of a ready buyer reflect a public consensus as to the law of pollution. The free market is seriously affected by the exercise or threatened exercise of eminent domain.

The fourth control postulated is injunction with compensation to the polluter. In our example, the landlord would be enjoined from using the furnace that emits soot but would be compensated for his economic loss and presumably could then purchase a new and more pollution-free furnace. But who would pay the damages? Should they be measured by the cost of the new furnace (very high) or the value of the old furnace which is depreciated by years of use (very low)? If the latter rule prevailed, the landowner might not be able to replace his furnace. Meanwhile, the tenants have a right to heat regardless of whether the furnace emits excessive smoke.

Clearly, existing law is inadequate to provide a satisfactory solution to this commonplace problem, despite the academic rules which are suggested. In fact, there are few, if any, laws that provide for payment of damages to the public or any members thereof especially inconvenienced by a polluter. There is no overall policy rationally arrived at and embodied in comprehensive legislation to provide a consistent declaration of rights, remedies, penalties and procedures with respect to a land-owning polluter. Even pollution has not been comprehensively defined by legislation. Instead we have a patchwork of zoning laws, condemnation laws, landlord and tenant laws, contract and real estate laws, many of which are in conflict with each other. There is no established order of priority, no determination of the rights or remedies of those inconvenienced by pollution or compensation to those whose property (or money) will be taken in order to abate the pollution.

This haphazard, piecemeal, incomplete legislation is characteristic of the law governing most of our day-to-day problems. It is safe to say that scarcely a single problem of contemporary life has been treated by a reasoned and complete legislative statement defining rights, prohibiting undesirable conduct, establishing penalties, creating remedies, and providing for access to the courts or other agencies for enforcement, and basing its conclusions on an adequate cost/benefit basis.

Whether a law is passed or defeated depends as much on political considerations as on policy. Many legislators do not have the time to read, much less to make a considered decision on, the laws they enact. There are few citizens' groups who undertake the difficult technical task of preparing comprehensive legislation on any subject. Statutes are often drafted by special-interest groups, both selfish and unselfish, which find a legislator willing to introduce their bill.

Perhaps the Uniform Commercial Code is the closest approximation we have to an ideal of reasoned and reasonable comprehensive legislation. It was the product of the labor of twelve hundred lawyers and law professors, with the advice of bankers, brokers and legislators who worked over a period of seven years. Significantly, the drafting of this code was possible because sophisticated, wealthy interests were concerned to have a law governing their operations which was contemporary, certain and uniform. The drafting of the code cost $400,000, which was contributed by charitable foundations. The successful completion of this code and its enactment in forty-nine states (with some modifications) was possible because it did not raise issues of great popular controversy. The need for a uniform law was well understood by large financial interests which did not want to rely upon chance determinations by judges who may or may not understand the problems of finance and by the uneven skills of lawyers representing a wide variety of clients before the courts. Such a powerful consensus backed by adequate funding is not available for most of the problems with which the legislatures must grapple. They improvise, act hastily, or simply do not take action because no organization has researched and drafted the necessary laws.

The failure of the legislatures to act upon many urgent problems gives rise to innumerable disputes that could have been avoided. If a statute clearly declares rights and no Constitutional or moral issue is involved, it is unlikely that the law will be challenged.

The law is clear that after an agreement for the sale of real estate is signed, and before title passes, the risk is on the buyer not the seller. When an agreement is signed the purchaser promptly takes out insurance. Rarely does anyone litigate a loss under these circumstances. On the other hand, the law with respect to loss or damage of a condominium apartment is decidedly unclear. In countless instances a fire in one apartment causes fire or smoke damage in adjacent apartments. Similarly a leak in the plumbing on the twentieth floor will most likely damage the apartments on the nineteenth and eighteenth floors and may, indeed, run through the entire building. Such daily inevitable occurrences are being slowly litigated in the courts on a case-by-case basis. A statute establishing rights and responsibilities would permit people to ensure against liability and avoid loss, irritation, uncertainty and litigation. No moral issue is involved. It really does not matter which party is liable so long as the law is certain. All persons can then protect themselves by obtaining adequate insurance. Sensible people will conform their conduct to what is required without litigation. Where the law is unclear or nonexistent, recourse to litigation is inevitable. These unresolved questions may be decided by the courts on the basis of inappropriate analogy to other laws, or may be governed by obsolete precedents or simply languish undecided for years.

Other problems fester and lead to demonstrations and overt hostility because there is no law applicable to the situation and no access to the courts to obtain a ruling. The conflict over the proposed construction of a gymnasium by Columbia University in an area used by the public erupted in demonstrations and riots. This was an issue that simply did not lend itself to judicial resolution under existing law because none of the protesters had a property interest that was affected and thus lacked standing to bring an appropriate lawsuit. Legislation giving members of the public who will be adversely affected in their enjoyment of life a standing to sue and defining their interests and scope of protection would permit many thorny problems involving the location of highways, housing projects, bars and taprooms to be decided in the courts in accordance with a legislatively determined set of priorities. The failure of the Congress and the state legislatures to provide access to the courts for people with real, although as yet legally unrecognized interests, raises the level of public discontent and dissatisfaction with the law.

The United States Supreme Court declared that the legislatures are "the main guardians of the public interest." Conceptually, under the Constitution they should be. But legislative inaction often plunges the courts into exacerbating litigation. Failure of the state legislatures to enact reapportionment laws decennially as mandated by the Constitution resulted in the famous reapportionment cases. The simplistic rule—"one man, one vote"—has been followed by other decisions clouding the rule and more uncertainty and more dissatisfaction. This is an issue which the courts should not have had to act upon. The Supreme Court finally ruled only when it seemed clear that the state legislatures would not assume their responsibilities.

Failure of state and local legislative bodies to abolish segregated school systems and to require racial integration of the schools has also resulted in slow, laborious and abrasive use of the federal courts to attempt to remedy these refusals to act. Similarly, failure or refusal of legislative bodies to enact laws protecting natural resources, prescribing appropriate penalties for crimes, repealing outmoded criminal statutes and inequitable rules of law has also forced the courts to improvise remedies or to find reasons for failing to grant redress for what are clearly wrongs in a moral, social or economic sense.

In the absence of adequate statutory law, both the citizens and the government resort to the courts for resolution of conflicting laws, interpretation of incongruities and what is called interstitial legislation, that is, judicial decisions to fill the gaps left in the legislation. When the legislatures do act, the results are often so complicated as to defy obedience to law. Interpretation is left to the courts in a multitude of separate and unrelated suits that result in ever more confusion and more litigation. Some litigants, raising social and political questions, use the courts as a forum to educate the public. Lawsuits are reported in the media. Delegations of citizens seeking an audience with a busy congressman or senator do not make headlines.

The courts recognize the untenable position they occupy. In the argument on the school desegregation case in 1953, Mr. Justice Jackson asked one of the attorneys, "Isn't the one thing that is perfectly clear under the Fourteenth Amendment is that Congress is given the power and the duty to enforce the Fourteenth Amendment by legislation?" But then the Justice answered his own question: "I suppose that realistically the reason this case is here is that action couldn't be obtained from Congress."

Effective action has not been obtained from Congress in many other situations. For instance, the pensions of millions of Americans have simply vanished. Over 135 billion dollars of pension funds have been collected by employers virtually without regulation by law or accountability to the employees. Elderly retired employees who have worked for decades for large and small companies in the belief that they were accumulating adequate pensions to sustain them after retirement find that they have no rights and no remedies. The United States Senate Subcommittee on Labor and Public Welfare in a 1972 report (S. Rep. No. 92-634) pointed out that 92 percent of more than 9 million people contributing to employee pension funds on retirement did not qualify for benefits. Aside from the gross inequities and personal hardships, the unjust enrichment of the few managers and the burden on the public in the form of public assistance, consider the disillusionment with law and government of these millions of people, their families and friends. The 1974 Federal Pension Law passed with such fanfare fails to provide security for the majority of the workers for the future. It does nothing to restore the savings of those who have already lost their pensions or to protect those about to retire. One must ask why congressmen and senators (most of whom are protected by federal retirement laws) failed to take any action whatsoever for decades.

Congress has not taken adequate action to provide a unified mass transit system for the nation. Special subsidies are granted to the airlines. The National Highway Act provides the necessary roads for buses. Both airplanes and buses are major sources of air and noise pollution. They use enormous quantities of gasoline, which is in short supply. Railroads, however, are permitted to go into bankruptcy and shut down needed services which, of course, leads to more use of private automobiles, more use of gasoline, and more pollution. These facts are obvious to everyone. But the problems of the railroads are not treated as one national issue requiring a comprehensive plan. Instead each railroad struggles with mounting debts and inefficiencies, under the aegis of a federal judge who is applying the bankruptcy law to a fragment of an essential national resource. The bankruptcy law was enacted to provide relief from debt for overburdened individuals and corporations. It was never contemplated that it be used to "bail out" a national industry like the railroads or to provide a preference for investors over users. The public interest is only tangentially affected by the usual bankruptcy. But in the cases involving the railroads, the needs of the passengers, the shippers, and the public at large are less well represented and less well protected than the interests of creditors. Because there is no legislation providing a sensible and appropriate means of dealing with the financially distressed railroads, the courts are proceeding under an inadequate law devised for other enterprises, other circumstances, and other times.

Most thoughtful people acknowledge the need for strict gun-control laws to stop the carnage on the streets, but Congress has failed to enact laws prohibiting the shipment of handguns in interstate commerce. Few states, especially those with severe violent-crime problems, have passed any meaningful laws prohibiting ownership of the "Saturday night special" handguns with which much street crime is committed.

There is no end to the need for updated, imaginative and practical laws establishing a national set of priorities and rights and remedies for individuals and organizations in the numerous situations of unresolved conflict in our social, economic and political order.

J. D. Hodgson, former Secretary of Labor, points out that the nation is forced to deal with railroad strikes under the 1926 Railway Labor Act, which is totally inadequate to meet contemporary needs. Neither the state legislatures nor the Congress have grasped the nettle of controlling strikes by public employees. The rights of perhaps one-eighth of the nation's work force is involved. So are the needs and rights of all the citizens. With respect to this problem as well as many others, there is a poverty of concepts and remedies. We are attempting to govern life in the 1970s with the obsolete theories and laws of the 1930s.

Legislative blindness or irresponsibility or incapacity leaves unanswered a host of critical questions. The Senate leadership complains of their inability to get the senators to attend sessions and enact legislation. Majority Leader Mike Mansfield declared, "The record we have is abominable and the situation is horrible." When Congress timidly acknowledged the prevalence of consumer dissatisfaction and proposed legislation giving consumers increased access to the courts, Chief Justice Burger protested that this would increase the burden on the courts. That, of course, is true. But what is the alternative? The options of the public are limited. If they lack appropriate laws to protect their interests, they will resort to the courts. If relief is not quickly available there, then they will act outside the law. The courts in a real sense are the last line of defense against anarchy and lawlessness when the legislature fails to provide appropriate remedies.

Much of the criticism of the courts for "legislating" arises from this willful failure of the legislative bodies to enact badly needed laws. As Roscoe Pound, former Dean of the Harvard Law School, pointed out, for the courts "to interpret an obnoxious rule out of existence rather than to meet it fairly and squarely by legislation is a fruitful source of confusion." It is also a cause of public disregard for "the law."

Courts cannot write laws or rules and regulations. That is the function of the legislature. Both congressmen and state legislators, many of whom are practicing lawyers, are far more knowledgeable in practical matters than the appellate courts. They are also in a position to observe the functioning of a new law and to amend it if it fails to achieve the desired end. An appellate court, which gleans much of its information from reports and studies, not first-hand observation, must wait for another suitable case in which to modify or overrule its prior decision if it proves to be unwise. Moreover, rapid reversals of court decisions create confusion and promote more litigation. When the public sees that decisions have a brief, ephemeral life, faith in the certainty and inevitability of law is eroded.

Courts rarely are able to establish a comprehensive scheme of regulation applicable to a broad range of variations in factual situations. This is, however, precisely the function of a statute. It establishes an abstract set of rules for dealing with a certain class of problems, setting forth not only legal rights but also remedies and procedures for enforcement. The legislature can take into consideration the social and economic ramifications of an entire problem, the costs of compliance, the necessity for allowing the affected industry, organizations or individuals time to adjust to the new rules. It can also set appropriate penalties for disobedience. In the absence of legislation a court can act only on an ad hoc basis. Usually the courts are limited to cases raising allegations of deprivation of Constitutional rights. Of necessity, a court deciding a specific case deals piecemeal and in limited fashion with a wider problem, considering only the limited issue presented by the chance operations of litigation. The facts of the particular case presented to the court may be anomalous. Yet the decision arrived at, not by a study of social needs or societal values but of a particular dispute, will become the law not only of that case but a precedent in countless other cases.

The Sunday blue-law cases illustrate the haphazard, aleatory methods of litigation in deciding questions of wide applicability. Blue laws, deriving from early eighteenth-century piety, which prohibit worldly employment and pleasure on the Sabbath, have not been repealed in many states. They were seldom enforced until the growth of shopping centers that stayed open on Sunday began to cut into the revenues of center-city stores. Then the old blue laws were dusted off and utilized to protect the income of the declining city stores and the tax returns of the hard-pressed cities. The first case to reach the United States Supreme Court involved a large discount store in the suburbs. It was decided on the First Amendment issue of establishment of religion, although real social and economic problems were involved in the case. Policy judgments between growth of suburban sprawl and protection of core cities, convenience of shoppers as opposed to rights of the general public to one noncommercial day in the week, government regulation of business and the rights of entrepreneurs should have been made. Religion had nothing to do with the real interests involved.

The parties, however, brought their action under the First Amendment. The discount store claimed that enforcement of the Sabbath as an official day of rest was an unconstitutional "establishment of religion." The center-city merchants were not parties to the case. Their position was upheld by the state and local governments, which feared the loss of tax revenues. They claimed that maintaining a day of rest was a secular matter, a proper concern for the health, welfare and peaceable enjoyment of the life of the community.

The Court held that the discount house could not prove that its religious rights under the provision of the First Amendment guaranteeing "free exercise" of religion were violated. Obviously a commercial corporation does not have a religion. Therefore, the discount store's claim that if it was required to close on Sunday it would not be able to observe the Sabbath on another day was specious.

Pious and observant Jews, Seventh Day Adventists and Muslims, who observe Sabbath on a day other than Sunday, were disadvantaged because they could operate only five days a week. Their rights, asserted by a small Kosher butcher who sued in court for the right to keep his store open on Sundays, were irretrievably lost because the bona fide religious issue which the butcher asserted was governed by the prior case involving a large commercial discount house. By chance the butcher's appeal was not heard until after the other case was decided.[4] For these small-business men to remain open on Sunday would not disturb neighborhood repose. To compel them to remain closed on Sunday, when their religion requires them to be closed on another day, permits them only five working days instead of six. For most of these people that is the difference between failure and solvency. This economic injustice was in some states, notably New York, reversed by the state legislature, which provided an exemption for individual religious entrepreneurs. In other states, non-Christians are bound by the harsh rule of the United States Supreme Court. This is another example of the more practical and understanding conduct of legislative bodies when compared with the rigid conceptualistic approach of appellate courts.

America lacks essential legislation governing the most fundamental and necessary subjects. The complicated relations between city and county, city and state, and state and national government require careful and comprehensive definition which cannot be provided by the random process of litigation. Almost every subject from the war in Vietnam to the regulation of offensive sexually explicit billboard advertising should have been decided by the appropriate legislative bodies as surrogates for the public. Their failure to act has imposed a staggering burden on the judicial system, which by default has assumed the determination of the rights and duties of individuals and governmental agencies.

The legislatures fail to act, not because they are incompetent, lazy and venal, although some individual members have these characteristics. Legislatures, like courts and the citizenry, are pressed by the enormous momentum of change, the wide variety and complexity of new problems and the inability of individuals and groups to obtain the information and acquire the understanding to cope with these problems.

The mythic belief in law assumes that legislative bodies have the wisdom, the capacity and technical assistance to cope with these problems. Even so knowledgeable a scholar as Professor Norman Dorsen of New York University Law School writes: "Legislatures are responsible politically to the electorate; they have committees and staffs equipped to make long studies and garner elusive facts as a basis for comprehensive treatment of broad subjects. . . ." The fact is that legislatures are not responsive nor are they equipped to make studies.

In 1970, the then Secretary of Health, Education and Welfare, Elliot Richardson, told the White House Conference on Youth, "We will listen to your recommendations. . . . Recommend with passion, but recommend a course of action which is lucid and tough-minded." Recommendations were made but they have not been translated into law. That is sadly true of recommendations made by countless studies, commissions and citizens groups. The Committee for Economic Development has called for systematic reform of law and law enforcement. The campaign laws are scandalously lax. But few meaningful amendments have been passed. Ralph Nader has demanded a host of legislative changes covering civil service, auto safety, nursing homes and the operations of Congress itself. The response has been inaction. Neither Congress nor the state legislatures will enact strict gun-control laws, although the need is obvious as slaughter on the streets continues.

The problems of state legislatures arise not only from unresponsiveness but also from inability to act. In part this is due to the overriding difficulty of states and local communities to obtain adequate revenue to finance the costs of existing government agencies. Naturally they are hesitant to embark on new projects, no matter how badly needed, if they cannot obtain funds to finance them. In addition, state legislatures simply do not have the resources in money or personnel to study the needs of society, to draft appropriate legislation, and to educate the legislators and the public so that the required laws will be enacted. Dean Abraham Goldstein of the Yale Law School points out: "Unless you've worked with state legislatures you can't realize how inadequate the staffing is." This gap is rarely met by foundations, academia, industry or professional organizations. Such groups as bar associations, medical societies and other bodies of experts seldom do more than lobby for their own special interests.

While there are hundreds of official government agencies with law-making powers, few have the time or talent or funds to under-take the long, difficult, and often unpopular tasks of examining the friction points of society and offering solutions. There is no agency to provide the unbiased expertise required to devise legislation covering innumerable contemporary social and economic problems. These problems are common to all state and local legislative bodies. Obviously our most pressing problems are basi-cally the same in all states. All big cities face the same crises. The suburbs in all states are afflicted with the same evils. But there is no interstate or national body charged with the duty of preparing legislation to meet these common problems.

Private bodies have been unable to meet this need. Since the promulgation of the Partnership Act in 1914, the Commission on Uniform State Laws has drafted only sixty-eight statutes, most of which have not been widely adopted. These model codes represent a very modest effort to meet an enormous problem. The American Law Institute in the 1930s undertook the monumental task of "restating the law" on a variety of subjects such as contracts, torts, property and agency. While the anonymous authors did advance certain changes in substantive law, they did not attempt to rewrite the law. They did not examine the operation of the established rules to see if they result in the fair and expeditious treatment of litigants. Amendment and repeal of old laws and enactment of new laws were left to the legislatures. They have not acted.

The legal system cannot function under obsolete laws imposing social and economic standards of past ages on a drastically changed and restless society. The legislatures have failed to meet these needs in part because they have abdicated their historic and constitutionally mandated function, in part because they simply are unable to cope with so many and complex issues, in part because it is politically expedient to avoid sensitive problems. Legislators, both United States congressmen and members of the state legislatures, are predominantly middle-aged or elderly mid-dle-class or wealthy white male lawyers. The recent election of a few young women and blacks has not substantially altered the pattern. Although some older men, such as Mr. Justice Douglas and former Senator Wayne Morse, have advanced views, in large part America's laws are enacted by an older generation and imposed upon a younger one. This combined with the slowness of governmental process results in laws which are at least two generations out of date. The predominance of lawyers undoubtedly influences the abstruse language in which legislation is written. The dearth of physical and social scientists in the legislative bodies acts as an inevitable limitation on the views and expertise of these bodies. When so many of our pressing problems involve scientific and technological questions or human behavior, the traditional training of the lawyer may not provide the breadth of background and understanding required for recognition of the problems and competent solutions.

The inadequacies of the Congress and the state legislatures cannot be compensated for by other agencies of government or private institutions.

Neither the executive branch with its enormous powers nor the courts ruling on a multiplicity of issues can supply a substitute for contemporary rational laws clearly declaring rights and obligations and prescribing suitable remedies.

Who killed Davey Moore,
Why an' what's the reason for?
"Not I" says the referee.
　　　Bob Dylan, "Who Killed Davey Moore?"

4: One Day in the Life
of a Trial Judge

When the legislature fails to provide clear, just and practicable rules to govern the everyday problems of the citizens, they must either turn to the courts or opt out of the system. Most Americans cannot afford to, or do not want to leave the country or move to a wilderness area where they can live without the restrictions and protections of society.

For most Americans, the courts are the agency to which they must turn for redress. And, of course, it is in courts that the hundreds of thousands of adults accused of crime, mental illness, alcoholism and drug addiction, and the children accused of everything from murder to receiving inadequate parental care, are tried. More than 19,500 of the 20,000 courts in America are trial courts. It is here that most people get whatever justice they will receive from the judicial system.

Professor Stanley Katz, writing about law in colonial America,

79

points out that "The real challenge is not to learn about the relatively infrequent intersection of law and political crisis, but to find out how legal institutions affected daily life." The challenge to those who would understand why the legal system has failed in America is to see its routine operations and how they affect the lives of the countless people who are subjected to it.

Only the lawyers and judges who are in these trial courts on a daily basis really know what happens there. Neither the leaders of the bar nor the legal scholars spend much, if any, time in these tribunals. Most treatises on law discuss legal principles, landmark cases and changing doctrines. They analyze the difficult issues presented to the appellate courts and focus primarily on their opinions.

There is one United States Supreme Court. There are ten appellate federal courts. Each state has a supreme court and one or two intermediary appellate courts. All of these courts pass upon only a very small fraction of the cases that are brought before the trial courts. The role of the trial courts in providing or failing to provide fair and just treatment for millions of Americans is a significant factor in creating a nation of scofflaws.

Our knowledge of what happens in these trial courts is fragmentary. We do not even know how many cases—criminal and civil—are brought to court or how many are actually tried.

Statistics with respect to the number of cases litigated are incomplete. Many cases are dropped or settled before trial. Many criminal prosecutions are withdrawn. No one knows why. No one knows whether justice was served by these abortive legal actions. The only certain fact is that the number of cases is enormous and increasing every year. The federal court system does maintain fairly complete records. In 1950, 44,454 civil cases and 36,393 criminal cases were commenced in the federal courts. In 1971, 93,396 civil cases and 41,290 criminal cases were filed in the same federal courts. Corresponding increases in numbers of cases seem to have occurred in state and local courts. The exact numbers are difficult to ascertain. One can, however, estimate from a limited set of statistics. In Philadelphia, which has a population of not quite 2 million, some 25,000 civil cases and 16,000 criminal prosecutions, excluding juvenile and domestic relations cases, were instituted in 1971. The national population in 1971 was in excess of 200 million. Extrapolating these figures, one concludes that probably at least 2.5 million civil cases and more than 1.6 million criminal prosecutions were instituted in the United States in 1971.

Few of these cases were noted by the scholars. They devoted the greater part of their attention to the four hundred cases decided on the merits each year by the United States Supreme Court. A single trial judge may decide four hundred cases in less than two months.

The emphasis upon appellate court decisions, and especially the opinions of the United States Supreme Court, obscures our very real ignorance of the operations of the law in more than 99 percent of the cases, those in which no appeal is taken. The number of major cases actually tried before judge and jury is relatively small. The vast majority of lawsuits are disposed of in brief hearings, unnoticed by the public, forgotten by all but the victim and the accused or the plaintiff and the defendant.

The press reports in considerable detail trials which involve great social, political or human interest. The public is shown giants of the bar contesting in lengthy proceedings under careful scrutiny, defending the rights of the accused, prosecuting industrial malefactors, litigating political issues. Plays and television dramas depict the clever lawyer winning, through skill and industry, the acquittal of the innocent. The daily press reports the prolonged legal battles resulting in the acquittal of Bobby Seale, Dr. Spock, Angela Davis, and the Harrisburg Seven and Dr. Shephard. Both literature and journalism foster the impression that the system is just and viable.

Such showcase spectacles of the American system of litigation present a false picture. Equally misleading are books about lawyers. Successful lawyers recount their victories in best-sellers. Journalists write about "superlawyers." Judges write about individual cases in which justice triumphs. Even the anti-establishment lawyers who represent the oppressed and unpopular, by writing about their victories, contribute to the belief that the legal system provides justice for the poor and the outcast. Few lawyers write about the overwhelming majority of cases, which are handled swiftly and routinely. The public does not know whether justice is done or can be done under these circumstances.

Occasionally the press reports chilling cases of miscarriage of justice; innocent people spending years in prison for crimes they did not commit; a young man imprisoned for seven years for two half-ounce sales of marijuana; a man in Texas sentenced to nine hundred years in jail by a jury which deliberated ten minutes; a woman obtaining a tax refund after six years of protests and appeals. These cases are treated as rare, unfortunate anomalies, all human institutions being subject to error. The critic of the American legal system is always asked accusingly: "What legal system is better than ours?"

The fact is that one cannot answer such a question. Not only are most lawyers, journalists and sociologists abysmally ignorant of other legal systems, they are also ignorant of the routine operations of the American legal system. Despite the overwhelming quantity of studies of the judicial process, the courts and the administration of justice in the United States, very little is known or written about the normal, uncelebrated processing of cases.

On a typical day in criminal motions court, fifteen to twenty cases are listed, of which two or three are "add ons" (matters that have come up at the last minute or that don't fit in any recognized category). In addition, there are applications for bail and reduction of bail. On the average, a judge in such a court must make decisions in twenty cases each day.

Even though the hearings are brief and hasty, a large corps of supporting personnel is needed to man any courtroom. There is at least one court officer to swear in the witnesses and take charge of opening court, maintaining order and calling the cases. There are also a clerk who brings in the files, keeps the records, enters the orders and returns the papers at the end of the day; a sheriff to bring in the handcuffed prisoners, remove the manacles while they testify, reshackle them and return them to the cell block; usually another sheriff or policeman armed with gun, nightstick and blackjack for security purposes (a courtroom is not a safe place). There are also: a court stenographer who must record every word of testimony; the prosecutor, the defender, and the policemen and detectives who will testify. Occasionally there are witnesses for the defense—poor, frightened people who sit waiting for they know not what. A few privately retained attorneys rush in and out to see when their cases will be reached. And there is the judge seated on a dais in a black robe. The judge has awesome powers over individuals but is subjected to many limitations. The judge is deferentially addressed as "Your Honor," but he can no more control the matters that are brought into court than the worker on an assembly line at General Motors can control the pieces of machinery that are borne along the conveyor belt in front of him. Fragments of human lives pass before the bench in unending procession.

The factory worker can only tighten or loosen a screw. He cannot change the shape or design of the product; he cannot see it whole. The trial judge, too, has a very limited function. He can only tighten or loosen the screws of the system very slightly. He can raise or lower bail; imprison or free the accused; suppress or admit a confession; permit or deny the defense information with respect to the alleged crime. There is little, if anything, a judge can do for the people he sees briefly each day.

For these cases, any old room will do. In many cities and counties the courthouse is an old, dilapidated building, too small and too antiquated to cover the needs of the community. The courtroom is often dirty, ill ventilated and depressing. It bears little resemblance to the spacious marble halls in which appeals are argued. An appellate court is composed of several members, usually seven or nine. Such a court hears argument by counsel and reads briefs in which the points of law have been carefully researched and analyzed. The court adjourns and deliberates, perhaps for weeks or months, and then ultimately files a written opinion which has been prepared by law clerks (often the most capable young law graduates), reviewed by the judges, revised, and finally issued after searching deliberation. The trial judge must rule on most matters from the bench, when a motion is made. Judge John Parker of the Court of Appeals for the Fourth Circuit is reported to have told this story. He, an appellate judge, said to a trial judge: "It has always been a matter of wonder to me how a trial judge who must decide so many questions on the spur of the moment makes so few mistakes." The trial judge replied, "I always marvel that appellate judges, who have so much time to consider, make so many damn mistakes."

A trial judge is under constant pressure to decide at once. For example, the sheriff and a guard from Kentucky are in the court room, ready to take a fugitive back from Pennsylvania to Kentucky. The judge cannot tell them to return in a few days after he thinks about the question and researches the law.

At nine thirty the court personnel begin to assemble. The crier opens court. "All rise. Oyez, oyez, all persons having business before the Court of Common Pleas Criminal Division come forth and they shall be heard. God save this honorable court. Be seated and stop all conversation. Good morning, Your Honor." The crier calls out the names of the defendants. Most of them are represented by the public defender. He checks his files. One or two names are not on his list. A quick phone call is made to his office to send up the missing files.

On one particular day when I was sitting in criminal motions court, three cases had private counsel. One had been retained by the defendant. The other two had been appointed by the court to represent indigents accused of homicide. Where are these lawyers?

As is customary, the court officer phones each of them and reminds his secretary that he has a case listed and he must appear. Several of the defendants are not present. The prison is called to locate the missing parties. The judge, if he wishes to get through his list, must find the lawyers and litigants and order them to come to court.

Frequently the prosecutor cannot find his files. When he does, he discovers that a necessary witness has not been subpoenaed. The case must be continued to another day. The other witnesses, who are present and have missed a day's work, are sent home. The defendant is returned to jail to await another listing. Often cases are listed five and six times before they can be heard. One day in motion court is like any other—filled with murder, rape, robbery, larceny, drug addiction, poverty and despair.

On this day there were three extraditions. Amos R. was wanted in South Carolina. Seven years ago he had escaped from jail and fled north. Since then he has been living in Philadelphia. He has married here and has two children. His wife and children are in the courtroom. He is employed. He has not been in trouble since leaving South Carolina. Ten years ago Amos was convicted of stealing a car and sentenced to nine to twenty years in prison. He had no prior record. In Pennsylvania, he would probably have been placed on probation or at most received a maximum sentence of two years.

Now he testifies that he didn't steal the car, he only borrowed it. Moreover, he didn't have a lawyer. When he pleaded guilty he was told he would get six months. It is probably true. Also, he was undoubtedly indicted by a grand jury from which Negroes were systematically excluded. All of these allegations would be grounds for release in a postconviction hearing for they are serious violations of Constitutional rights. But they are irrelevant in extradition hearings. The only issues that the judge may consider before ordering this man to leave his family and shipping him off to serve eighteen more years in prison are whether he is in fact the Amos R. named in the warrant and whether the papers are in order. There is little judicial discretion. One is often impelled by the system to be an instrument of injustice.

This is the dilemma of a judge and of many officials in the legal system. Following the rule of law may result in hardship and essential unfairness. Ignoring the law is a violation of one's oath of office, an illegal act, and a destruction of the system. Some choose to ignore the law in the interests of "justice." Others mechanically follow precedent. Neither course is satisfactory. The judge who frees a defendant knows that in most instances the state cannot appeal. Unless there is an election in the offing and the prosecutor chooses to use this case as a political issue, there will be no repercussions. But it is his duty, as it is that of the accused, to obey the law. If the judge is not restrained by the law, who will be? On the other hand, it is unrealistic to say, "Let the defendant appeal." In the long period between the trial judge's ruling and that of the higher court, if it hears the appeal, a human being will be in jail. One does not easily deprive a person of his liberty without very compelling reasons. Almost every day, the guardians of the law are torn between these conflicting pulls.

After hearing the life story of Amos R., as reported by the prosecutor, the young defender said, "Mr. R. wishes to waive a hearing."

I looked at the lawyer. "Mr. R., do you know that you have a right to a hearing?"

"Yes."

"Have you consulted with your attorney about waiving a hearing?"

"My attorney?" R. looks bewildered.

"Your lawyer, the defender," I pointed to the young man.

"Oh, him," R. replies. "Yes, I talked to him."

"How long?"

"'Bout two minutes."

"Your Honor," says the defender, "I have spoken to the sheriff. There is no question that this is the Amos R. wanted. The papers are in order."

I search through the official-looking sheaf of documents with gold seals and red seals and the signatures of two governors, hoping to find a defect, a critical omission. At last I discover that Amos R. was arrested in New Jersey on a Friday night. He was not taken to Pennsylvania until the following Monday. It is eighty-nine days that he has been in jail in Pennsylvania. The extradition hearing must by statute be held within ninety days of arrest. By adding on the three days he was in custody in New Jersey, I conclude that the ninety-day time limit has not been met. Amos R. is once again a free man. This happy ending is unusual. Bureaucratic inefficiencies seldom redound to the benefit of the individual.

The next four matters are bail applications. All the defendants fit the stereotype. They are black males under the age of thirty. Only one is in the courtroom. The others are in the detention center. It is too much trouble and too expensive to transport them to court for a bail hearing. I must decide whether to set free or keep locked up a man whom I cannot see or talk to. If I do not release him, he may be in jail for as long as a year awaiting trial. The law presumes that he is innocent. I look at the applications. This is not the first arrest for any of them. There are records going back to age nine, when Daryll was first incarcerated for truancy.

"The defendant's juvenile record may not be used against him in adult court," I remind the prosecuting attorney.

"I know, Your Honor," he replies apologetically, "but the computer prints out all the arrests."

"How many convictions?"

The computer does not give the answer to that question. So knowing only the number of arrests and not the number of acquittals almost creates a presumption of guilt rather than of innocence.

One man is accused of rape. The record shows that his prior offenses were larceny of an automobile and, as a child, running away from home. The police report indicates that when the police arrived the defendant was in the complainant's apartment with his clothes off. He left so quickly that he abandoned his shoes and socks. The complainant admitted knowing him and gave his name and address to the police. No weapon was involved.

My usual rule of thumb is a simple one: "If he had time to take off his shoes, it isn't rape."

Before releasing an alleged rapist from jail, possibly to prey on other victims, I want to see him. Although Lombroso's theory that one can tell a criminal by his physical appearance is out of fashion, I still want to see and speak to the accused, but he is not in the courtroom. Perhaps his lawyer, the defender, can give some helpful information. However, the defender has never seen the accused. Someone else interviewed him on a routine prison visit. No one knows whether he has a family, a job, a home.

"Please have this defendant brought to court tomorrow and get me some information on him," I tell the defender.

He replies, "I'm sorry, Your Honor. I'll be working in a different courtroom tomorrow. There is no way I can find out about this man."

"We're dealing with human beings, not pieces of paper," I expostulate. "You are his lawyer. You should know him."

The young defender sadly shakes his head. "Your Honor, I work for a bureaucracy."

So do I, I remind myself, as I look at the clock and see that it is past 11:00 and there are fourteen more matters to be heard today.

I refuse bail for a fourteen-year-old accused of slaying another child in a gang rumble. Will he be safer in jail than on the street, where the rival gang is lying in wait for him? I do not know. The boy is small and slender. The warden will put him in the wing with the feminine homosexuals to save him from assault. I mark on the commitment sheet that the boy is to attend school while in prison awaiting trial. But if the warden does not honor my order, I will not know it.

A twenty-three-year-old heroin addict tells me that there is no drug treatment program in prison. "It's just like the street. Nothin' but drugs," he says. I try to move his case ahead so that he can plead guilty at an early date and be transferred to the federal drug treatment center. He, like so many of the others up for robbery and burglary, is a Vietnam veteran. He acquired his habit overseas and now must steal in order to pay for his daily fix.

The next matter is a petition to suppress a confession. Court-appointed counsel alleges that the defendant did not make a knowing and intelligent waiver of his rights when he confessed three murders to the police. Cornelius takes the stand and describes his life. His is a typical history. He was sent to a disciplinary school at eleven, runaway at twelve, and a year in juvenile jail. At seventeen, a conviction for larceny and another period of incarceration. He is married, two children, separated from his wife. He is vague about the ages of the children. Cornelius works as an orderly in a hospital earning $80.00 a week take-home pay. At the end of each week he divides his money in two parts: $40 for living expenses and $40 for methadrine. It costs $20 a spoon.

Where does he buy it? On any corner in the ghetto. He steals the syringes from the hospital. His expenses are minimal except for the precious methadrine. He is riddled with V.D. He seldom eats.

While on a high, he shot and killed three strangers. Why did he do it?

"There are these voices I hear. They're fightin'. One tells me to kill; the other tells me not to. Sometimes I get so scared I run out into the street. That's when I'm in a low. But when I'm in a high, I feel I can walk in the rain without getting wet. I don't feel sad, I ain't lonely. When I'm comin' down from a high, I got to get another shot."

Now he is in a low—sad, soft-spoken, withdrawn, disinterested in his own fate. I see his skinny brown arms pocked with little needle scars. The psychiatrist says that when Cornelius is on drugs he cannot gauge reality. He could not understand the meaning of the privilege against self-incrimination and make a knowing and intelligent waiver of his rights.

The earnest psychiatrist explains patiently. I watch Cornelius, wraith-thin, sitting in withdrawn disinterest, lost in some dream of flight. Is he mad or are we—the prosecutor, the defense lawyer, the psychiatrist and the judge? After five hours of testimony, I rule that the confession must be suppressed. There are dozens of eyewitnesses. The confession is not necessary to convict Cornelius. After this hearing, and before trial, a psychiatrist for the defense will testify that Cornelius is not mentally competent to stand trial; he cannot cooperate with his lawyer in preparing his defense. A psychiatrist for the prosecution will testify that when Cornelius has withdrawn from drugs he will be able to participate intelligently in his defense. The motion to defer trial will probably be denied. At the trial itself, one psychiatrist will testify that at the time of the shootings Cornelius did not know the difference between right and wrong and the nature and quality of his act. Another will testify that he did. Neither psychiatrist saw Cornelius at the time of the crimes. Both of them examined him in prison months later. They are certain of their opinions.

All of us know that Cornelius cannot live without drugs, that if he is released from jail he could just as likely kill three more people tomorrow. But he is entitled to reasonable bail pending trial. Why are we going through this endless procedure? Because the law requires it. Counsel, sworn to defend his client, must take every step to prevent him from being electrocuted. If there were no death penalty,° it would be easier for him to plead guilty and be incarcerated in an institution for the criminally insane for the remainder of what will undoubtedly be a very short and wretched life. Meanwhile, the prosecution, defense and all of the court personnel must play out their appointed roles according to the script prescribed in a long series of opinions involving other men, other crimes, other conditions.

A middle-aged, white, epicenely soft man is next on the list. His face is a pasty gray. He mutters under his breath. He is accused of committing sodomy on three teen-aged boys. Most of his meager salary he spent on these boys and now they have turned on him. I order a psychiatric examination simply because I don't know what else to do. A month later the report was sent to me. It follows a standard format: facts (gleaned from the accused), background, diagnostic formulation and summary, and recommendation. This

---

° This hearing took place before the opinion of the United States Supreme Court outlawing the death penalty under certain circumstances. The local prosecutor is seeking to reverse the ruling. In many states, the legislators are enacting mandatory death penalties in an effort to skirt the Supreme Court ruling. No lawyer can relax in the certainty that his client will not, if convicted, be sentenced to death.

report states: "Probable latent schizophrenia. We recommend a full examination sixty-day commitment." At the end of sixty days and the expenditure of hundreds of dollars, the doctors will decide that he is or is not schizophrenic, possibly sociopathic. A long period in a "structured environment" will be recommended. But what will the judge do with him? There are only two choices: prison, where he will be tormented and perhaps beaten by strong young thugs, or the street.

As the silent, defeated prisoners are brought before me I think of Emma Lazarus' hopeful words: "Bring me . . . the wretched refuse of your teeming shores." These people—almost all native-born Americans (Puerto Ricans are Americans, too)—are our wretched refuse. But they have no promised land across the seas. They have only the cell block at the detention center from which they are brought to me, or the cell block at another prison to which they will ultimately be sent.

Most of them are young—under thirty. I also see children who are charged with homicide. They are denied even the nominal protections of the juvenile court and are "processed" as adults. The fourteen-year-old accused of slaying another child in a gang rumble; the sixteen-year-old dope addict, surprised while burglarizing a house, who panicked and shot the unwary owner; the girl lookout for the gang, who is accused of conspiracy and murder. Many of these children are themselves parents. Can they be turned back to the streets? I refuse bail for an illiterate fifteen-year-old accused of murder and note on the bill of indictment that he be required to attend school while in detention. I ask the court-appointed lawyer to check with the warden and see that the boy is sent to class. But is there a class in remedial reading at the detention center? Who will pay for it? Not the overburdened public schools or the understaffed prisons. It is not a project likely to find a foundation grant. What startling research can be developed from teaching a fifteen-year-old illiterate slayer to read?

A perplexed lawyer petitions for a second psychiatric examination for his client. The court psychiatrist has found him competent to stand trial but the lawyer tells me his client cannot discuss the case with him. Randolph, who is accused of assault with intent to kill, attacked a stranger in a bar and strangled the man, almost killing him. Fortunately, bystanders dragged Randolph away. I ask to speak with Randolph. A big, neatly dressed Negro steps up to the bar of the court. He speaks softly, "Judge," he says, "I'm afraid. I need help."

Randolph is out on bail. This is his first offense. He has a good work record. He is married, has two children, and lives with his family. It is Friday morning. I fear what may happen over the weekend. The court psychiatric unit is called.

"We've got people backed up for a month," the doctor tells me. "Even if I took Randolph out of turn I couldn't see him until next week." When he does see Randolph it will be a forty-five-minute examination. A voluntary hospital commitment seems to be the only safeguard. But at least he will be watched for ten days. Gratefully, Randolph promises to go at once to the mental health clinic. What will happen to him after the ten-day period?

There is no time to wonder. The next case is waiting. The parade of accused muggers, robbers and thieves continues.

It is a sultry day. When the ancient air-conditioner is turned on we cannot hear the testimony. When it is turned off the room is unbearable. No bank teller or sales clerk would work in such surroundings. At 4:45 P.M., I ask hopefully, "Have we finished the list?" But no, there is an application for a continuance on an extradition warrant. The papers from the demanding state have not arrived. It is a routine, daily occurrence.

I look around the courtroom. By this hour only the court personnel and a few policemen and detectives are present. "Where is the defendant?" I inquire. The prosecutor does not know. He is not responsible for producing him. The defender does not have him on his list. "Is he in custody?" I ask. We all search the records and discover that he was arrested more than five months ago. There is no notation that bail has ever been set. No private counsel has entered an appearance. A deputy sheriff checks and reports that he has not been brought up from the prison. The computerized records show that this man has never had a hearing. Hardened as we are, the prosecutor, the defender and I are horrified that someone should be sitting in jail all this time without ever having had an opportunity to say a word. Is he, in fact, the person wanted for an offense allegedly committed years ago and hundreds of miles away? Was he ever there? Is he a stable member of society? Has he a family, a job, a home? Is he a drug addict? No one knows. The papers do not indicate. No one in the courtroom has ever seen him. Each of us makes a note to check on this forgotten prisoner whom the computer may or may not print out for appearance on some other day in some other courtroom.

The scene in criminal trial court is similar. Most of the cases are "waivers" and guilty pleas. The accused may waive his Constitutional right to be tried by a jury of his peers and be tried by a judge alone. Fewer than 5 percent of all cases are tried by jury. In most cases, the accused not only waives his right to a jury trial but also to any trial and pleads guilty. Before accepting a waiver or a plea, the accused is asked the routine questions.

Day after day defense counsel recites the following formula to poor, semiliterate defendants, some of whom are old and infirm, others young and ignorant. Read this quickly:

Do you know that you are accused of [the statutory crimes are read to him from the indictment]?

Do you know that you have a right to a trial by jury in which the state must prove by evidence beyond a reasonable doubt that you committed the offenses and that if one juror disagrees you will not be found guilty?

Do you know that by pleading guilty you are giving up your right to appeal the decision of this court except for an appeal based on the jurisdiction of the court, the legality of the sentence and the voluntariness of your plea of guilty? [The accused is not told that by the asking and answering of these questions in open court he has for all practical purposes also given up this ground for appeal.]

Do you know that the judge is not bound by the recommendation of the District Attorney as to sentence but can sentence you up to ―――― years and impose a fine of ―――― dollars? [The aggregate penalty is read to him. Judges may and often do give a heavier penalty than was recommended. They rarely give a lighter sentence.]

Can you read and write the English language?

Have you ever been in a mental hospital or under the care of a psychiatrist for a mental illness?

Are you now under the influence of alcohol, drugs, or undergoing withdrawal symptoms [from being off the use of drugs]?

Have you been threatened, coerced or promised anything for entering the plea of guilty other than the recommendation of sentence by the District Attorney?

Are you satisfied with my representation?

All this is asked quickly, routinely, as the prisoner stands before the bar of the court. He answers "Yes" to each question.

If it were read aloud to you in the frightening atmosphere of a courtroom by a lawyer whom you had not retained, whom you had seen for the first time that day, would you be able to reply "Yes" knowingly and intelligently?

The final question is: "Are you pleading guilty because you are guilty?" The defendant looks at the defender, uncertainly.

"Have you consulted with your lawyer?" I inquire.

"Right now. 'Bout five minutes."

"We'll pass this case until afternoon. At the lunch recess, will you please confer with your client," I direct the defender.

I am not being fair to the young lawyer. He is entitled to eat lunch. He seldom has a chance to do so because he must call for missing files, check to see what has happened to the clients he has never seen and who have not appeared. Now I am ordering him to confer with this man. It is an exercise in futility, like so much that we do.

In the afternoon, the accused, having talked with the lawyer for another ten minutes, again waives his right to a trial. He has been in jail more than eight months. The eight months in jail are applied to his sentence. He will be out by the end of the year—sooner than if he demanded a trial and was acquitted.

The plea has been negotiated by the assistant defender and the assistant prosecutor. The defendant says he was not promised anything other than a recommendation of sentence in return for the guilty plea. But the judge does not know what else the defendant has been told, whether his family and friends are willing to come and testify for him, whether his counsel has investigated the facts of the case to see whether indeed he does have a defense. The magic formula has been pronounced. The judge does not know what the facts are. Did the man really commit the offense? Even if there were a full-scale trial, truth might not emerge. Many of the witnesses have long since disappeared. How reliable will their memories be? The policeman will say he did not strike the accused. The accused will say that he did. Friends and relatives will say that the accused was with them at the time of the alleged crime. The victim, if he appears, will swear that this is the person whom he saw once briefly on a dark night eight months ago.

The lawyers are in almost equal ignorance. The prosecutor has the police report. The defender has only the vague and confused story of the accused. The judge is under pressure to "dispose" of the case. There is a score card for each judge kept by the computer. The judges have batting averages. Woe betide those who fail to keep pace in getting rid of cases. A long trial to determine guilt or innocence will put the judge at the bottom of the list. The prosecutors and public defenders also have their score cards of cases disposed of. Private defense counsel—whether paid by the accused or appointed by the court and paid by the public—has his own type of score card. For the fee paid, he can give only so many hours to the preparation and trial of this case. He must pay his rent, secretary and overhead. All of the persons involved in the justice system are bound by the iron laws of economics. What can the defendant afford for bail, counsel fees, witness fees, investigative expenses? All of these questions will inexorably determine the case that is presented to the court.

The National Conference on Criminal Justice, convened in

January, 1973, by Attorney General Kleindienst, recommends that plea bargaining be abolished within five years. What will replace it?

Motions in civil court are disposed of even more quickly and casually. The defendant files a motion for judgment on the pleadings. If it is granted, the plaintiff has lost his cause of action. He is out of court and can never get a trial on the issue involved.

A motion to take off a judgment is filed and opposed. There was never a trial. The plaintiff had simply signed a note when he bought his appliances on time. The TV didn't work and so he stopped paying. Now there is a judgment against him for the balance of the payments plus interest and costs of the proceeding. It amounts to more than the retail price of the TV set. The federal courts have ruled that judgment notes are, in certain circumstances, unconstitutional. By artful pleadings the plaintiff's counsel must try to bring his client within the scope of those decisions and also meet the onerous conditions for taking off a judgment. The seller asserts that the pleading fails to meet the rules.

A couple who bought a house ten years ago now want to move but they find that there is a lien against their property and they cannot sell the house. A motion to quiet title is filed. Have the necessary elements been pleaded?

A woman badly injured in a collision between a train and a bus brought suit against both companies. Her lawyer wants the accident reports of the company investigators. They will not turn them over to him, so he files a motion. Both companies resist. Without the reports the woman cannot prove negligence.

In all these matters and hundreds of others the disposition of the motion will decide whether the parties can legally or feasibly pursue their claims. Oral arguments are brief—perhaps ten or fifteen minutes. The judge, with the help of a law clerk—who is usually young, inexperienced and often unaware of the critical significance of the decision—disposes of twenty or thirty motions a day. Many of them raise questions, like the confession of judgment note, which will ultimately be decided by an appellate court in another case years later. When there is a concurrence of public outrage, a flagrantly unfair case, and a judge willing to overturn decades or centuries of precedent, the harshness of the common-law rule that governs the disposition of such cases will be set aside. Meanwhile, there are countless people whose rights and economic existence are determined by whether a document filed in court fits within the Procrustean bed of the law.

At the end of a long day in court, even the crier remarks despairingly, "There must be a better way." But we go on day after day in the same old unsatisfactory way.

At the end of a day in which as a judge I have taken actions affecting for good or ill the lives of perhaps fifteen or twenty litigants and their families, I am drained. I walk out of the stale-smelling, dusty courtroom into the fresh sunshine of a late spring day and feel as if I were released from prison. I breathe the soft air redolent of lilac, but in my nostrils is the stench of the stifling cell blocks and detention rooms. While I sip my long, cool drink in the quiet of my garden, I cannot forget the prisoners, with their dry bologna sandwiches and only a drink of water provided at the pleasure of the hot and harried guards.

Was Cottle really guilty? I will never know. Fred made bail. Will he attack someone tonight or tomorrow? One reads the morning paper with apprehension. It is safer for the judge to keep them all locked up. There will be an outcry over the one prisoner released who commits a subsequent offense. Who will know or care about the scores of possibly innocent prisoners held in jail?

This brief description of an ordinary average day in a trial court sheds no new light on the legal system. Small-time lawyers, trial judges and court personnel have seen it all hundreds of times. But the public, especially the educated, more affluent citizens, never go to these courtrooms. Neither do the leaders of the bar or the legal scholars.

Before the reader can consider possible alternatives or remedies, he must see, hear and smell the squalor and despair of the nation's trial courts. He must understand the haste, the "speed up," in which disposing of cases is more important than doing justice. This chapter is only one day in a diary. Replicate this by 260 times a year, at least 15,000 courts, and ten or twenty or thirty years in the past. Can one doubt the thesis of this book: that the operation of the legal system is slowly but surely strangling the law?

I must sit only three and a half more weeks in criminal court. But there is a holiday. So with relief I realize that it is really only seventeen more days that I must sit there this term. Next year I shall again have to take my turn.

As I turn out the light, waiting for sleep, I am reminded of Ivan Denisovich. Solzhenitsyn describes Ivan's bedtime thoughts in a Soviet prison. "Ivan Denisovich went to sleep content. He had been fortunate in many ways that day—and he hadn't fallen ill. He'd got over it. There were three thousand and six hundred and fifty-three days like this in his sentence. From the moment he woke to the moment he slept. The three extra days were for leap years."

This chapter does not propose remedies, although it is apparent that fewer numbers, better preparation by prosecutor and defense in criminal cases might reduce the likelihood of error. Similarly, in civil cases, better preparation and more thorough consideration of legal issues would be desirable.

The trial judges, who know intimately what is so wrong and so unjust, have rarely spoken out. Many of them cannot afford to resign from a position which they find brutalizing and degrading. A few judges have done so. Their resignations and condemnations have passed almost unnoticed—one cog in the machine replaced by another. The majority of us know that and we are simply too tired to speak out.

We know that the critic is asked accusingly: "If things are so bad, what remedy do you propose?" The honest answer—that the problems are enormous, complex and interrelated, that it is not possible for one person in his spare time to devise a new approach that will meet so many diverse and competing interests, that much more information, skill and expertise are required—seldom satisfies. With unconscious Panglossian chauvinism, most members of the legal profession continue to proclaim that ours is the best of all legal systems. Those of us who daily see the law in action know that, whether or not it is the best of all existing systems, it certainly cannot be the best of all possible systems. On the whole we limit our discussions and proposals to small specifics because we can suggest feasible, immediate remedies only for such matters and we are obsessed with the need to get through the day, doing as little harm and as much kindness as the system permits.

Crime: A positive or negative act in violation of penal law.

Black's Law Dictionary

5: The Manufacture of Criminals

By the time the accused is brought before the trial judge, the long process known as criminal justice is almost half over. What precedes the trial and what happens afterward are largely ignored.

Public attention has focused primarily on the courts. This is natural because the courts are required to operate in public. The secret star chamber trial, with few exceptions, has been abolished. It is easier to criticize what we see than operations of which we are largely ignorant. It is commonly said that the criminal justice system consists of the police, the courts and corrections. (Corrections is the fashionable euphemism for prison.) The process is much longer and more complicated. It begins with the legislative determination to make certain acts or behavior crimes. It does not end until the criminal is returned to society and enabled to obtain gainful employment.

The first question, of course, is, "What is a crime?" Crime is an elastic term. It includes anything the legislative bodies of cities and states and the United States Congress choose to declare illegal.

A conference of European criminologists held in Strasbourg in December, 1971, concluded that there was no sharp difference between criminals and other people. "What makes a person a criminal," they concluded, "is not the fact that he has committed a crime—because noncriminals have also done that—but the fact that he has been caught, tried, convicted and punished." It is the law which makes the criminal.

Dr. Thomas Szasz, a psychiatrist, suggests that the profession of psychiatry is engaged in manufacturing madness by certifying people as mentally ill when such people are not dangerous or incapable of functioning. Dr. R. D. Laing also points out that frequently the person who is committed to a mental institution by his relatives may be perfectly competent but simply refuses to accept the norms of behavior of his family. It is significant that some psychiatrists are questioning the propriety and utility of their decisions in classifying people as mentally ill.

But few lawyers and judges doubt the validity and propriety of the legal system's classification of people into two categories: criminals and noncriminals. After regularly observing large numbers of people who are arrested, and examining the offenses with which they are charged, I cannot avoid the disquieting thought that the American legal system is engaged in the manufacture of criminals.

This view was expressed bluntly by Daniel R. Turner, a lifer who is reported in the *New York Times* as saying: "The lawyers and the judges and the prison authorities are breeding criminals for financial gain." Obviously no one is deliberately creating criminals, but the effect of the criminal justice system is to criminalize those who are caught up in it. The lawyers, the judges and the prison authorities know this, and recently schemes to "divert" arrestees from the system have been devised. First offenders are released without trial on probation, in the hope that they will not return. But these programs simply turn a blind eye to the law, a kind of establishment scofflawism.

Those who are not kept out of the criminal justice system are all treated alike: as criminals. Some of them—prosecuted, convicted and imprisoned under law—have done nothing violent or intrinsically evil. They simply refuse to accept the norms of behavior set forth in legislation enacted fifty or a hundred years ago. Others have committed vicious, dangerous and violent acts. They are all included in the crime statistics. They are all arrestees processed through the criminal justice system.

The common denominator of most people the legal system declares criminals, or treats as criminal, is poverty. With few notable exceptions, persons accused of crime are poor. In 1883, Sir James Fitzjames Stephen, in his monumental study of the criminal law,[1] wrote: "It must be remembered that most persons accused of crime are poor, stupid and helpless." This is equally true today when at least two-thirds of all adults accused of crime and more than 90 percent of the juveniles are represented at public expense because they are indigent. Other poor, helpless people who are not accused of crime are treated as criminals but with few of the Constitutional rights and protections of those accused of crime. These vulnerable people include homeless children, truants, old people, derelicts, alcoholics, drug addicts, mentally ill and emotionally disturbed children and adults, who are thrown in jail with murderers and rapists. Many adult criminals learned their trade when they were children incarcerated for months or years for the social offense of being poor, homeless, unloved or difficult. Mrs. John A. Willis, Chairman of the Task Force of the Citizens Committee for Children of New York warned: "If we do not improve conditions for these children [in detention centers], we will get compassionless, alienated brutal adults who are the logical end of our own work."

In the United States today there are tens of thousands of acts that have been made criminal, many of which do not require knowledge of their illegality or intent to commit an offense. The National Conference on Criminal Justice reports: "Americans are, nevertheless, regulated by the most far-reaching and detailed collection of federal, state and local laws found anywhere in the world." Among these countless crimes are such violations of statute law as possession of a marijuana cigarette, sale of a pornographic book to an adult, ownership of an automobile with a defaced serial number, sale of a glass of wine in one's home without possessing a liquor license, sale of a numbers ticket or operation of a bingo game, acts of fellatio or cunnilingus by consenting adults in private, sexual intercourse by consenting adults who are not legally married to each other, drunkenness and vagrancy. These and countless other nonviolent acts that are not dangerous to others have been made crimes. At least one-third of all arrests, according to former Attorney General John N. Mitchell, are for public drunkenness. Tens of thousands of Americans are arrested, prosecuted and convicted for committing such acts. They make up a sizable portion of the 6 million people arrested annually. The prosecution of people accused of these offenses occupies a large part of the time of police and courts and a great deal of the taxpayers' money. People accused of such acts constitute a large proportion of those incarcerated *before* trial, and many of those jailed after conviction.

George Jackson, one of the Soledad Brothers, is an archetypical child who was manufactured into a criminal by the justice system. He was imprisoned on an indeterminate sentence of one year to life for robbing a gas station of $70.00. He pled guilty on advice of counsel. As a juvenile he had had two prison convictions for thefts of motorcycles. His contact with the law did not rehabilitate him, contrary to the theoretical basis of the juvenile court philosophy. Nor was the indeterminate sentence conducive to good behavior, but rather its severity engendered a feeling of hopelessness.

Tyrone R. is another youngster who was criminalized by the system. Although he was never accused of committing a crime, he spent several years in juvenile lockups. He was poor, unlovable and unwanted. There was no home for him, no foster home, no place but a juvenile jail. After a court hearing, the judge, having no other place to send the boy, returned him to a correctional institution. This child's lawyer wrote me despairingly: "It seems to me that we are witnessing an irremedial tragedy in this boy's life but, frankly, I don't know what to do about it. When I spoke to Tyrone at the hearing his reaction was almost one of indifference." There is widespread indifference among judges, social workers and those involved in the criminal justice system, an indifference not of callousness but of helplessness. For the problems of lives like Tyrone's and countless others are beyond the capacity of the law to solve.

Those who are caught up in the criminal justice system are all powerless. The prisoners who are not accused of crime, the prisoners who are accused of crime and the prisoners who have been convicted of crime have all lost control of their lives. Those who administer the system are powerless to change it. All are corrupted by the hypocrisy and indifference of a system that proclaims equal justice under law but patently operates unequally. The famous aphorism of Anatole France that the law punishes rich and poor alike for stealing a loaf of bread is still true. But it has a new corollary. The law fails to punish rich and poor alike for stealing a railroad or an election.

My own experience as grand jury judge confirms that the vast majority of state indictments and prosecutions are for relatively petty crimes. Of 1,408 bills of indictment in a random month, more than two-thirds were for some sort of stealing—larceny, burglary, robbery. Many were for numbers writing, drunkenness and drug abuse. Significantly, not a single bill of indictment in the entire month was presented against a professional criminal. Thieves are regularly prosecuted, but fences are very rarely arrested. Neither are drug lords and vice kings. Of course, it is apparent that political corruption, the widespread availability of narcotics, and large-scale larceny exist because there are wealthy professional criminals. These people are seldom arrested and rarely tried.

In this same random month there was not a single indictment against a slumlord, an industrial polluter, or manufacturer of unsafe products. Many large-scale frauds and illegal acts by large businesses and major tax evasions are, of course, prosecuted in federal court rather than state courts; nonetheless, the relative absence of prosecution of white-collar and professional criminals in state courts is startling.

Many business crimes—violations of blue laws, sales of defective merchandise, misrepresentation, excessive finance charges, and the like—never come to court. It is cheaper for the guilty party to pay the fine and continue his illegal practices than to fight the charges or comply with the law.

Columnist Russell Baker humorously points out that the cost of everything has gone up except the cost of committing crimes. The penalties have not risen. The maximum fine for making illegal campaign contributions, for example, is $5,000 for a corporation and $1,000 for the executive officer of the corporation. The benefits to the corporation in favors, special legislation and price raises are astronomical. This wealth, of course, is taken from the public for the benefit of corporate officers and insiders. Such bargain-basement penalties have little, if any, deterrent effect. Certainly the suspended sentences and light penalties imposed on Vice-President Agnew and "the President's men" do not even deprive them of their ill-gotten gains.

The routine operations of the criminal law are largely concerned with small criminals, not those who loot the public of millions.

A number of bills of indictment which I routinely examined were for the theft of a few postage stamps and items of property valued at less than $10.00. For example, individuals were indicted for stealing such objects as three bottles of whiskey, or one cigar, or groceries valued at less than $5.00. One individual was indicted for stealing 40¢ from a poverty office, another for receiving stolen goods valued at $4.00. Two people were indicted for malicious mischief: one broke a window, the other a trellis. Of all the larcenies and burglaries for which indictments were returned that month only twelve involved money or goods valued at $1,000 or more. Obviously, these crimes were committed by poor, stupid people. For who, if he exercised any intelligence, would risk imprisonment for such small gain?

When one compares the numbers of arrests with the nature of the charges, it is yet more apparent that the law is manufacturing criminals. Of the 6 million arrests in 1970, 73,300 were for serious offenses against the person, such as homicide, robbery and rape.

Many arrestees accused of rape are known to the alleged victims. Whether the act was forcible or consensual is often a serious question. The cases of brutal, forcible rape by strangers have a much lower percentage of arrests because the police have great difficulty in finding these unknown rapists, and moreover the victims are often unable to identify their assailants.

There were 484,800 arrests for serious crimes against property. Even this figure is subject to revision downward since it includes all larcenies over $50.00. With inflation and perhaps some exaggeration of the value of the property taken, many of these thefts may not actually involve large sums.

The value of the property taken does not, of course, indicate the viciousness of the crime. People have been shot to death in hold-ups which netted the robber less than a dollar. I see many people accused of committing brutal, cruel and senseless crimes. Often I ask for psychiatric examination of such defendants, for it would appear that any rational person would not risk killing or maiming another human being for such a small chance of gain. With few exceptions, the psychiatrists report that these defendants know the difference between right and wrong, that they are in touch with reality, that they are not under a delusion or hallucination or subject to uncontrollable impulses. Medical labels such as socio-pathic personality, schizoid, or paranoid may be ascribed to them, but in essence the doctors find that regardless of medical diagnosis these people knew they were committing crimes and were capable of choosing whether or not to do so. The assumption that people who are not certifiably insane have a calculus of harm to others and benefit to themselves is evidently not valid.

The operation of law may well have induced many people to substitute a different calculus—the risk of imprisonment as opposed to the chance of gain. It is estimated that of every 100 crimes committed, 50 are reported, 12 result in arrests, 6½ are convicted, and 1½ go to prison. Obviously, the chance of being caught and imprisoned is very slight. There is also the cynical attitude of those who have been arrested repeatedly for crimes they did not commit: that innocence and guilt are irrelevant. Ninety percent of

inner-city nonwhite males are arrested at least once before
reaching the age of eighteen. Many of them were simply picked
up in a dragnet search. Earl R. had already been arrested eleven
times between the ages of twelve and twenty-three when I saw
him. Nine of those times he had been discharged. But he served
more than a total of two years in jails for crimes of which he was
acquitted.

I do not know what motivated Vernon, a hostile black high
school graduate. He exercised a tight control over himself in the
courtroom. He looked balefully and inscrutably at me behind dark
glasses during the nine days of hearing. He had a record of six
arrests, but no convictions. The facts of the case being tried before
me were incredibly simple. Vernon was the ring leader and mas-
termind. He does not use drugs or alcohol. He is intelligent and
good-looking. Vernon and two companions, Loraine and Elwood,
regularly held up specialty shops. While Loraine tried on clothes,
Vernon and Elwood would simply empty the cash register and the
pocketbooks of the shoppers at gunpoint. On the sixteenth or
seventeenth robbery the plans miscarried. Loraine and Elwood
were both high on heroin. In the midst of the holdup a
fifteen-year-old girl walked into the store, unaware of what was
happening, and inadvertently jostled Elwood. He panicked and
fired the gun. The girl is totally and irreversibly paralyzed from
the neck down for life.

Elwood and Loraine dozed during the trial. They were examined for drug use but found not to be under the influence. They
appeared to be remote from everything around them, totally
indifferent to the fate of the paralyzed girl or their own lives.

Vernon, however, was alert, taking notes and occasionally
whispering to his lawyer. His testimony was precise and clear. The
only emotion he displayed was anger at Elwood's stupidity in
shooting. "It wasn't necessary," he said. Neither of Vernon's parents came to court. He was alone in a hostile world with only a
lawyer—a stranger appointed by the court—to defend him. Is
Vernon one of the 10 percent of children abused, beaten—psychically scarred for life? Has he been the victim of police brutal-

ity? Is he enured to death and violence by his year in Vietnam? Is he a "bad seed"? The judge will never know. And if the court could find out, it would make little difference. He will go to the same jail regardless of the etiology of his behavior, and he will receive the same treatment in prison regardless of the psychiatric findings. Is he repentant? Has he hope for himself? What does he expect of this long series of judicial proceedings—preliminary hearing, bail hearing, suppression hearing and trial—brought against him by the state which also provided him with a lawyer and the right to appeal? The judge can only wonder.

Kenneth R. let me know what he was thinking. Kenneth was also on trial for armed robbery. With a group of his friends—all in their late teens or early twenties—Kenneth went down to the subway station late at night. There he saw a young man, Mr. I., dressed in a very expensive suede fur-lined coat and wearing a gold watch. Mr. I. was accompanied by his wife and her girl friend, Loretta, both young, pretty and well dressed. Kenneth and his friends made several very pointed remarks about Mr. I. having two girls and they having none. The subway came and they all boarded it. When Mr. and Mrs. I. and their friend got off the subway, Kenneth and his pals followed them. As Mr. and Mrs. I. and Loretta started to cross a dark alley, Kenneth and his pals jumped them. At knife point, Kenneth seized Mr. I.'s coat and his watch. Others grabbed the girls and snatched their pocketbooks.

In court, Mr. and Mrs. I. positively identified Kenneth, who had been found wearing the fur-lined coat and the watch. After Kenneth was convicted and was being led away by the sheriff, he muttered loudly, "I shoulda slit the motherfucker's throat."

These cases are exceptional for several reasons. First, they were actually tried. Fewer than 5 percent of all cases come to trial. Second, the facts were fairly clear. Although the law requires the prosecution to prove the defendant's guilt beyond a reasonable doubt, this is not often done. The jury often finds guilt when most lawyers would have more than a reasonable doubt. For example:

Nelson was convicted of burglary. Mrs. Ferrara testified that she was asleep in her living room on the sofa. The only light was from the TV set and a street light shining through the venetian blinds. Mrs. Ferrara had dozed off during the late show. Her door was locked. She awakened to find a young man standing over her demanding money. She handed him her social security check, which was in her pocketbook next to her on the sofa. The man took the check, threw it on the floor and said, "I want cash." She told him there was a $20 bill in a table drawer. He took it and left. A half hour later Nelson was picked up almost a mile from Mrs. Ferrara's home. The description Mrs. Ferrara had given the police did not match Nelson's appearance. But when the police brought him back to her home, she positively identified him. The police did not find a $20 bill on Nelson. No fingerprints were taken. There was no evidence of how the burglar had gotten into the house. Mrs. Ferrara had seen him only a few moments in uncertain light at a time when, she admitted, she was terrified. The jury deliberated less than two hours and found Nelson guilty of burglary and larceny.

These cases are not unusual among those which actually go to trial. But more than 95 percent of people arrested do not have a trial by jury. Only 85 percent of all arrestees have any trial. This is what happens to them: After arrest the suspect is interrogated. This procedure may last as long as twenty-four hours. After the police have sufficient evidence, through the confession of the suspect or one of his friends or companions, he is slated—formally charged with a crime. The next step is the setting of bail.

Unlike the decision to make an arrest, the interrogation, and the decision to file charges—all of which take place in closed rooms to which the public is not admitted and for which there is no judicial review—the setting of bail is done in open court and is subject to Constitutional standards. Bail is fixed to ensure the appearance of the accused at the trial. The Constitution prohibits excessive bail. Although the nature of the crime and the likelihood of guilt are not supposed to be considered as factors in setting bail, obviously they influence every judge. Judges, like all human beings, vary in their responses. Some judges are more inclined to be severe with the young. Some find certain offenses more odious than others.

There is little consistency in bail. Often the prosecuting attorney makes a recommendation as to the amount of bail. Since he has the police and investigative reports, he is far better informed than the judge of the strength of the evidence against the accused. These recommendations have little uniformity. The same prosecutor has recommended to me bail as low as $300 in a murder case and as high as $50,000 in a larceny case. Nominal bail is frequently set for child abuse but high bail for robbery.

A bail hearing usually lasts no more than ten or fifteen minutes. On the basis of a police report, the prior record of the defendant and a few words about his family history, education and employment, a decision is made that may affect the accused more profoundly than the trial. If he cannot make bail, he will stay in prison until the time of trial. Despite the expenditure of great amounts of money and the establishment of a variety of bail projects to provide for release of indigents accused without bail, more than half, possibly two-thirds, of all the people in prison are there *awaiting* trial. Many stay in jail for months for want of sums as little as $30 or $50. Obviously bail works a severe discriminatory hardship on the poor.

If the defendant has no friends or family who can and will put up bail for him, if he has no job and no home, it is likely that he will flee the jurisdiction if released. What reason has he to stay? The fact that the defendant has been refused help by the various bail projects may weigh heavily against him. A judge may be likely to conclude that if the bail project, designed to get people out of jail, is unwilling to help this person, he must be a bad risk. And so, many poor, untried prisoners wait for months and years in the various tombs throughout the nation. It is difficult to evaluate bail projects. Many of those released under the projects could have made bail. Those not recommended by the project are worse off than before. But bail is not the answer to the problem. The only solution fair to rich and poor, to the defendant and to the public, is a very prompt trial. There are now rules in many states requiring that an accused be released if he is not tried within six or nine months. If these rules are strictly adhered to, dangerous and vio-

lent people will be back on the streets, because in many communities it is a physical impossibility to bring every person to trial
within a limited period of time.

In many states there are laws which require that a person be
brought before a judicial authority for bail setting within a specified period of time. Those arrested for violation of probation are
entitled to a hearing within forty-eight hours. Frequently, such
people are brought before me two and three weeks after arrest.
There is nothing a judge can do to right this wrong. The individual
has been illegally detained for weeks. But he has no remedy,
although there are laws in some states which require that a
prisoner awaiting trial *who has requested that he be tried promptly*
be released from jail if he is not brought to trial six months after
the request. Again, the poor and ignorant do not know that they
have a right to request a speedy trial, while the wealthy, who have
able counsel, are, of course, informed of this right. Frequently I
encounter indigent defendants who have been in jail for a year or
two *before* the public defender requests a trial on their behalf.
There is nothing anyone can do to compensate a poor accused
person in jail for his long incarceration or to ensure that other
hapless people are not held for equally long periods without trial.
The New York rule requiring discharge of accused persons held
for excessive periods is also unsatisfactory since, again, it results in
the release of many who may be guilty of serious offenses and who
will likely commit other dangerous crimes.

After arraignment and setting bail, the next step is indictment
or information. This is the formal action taken to initiate the
prosecution of the accused. The prosecutor has really unlimited
discretion to present or not to present cases to the grand jury for
indictment. This decision is also taken in secrecy and is rarely
subject to effective review by the judiciary.

Occasionally the victim of a crime will protest failure to
prosecute the perpetrator and bring action to compel his prosecution. This is an expensive, long and usually futile effort. For
while the victim pursues the alleged criminal through the ill-
defined mazes of the prosecutor's office and the courts, the statute

of limitations is running on the crime. By the mere lapse of time, the alleged criminal will go free. The victim may be motivated by vengeance. He may also be moved to act by a sense of outrage and belief in equal enforcement of the law.

Prosecutorial discretion is not controlled by the courts. Few courts will order the prosecutor to take action against a suspect. Many prosecutors are reluctant to press charges against policemen who are accused of brutality, shooting civilians or other serious charges. Often a prosecutor fails to press charges against politicians of the same party. The control over these decisions is virtually unfettered. I often think of Juanita, who complained to the prosecutor that she had been raped by two policemen. She was then arrested for making false charges. With much difficulty her lawyer managed to get the charges against her dropped. "But when are they going to prosecute the rapists?" she asked me. The truthful answer is, "Never."

Between indictment and trial, there may be a series of costly and time-consuming procedures that are mandated by law. The accused is given a copy of the charges against him, which usually tells him the crime of which he is charged, the name of the victim, the date and the place, but nothing more. Often some of these facts are omitted. At the preliminary hearing, if the accused is represented by competent counsel, he may through skillful cross-examination find out more about the crime and the evidence against him. Often, the hearing is perfunctory. A policeman or detective presents very brief testimony, giving only the bare bones of the charge. The defendant, especially if he is innocent, has little knowledge of the witnesses who have accused him or the nature of the evidence. Is it an eyewitness, fingerprints, bloodstains, circumstantial evidence? If he does not know the exact time of day when the offense is alleged to have occurred, how can he establish an alibi?

Months or years may pass between arrest and trial. Meanwhile the state, with its resources of police, investigators, crime laboratories, the cooperation of federal and other state agencies, is supposed to be gathering evidence. Often the file is gathering dust while the accused sits in jail. Six months after arrest a stolen-car case came before me for trial. The prosecutor asked for a continuance. He said the state needed more time "for research" to make out a case against the defendant. Six other judges in the preceding months had granted the prosecutor more time. I refused to do so and held that the defendant was entitled to a speedy trial under the Constitution. The prosecutor then dropped the charges. Was the defendant guilty? No one will ever know.

The accused is also supposed to be gathering his evidence prior to trial. Often he is in jail from the date of his arrest until trial, and must rely on the ingenuity of a lawyer whom he does not know and whom he did not select to make the investigation and persuade reluctant witnesses to testify. These are often marginal people with criminal records, who are reluctant to come to court. From such inadequate fragments of evidence defense counsel must attempt to find the facts and construct a plausible and legally sound theory of defense.

Prior to trial defense counsel may file a variety of motions—to quash the indictment for failing to charge a crime or being improperly returned, to suppress an illegally obtained confession or illegally seized evidence, to exclude the testimony of identification witnesses that was illegally obtained in that the defendant was not put in a fair line-up. For example, if the criminal is described as a tall, thin Negro about thirty-five years old and the accused who fits this description is placed in a line-up where the other people are either white, teen-agers, old or short or fat, obviously he will be promptly selected as the perpetrator of the crime. For this reason, a defendant is entitled to demand that his counsel be present at a line-up. Frequently he does not know his rights or fails to understand the importance of the line-up and waives his right to have counsel present.

In a typical case the state will claim that before the defendant made a confession, his Constitutional warnings were read to him, that he answered the seven questions indicating that he did not want a lawyer and that he wanted to talk to the police. This requirement that an accused be "warned" of his Constitutional rights was mandated by the notorious *Miranda* case.

The facts in the celebrated case were simple. Miranda, a poor, ignorant man, was arrested in connection with a kidnapping and rape. Without advising him of his right to counsel or his right to remain silent, police questioned him. Within two hours Miranda confessed. Under the prior doctrine governing confessions it was required that the court examine the "totality of the circumstances" under which the confession was obtained. Unless the entire situation was such that a court could find by a preponderance of the evidence that the accused's will was "overborne," the confession was admissible. The Supreme Court, Chief Justice Warren writing for the majority, reviewed a parade of horribles: cases in which suspects had been beaten, abused, threatened, subjected to psychological pressures and physical indignities. All of these things had happened for years in scores of cases. The Supreme Court had shown little interest in the problem until 1943, and then only with respect to federal prisoners. Of course, the overwhelming majority of persons accused of crime are prosecuted by the states, not the federal government.

In seeking definitively to dispose of the vexations and continuing problem, the Court ruled that henceforth every person taken into custody on suspicion of a crime must be advised of his Constitutional right to remain silent and to have counsel present when he is questioned, and if he cannot afford to have counsel to be informed that counsel will be provided for him at state expense if he so desires. The Court specified the exact language of the warnings every suspect must be given before the police can interrogate him.

Few recent decisions of the Court have been subjected to such scathing criticism. Some say it favors the rights of the criminal over those of society and the victims of crime. Others maintain that it has added an unnecessary burden to the overworked police. Legal scholars find the decision represents an unwarranted change in Constitutional interpretation, a use of the due process clause instead of the privilege against self-incrimination. More cynical observers called it a new "license to lie" for the police.

Neither the fears of the critics nor the hopes of the majority of the Supreme Court have been realized. Miranda's conviction was set aside and he was given a new trial in which he was again convicted. The percentage of poor, ignorant people who confess to crimes without the presence of a lawyer has not appreciably decreased. The use of physical and psychological coercion on suspects has become a little more sophisticated but no less effective in getting statements. Confessions are routinely given after the warnings. Often the defendant will claim that he was not advised of his rights until after he had given the confession. The number of convictions has not been affected by the decision.

However, court procedures have been changed. Between preliminary arraignment and trial an additional hearing has been added. This is a suppression hearing, a proceeding in which a judge without a jury hears evidence detailing the steps taken by the police to obtain a statement—usually a confession—from the suspect. In countless courtrooms all over the country on any day at any moment, a policeman will be reading into the record the contents of the police card, and a court stenographer will be transcribing in stenotype the policeman's reading of the card. The court stenographer will later read from his stenotype tape into a dictaphone and still later a typist will transcribe into the notes of testimony the contents of the little card.

[On the face of the card are these warnings:]

1. You have a right to remain silent and do not have to say anything at all.

2. Anything you say can and will be used against you in Court.

3. You have a right to talk to a lawyer of your own choice before we ask you any questions, and also to have a lawyer here with you while we ask questions.

4. If you cannot afford to hire a lawyer, and you want one, we will see that you have a lawyer provided to you, free of charge, before we ask you any questions.

5. If you are willing to give us a statement, you have a right to stop any time you wish.

[On the reverse side are the seven mandated questions:]

1. Do you understand that you have a right to keep quiet, and do not have to say anything at all?

2. Do you understand that anything you say can and will be used against you?

3. Do you want to remain silent?

4. Do you understand that you have a right to talk with a lawyer before we ask you any questions?

5. Do you understand that if you cannot afford to hire a lawyer, and you want one, we will not ask you any questions until a lawyer is appointed for you free of charge.

6. Do you want to talk with a lawyer at this time, or to have a lawyer with you while we ask these questions?

7. Are you willing to answer questions of your own free will, without force or fear, and without any threats or promise having been made to you?

The lawyers, the policemen, the judge and the court stenographer can recite the warnings from memory. They know them as well as their own names, but the law requires that the policeman testify as to what he told the defendant and that a verbatim transcript of the testimony be made. All of this is expensive. It also causes considerable delay. In clear-cut cases, a judge can rule from the bench at the close of testimony. But in many cases the situation is borderline; a conscientious judge will want to review the evidence and the law. Until the notes of testimony have been transcribed, the lawyers cannot write their briefs. The judge must then read the briefs and the notes of testimony. Two or three months after he has heard the evidence in the suppression hearing, the judge will render his decision. Meanwhile his memory has dimmed. He has heard dozens of other similar cases. He has the notes of testimony but he cannot be sure of the identity of the person, his impression of truthfulness, intelligence. He wonders, Was this defendant the drug addict, the illiterate, the man with the nervous tic? Unless the judge makes notes of these little impressions, which do not appear in the transcript, he often has no clear picture of the person on whose fate he is passing.

At the suppression hearing, a series of policemen and detectives testify that the warnings were given, that the defendant was fed, taken to the lavatory at regular intervals, that he was alert, not drunk or under the influence of drugs, that he was not threatened or coerced, and that he knowingly, intelligently and voluntarily made the confession which is then read from one piece of paper, transcribed by the court stenographer, redictated by him, and typed by his typist on another piece of paper. The defendant testifies that he was not warned of his rights until after he was interrogated, that he was manacled to a chair for six or ten or twenty-four hours with the light on continuously, in a windowless room without a clock, and that he finally signed the confession, which was typed by a policeman. The defendant testifies that he signed the confession without reading it because he was too exhausted, or was not given the opportunity to read it, or because he was beaten or threatened, or had been told that he was accused of the crime by his friends (which may or may not have been true). Meanwhile defense counsel has obtained a copy of the statement, has learned the circumstances of the arrest and the probable cause (the information leading the police to arrest this defendant).

After hearing such testimony for three, four or five hours or days, the judge must decide, not whether the defendant is guilty or innocent, but whether the defendant voluntarily made the statement. The judge is really deciding whether the police or the defendant is lying. In 1974, eight years after the Miranda decision, I am hearing cases in which it is admitted that the defendant was held in custody, manacled to a chair for twenty-eight hours, until he signed a confession. But he was given his warnings!

Thoughtful people recognize that a coerced confession is not reliable evidence. We know that every person has a breaking point. Except for saints and martyrs, people will confess to crimes they did not commit when sufficient physical torture or psychological pressure is exerted. The political trials in dictatorships give ample evidence to the untruthful confessions that even learned and sophisticated people will make. Ignorant, poor, semi-literate people, who constitute a large proportion of defendants, are likely to have a low breaking point. But how does a judge decide when this particular person reached that breaking point and, in the language of the Supreme Court, his "will was overborne"?

All of these pretrial hearings require the presence of counsel and of the defendant. It is obvious that since lawyers, like all people who perform services, whether doctors or plumbers, are paid for their time, defense of a criminal charge is very expensive. Frequently, if a defendant is employed and out on bail, he cannot afford to attend all these hearings (even though counsel is being paid by the public). The accused has to go to work or risk losing his job. Consequently he waives some of his rights. At present in many cities the average delay for defendants *in custody* is one hundred fifty to more than two hundred days, and in many cases a defendant is in jail more than a year before trial. More than two-thirds of the prisoners in most city jails have not been tried.

After the suppression hearing, when the case is finally listed for trial, the negotiations between the prosecutor in charge of the case and the defense attorney, known as plea bargaining, take place. Many imponderables influence the result, but only a few of them involve the defendant and the evidence against him. The prosecutor must consider the record of the office—how many victories and how many defeats. Is defense counsel a formidable opponent with whom it would be better not to joust? Or is it an inexperienced public defender, a starry-eyed do-gooder, or a lazy political appointee glad to receive his fee from the public exchequer for doing a minimum of work? The prosecutor must also take into account the public temper of the moment. Is this a case that has aroused great public indignation, such as the stabbing of a white citizen by a nonwhite hoodlum, or is it just a fatal shooting of one slum dweller by another? The defendant is always accused of a great variety of offenses so that a number of charges can be dropped without endangering the trial. The theft of a TV set, a common offense, is usually prosecuted under four indictments charging burglary, larceny, receiving stolen goods, and conspiracy. A purse snatching, especially if the thief has a gun or a knife, often is charged as robbery, larceny, assault and battery, assault with intent to kill, violation of uniform firearms act, and carrying a concealed deadly weapon. The multiplication of charges for a single incident also has curious effects on statistics. Five charges can be cleared by one arrest. One crime mushrooms into five. Often eight or nine people are arrested for a holdup which eyewitnesses state was perpetrated by only two.

In most jurisdictions the judge is not supposed to participate in the plea bargaining. In some states he is not in any way bound by the deal which the lawyers make. The defendant is brought before the bar of the court and pleads guilty. He is asked the routine questions to determine voluntariness of the plea. The law requires that one who waives his right to a trial must do so knowingly, competently, intelligently and voluntarily without threats or promises and with a full understanding of the rights he is giving up and the penalties he may receive.

Few defendants are able to survive, financially and emotionally, to utilize all the procedures that due process mandates. If any appreciable number of persons did exercise all these rights, refused to plead guilty and demanded a jury trial, the entire system of criminal justice would grind to a halt. Approximately 80 to 85 percent of all accused persons plead guilty to some charge and avoid trial.

Take the case of Willie J.—young, black and poor. He had a record of five or six convictions for minor charges. If he went to trial and testified in his own defense, his prior record would be revealed. If he did not testify, he would have no defense other than to try to cast doubt on the prosecutor's case. It is difficult to persuade a jury that all the prosecution witnesses are lying or mistaken if no one tells a contrary story. Willie was unable to make bail and spent some eight months in jail before he was brought to court for trial. Like all persons in jail he was taken from his jail cell to court in handcuffs. He "waived" his right to a jury trial because counsel suggested that he do so. The young defender must "dispose" of his quota of cases. In fact, an accused may have a better chance of acquittal before a judge who understands the uncertainty of eyewitness identification than before a jury whose only knowledge of law is gleaned from the press and TV aside from the charge by the judge.

When Willie was brought into the courtroom the defender asked for five minutes to confer with his client. He had never seen Willie. A different lawyer interviewed Willie in jail. Another one was at the preliminary hearing, a third at the motion to suppress. This was Willie's fourth appearance before a judge or magistrate. This was his fourth different attorney. After a brief whispered conference Willie pleaded guilty to a lesser charge.

And so the case of Willie J. was disposed of. But this was not the end. In prison Willie learned about postconviction remedies. With the help of a more knowledgeable convict, he filed a petition for a postconviction hearing, alleging that he was not properly and adequately represented by counsel, that he did not have time to discuss his case, to get witnesses, and that he was told to plead guilty or he might get a stiffer term. In due course, a private attorney was appointed by the court to represent Willie at public expense. There was another hearing at which the defender testified. He testified truthfully that he could not remember Willie. His file indicated that he recommended a guilty plea; that Willie could have gotten more than sixty years on all those counts. (Willie had received a sentence of three to ten years.) He thought then and he thinks now that this was a fair result. He is sure that he explained the significance of a guilty plea to Willie; it is his practice to do so in all cases. Relief was denied. Private counsel took an appeal. At oral argument one of the Justices of the State Supreme Court plaintively remarked to the attorney, "But they always say that they were not adequately represented by the defender." And counsel replied, "Yes, Your Honor, they always say so because it is true." Willie's appeal was dismissed.

Willie's case had been before various courts six times. All of the technical requirements of due process were complied with. But Willie never had a trial of the facts: did he or did he not commit the robbery? At public expense he was represented by the defender at four different hearings and was interviewed once. Private counsel, who was paid $450.00, appeared at a hearing and took an appeal. How much did all this cost? No one knows. Is Willie satisfied that he has had his day in court, a fair hearing on the charges? Of course not! In fact, he has never had a hearing on the substantive issue, guilt or innocence. And yet all the procedures have been followed to the letter if not the spirit of the law.

Willie and tens of thousands of people like him are in jail awaiting trial or serving sentences. Mr. Chief Justice Burger rightly points out that "Today the American system of adjudication of guilt or innocence in criminal cases is the most comprehensive—and indeed the most complex in terms of retrials, appeals and postconviction reviews—that can be found in any society in the world. No nation can match the United States in these manifestations of profound concern for the rights of accused persons. Yet with all this development of the step-by-step details in the criminal adversary process, we continue, at the termination of that process, to brush under the rug the problems of those who are found guilty and subject to criminal sentence." [2]

We also ignore the beginning of the process—the unfettered discretion of the prosecutor to bring charges against the accused, which sets in motion the entire criminal justice process. We ignore the end of the process, the prison system which, in the telling phrase of Justice Burger, has a two-thirds reject rate. Two-thirds of those who are imprisoned, after release, are arrested for new crimes. The criminal justice system continues the manufacture of criminals in the jails which are, with unconscious irony, called "correctional institutions."

Specific proposals for changes in the substantive law, the procedural law, the type of legal representation and the prisons abound. Everyone, from the prisoners themselves to the President, manifests concern. Prisoners riot to call attention to their plight. Many of them are shot and killed in these futile uprisings. Commissions and committees investigate and make reports. Criminologists, psychologists, sociologists and psychiatrists make studies of crime and delinquency. Both President Johnson and President Nixon appointed commissions to examine the criminal justice system. The Johnson Commission report, "The Challenge of Crime in a Free Society," is a careful statistical and descriptive study. Criminologists, sociologists, psychologists, lawyers, judges and public officials participated in the research, deliberations and recommendations. President Nixon's National Conference on Criminal Justice was held in Washington, January 23–26, 1973. This body also made many recommendations for procedural changes.

After centuries of ignoring the criminal law, the legal profession has during the past two decades taken an intense interest in the problems of criminal justice. With all the current public concern and activity, it is easy to forget the long years of disinterest and neglect when criminal law was treated as the stepchild of the legal profession. Law schools customarily offered one course out of a three-year curriculum in criminal law. Few of the leading graduates of the leading law schools entered this branch of practice. The reasons are obvious. It is difficult and emotionally wearing to have the responsibility for a client's life [3] or liberty. Neither the clients nor the witnesses, on the whole, are people whose company one would enjoy. Before the landmark decision of the United States Supreme Court, *Gideon v. Wainwright*,[4] in 1963, holding that the Constitution required that persons accused of crime be provided with legal counsel and if they are indigent at public expense, the prospects of earning a living as a criminal lawyer were decidedly limited. Criminal law was not a promising field for an ambitious young lawyer, except for those who sought a political future through the office of prosecutor.

Until recently, the law itself was static and not very challenging. Criminal law was largely ignored by the appellate courts. In the 1950 term of the United States Supreme Court, of 192 cases decided on the merits only 16 involved criminal law and habeas corpus. In the 1970 term of court, however, of 141 cases decided on the merits, in which there was a full opinion, 35 involved criminal law and habeas corpus.

In part, this reflects the rising crime rate, a recognition that perhaps half of the cases in the trial courts today involve prosecutions for crime. One would also like to view this increased concern with the criminal law as an indication that the law has developed a greater awareness of the rights and needs of those accused of crime. The evidence on this point is conflicting. In a nation in which 6 million crimes are reported annually, no one can ignore the problems of criminal law.

Many of the recommendations for reform or change are sensible and practical. However, they deal with specifics and ignore the underlying fact that this is a lawless society. The so-called radicals propose the elimination of poverty, war and racism. These are desirable ends in themselves. It must be remembered that the vast majority of poor white and poor nonwhite Americans are not convicted of crime, and that much lawlessness is found in affluent, white America.

Those who look at the crowded court system recommend the repeal of victimless crimes and "sin" crimes, such as drunkenness, drug addiction, prostitution, irregular sexual behavior among consenting adults and gambling. This would reduce the police and court load by at least half and also drastically reduce the jail population. Obviously these are desirable proposals, beneficial to those now manufactured into criminals and to the taxpayers. It costs on an average $4,000 to $10,000 a year to keep one person in jail. It costs, depending on the community, $500 to $1,500 a day to operate one court room. The removal from the criminal sanction of behavior which is acceptable to a large proportion of the population would lessen the dysjunction between legal and societal standards, relieving in part a burden which law, qua law, can no longer sustain.

Other practical recommendations include a rigorous screening of arrests before prosecution to eliminate cases which are of marginal public concern, and cases in which there is insufficient evidence to sustain a conviction. Requiring disclosure of prosecution witnesses and evidence against the defendant prior to trial would measurably shorten the proceedings and make the trial itself fairer. Appeal of sentences is another long overdue reform. At present, the only way a convict can obtain a review of an unduly harsh sentence is to try to find an error in the trial—a long, expensive process for the appellant and an unnecessary and time-consuming one for the courts.

An ombudsman or civilian review of police practices, not only to protect the public against police brutality and corruption but to oversee the fairness and legality of arrest procedures, is desirable and will save much court time.

Prison reform is also long overdue. We are aware of the "Crime of Punishment" [5] as it is administered in our prisons. This book does not discuss the problems of prisons, capital punishment, and alternative forms of jails. In some prisons convicts attend college and obtain degrees at public expense while honest working people cannot afford to go to college. Other prisons are brutal and inhuman. While under the common law a convict was sentenced to hard labor, the average prisoner spends months and years in idleness or meaningless prison chores. The evils of the prison system have been documented again and again.[6] The failure to consider any alternatives to the existing range of penalties—fine, imprisonment (either in a conventional jail or a new community-based facility) and probation—indicates a poverty of imagination and an unwillingness to question the validity of traditional concepts. There are countless proposals for new types of prisons, new types of therapy, vocational training, job placement for parolees, and help in making the return to society. But these proposals are concerned only with the convict and his rehabilitation. The rights of the victims of crime are largely ignored by those concerned with corrections—prison and probation. The notion that the law violator owes a duty to the victims of his wrongdoing has disappeared from the common law. Under Anglo-Saxon law, before the Norman conquest, the criminal slayer was required to pay compensation to the victim's family. This was known as "wergild"—or, the price of a man. This is similar to the present law of negligence. If Jones negligently runs over and kills Smith, the family of Smith can sue and collect as civil damages the amount of the estimated earnings of Smith during the period of his life expectancy. If, however, Jones kills Smith in the course of a holdup, Jones will be prosecuted for murder. Most likely he will be imprisoned for a period of years at a cost of perhaps $7,000 a year to the taxpayers. But the family of Smith will not be compensated. Under our law, they are nonpersons, without standing to sue. Only the state can prosecute the criminal. The victim and his family have no rights or remedies.

Several states, responding to the public demand for consideration of the victims of crime, have enacted statutes providing for limited compensation from public funds for such victims, an additional burden on the taxpayers. The nexus between the criminal and the victim, the old idea of the responsibility of the wrongdoer to the victim, has not been restored by these laws.

In most states the maximum fine is set by statute and bears no relation to the harm done or the criminal's ability to pay. For example, the maximum fine permitted in Pennsylvania is $25,000, in Michigan $10,000, and in California $15,000. Many crimes, such as fraud and forgery, net criminals hundreds of thousands of dollars. The maximum fine in no way removes the profit from crime. New York permits a fine not to exceed double the accused's pecuniary gain from the crime. But corporations are exempted from this provision. Such fines are not payable to the victims but to the state. There is no reason why convicted criminals should not be made to labor at minimum wages and pay over a period of years into a revolving fund which would be used to compensate the victims. As under insurance policies, the risk would be spread so that all criminals would pay into the fund according to their financial ability and earning capacity, and the fund would make disbursements to the victims in accordance with the damages suffered. A public works program to employ the convicts would be required to implement such a program since many are unemployed and unemployable in the open work force. This is but one suggestion of many possibilities to restructure the principles of the criminal law to meet the needs of society. There is no Constitutional inhibition against changing the penalties for crime or establishing compensation for victims of crime. Little thought is being given to such basic matters as the ethical relationships among state, criminal and victim or a more just equation.

Many new and costly programs within the existing criminal law and prison system are being proposed and tried with questionable success. These range from rap sessions to changing the personality of convicts by chemical or surgical means. The legality, the efficacy, and the morality of such plans are highly questionable. Assuming for the sake of argument that personality-altering procedures were medically safe and effective, and that there was a truly voluntary consent on the part of the convict, do we know what constitutes a normal, law-abiding, nonviolent person? Is there such a standard or norm in American life today? Is there a consensus as to moral, acceptable behavior? One looks in vain among the brightest and the best for a recognition of law as a force or principle governing the behavior of the governors. The scientists themselves who propose these experiments often reveal a shocking insensitivity to the legal rights of their subjects and an almost total lack of awareness of law which should limit their experimentations. Similarly, false reports of allegedly successful studies by scientists indicate that illegal behavior extends throughout the entire spectrum of American society—from illiterate slum dwellers to Ph.D.'s and university professors.

If all of these proposed reforms were instituted at once, and if they were wisely, lawfully, and effectively administered, it is apparent that the court backlogs and the prison populations would be somewhat reduced. The victims would receive some help. Some of the hostility toward the legal process would abate simply because fewer people would be involved. Possibly some forms of violent behavior would be reduced. *But the basic problem of governing a lawless society based upon a rule of law would remain.*

It is an undeniable fact that law fails to provide satisfactory normative behavioral controls. Lawless violence is accepted and condoned by wide segments of society, from the highest levels of government to the average citizen. The grand jury that refused to indict the law-enforcement officers who shot the Kent State students were average members of the community in Ohio. Average citizens of East Meadow, Long Island, also refused to indict George Diener, who killed his seventeen-year-old son, Richie. Richie wore his hair long and took drugs. He was an alienated youth. But there are hundreds of thousands like him. His father, who is described as a "decent man," shot and killed the boy.[7] One wonders how many decent George Dieners there are in America. The members of the grand jury that condoned the slaying doubtless considered themselves decent persons, far removed from "criminals" like Vernon and Kenneth and poor, black Mrs. T., who shot the boy who raped her daughter.

In pluralistic America there is no single law to which the population as a whole assents. The National Advisory Commission on Civil Disorders reported in 1968: "Our nation is moving toward two societies, one black, one white—separate and unequal." Our administration of criminal law is also separate and unequal. It bears more heavily on the poor, the nonwhite, the young and the dissident who make up the vast majority of arrestees and prisoners. A young hood, interviewed by Jerry S. Cohen and Morton Mintz, authors of *America, Inc.* declared the law is "an instrument for the rich. When did you last hear of one of those big old corporations going to jail for fixing prices or selling rotten meat or evasion of income taxes?" Former Secretary of the Interior, Hickel, plaintively and profitably wrote *Who Owns America?* He answered that we do. But even a young hood knows better.

America in the sixties was explosive, volatile, conscience-stricken and seeking change. The dominant white, affluent American society in the seventies is withdrawn and self-centered. The poor are relegated to benign neglect and the criminal justice system. Our leaders openly flout the decencies and amenities of the law. The series of illegal actions revealed in the Watergate hearings clearly demonstrate that crime flourishes among the educated, wealthy and powerful as well as among the semiliterate, poor and outcast.

All Americans are scofflaws. All Americans are afflicted with anomie, which Emile Durkheim described as characteristic of our age. Alienation and loss of common moral beliefs have resulted in a general disregard of law. The entire criminal process from arrest through trial and imprisonment, regulated by Constitutional doctrine and premised upon the recognition of good and evil by the accused, has become an elaborate, unending exercise in futility.

Unless the American people believe in the justice and efficacy of law, we shall continue to be a nation of scofflaws operating an expensive criminal justice system which simply cycles and recycles those defendants unlucky enough to have been caught through the assembly line of arrest, trial and imprisonment. When law as an animating principle of behavior is dead, procedural reforms in trials, updating the definitions of crime, and humanizing prisons —all worthy ends in themselves—will not induce a lawless people to become law abiding. Every literate American knows that it is illegal and immoral to "bug" conversations, to use the processes of government to harass one's "enemies" and make profits for one's friends. Similarly all Americans know that it is illegal and immoral to kill. A study of prisoners convicted of murder revealed that all who were questioned knew that it was wrong to kill. Killers, conspirators and misfeasors in public office know that they are violating the law. We must acknowledge the obvious fact that law no longer has the vitality or force to deter crime in America.

From the sordid stuff of litigation,
shining truths emerge.

Benjamin Nathan Cardozo, *The Nature*
of the Judicial Process

As the wheels of justice grind on,
innocence becomes progressively less
relevant.

F. Lee Bailey,
The Defense Never Rests

Less is more.

Mies van der Rohe

6: The Nature of Litigational Process

Most of the criminal prosecutions in the United States are directed against poor people. Most of the civil litigation involves money. These are simplistic statements. Nonetheless they are true. One can point to wealthy and powerful people who have been prosecuted and convicted; there are lengthy cases involving prosecutions of dissidents and political figures which raise great Constitutional issues of freedom of speech, due process of law, equal protection of the laws and limitations on governmental powers; similarly, some civil litigation also involves important issues of governmental power, individual rights and the protection of the public; much of the litigation involving the environment, unsafe products, integration of schools and public facilities and voting rights is in the form of civil suits. However, conservatively estimating the various types of litigation in the state courts, one can safely say that 85 percent of all criminal prosecutions and juvenile cases involve poor if not indigent people and that 85 percent of all civil cases involve disputes over money. Such cases include damage suits for personal and property injuries arising out of accidents, unsafe products, medical malpractice, contracts, landlord and tenant cases, will contests, and even family problems, which ultimately come to a question not of love and fidelity but of money.

All of these cases, whether they involve a purse snatching or the parameters of Presidential powers, whether they involve a private dispute over $50 or the defrauding of the public of millions of dollars, are tried under the same form of adversary contest under our system of litigation. The Anglo-American trial is often depicted by the hackneyed symbol of the blindfold goddess weighing the merits of the opposing parties in the scales of justice. The judge in charging the jury often refers to this symbol, telling the jury to weigh the claims of the opposing parties without bias or favor, considering only the evidence, being blind to the wealth, poverty or other characteristics of the litigant, and that the judge or court is merely the fulcrum on which the scales are balanced. The fairness and justice of such a rule is not seriously questioned, although, in fact, the scales are heavily weighted against the poor.

Colonel Wigmore, the great authority on evidence, used a different metaphor to explain the theory of Anglo-American trials. He called it the "sporting theory" of justice. Under this view, the courtroom is an arena in which the two lawyers slug it out, with the judge acting as referee—blowing the whistle only when one side or the other hits below the belt, kicks or gouges. The fairness of this sport known as litigation is seldom questioned even though the average civil litigant and the average indigent defendant have about as much chance as the unarmed Christians had in the gladiatorial combats with the lions in the Coliseum of ancient Rome. In both civil and criminal cases, the sporting theory of litigation gives too great an advantage to the skill and resources of counsel. The poor defendant with a lawyer whom he does not know usually pleads guilty. A poor plaintiff who cannot afford to wait for trial settles for a fraction of his losses. In those cases which are tried, all too often, referring to the athletic analogy, one sees a bantamweight amateur sparring with a heavyweight champion. There is little that the judge, as referee, can do to equalize the combat. The theory of trial and the rules governing the conduct of judge, counsel and the presentation of evidence do not permit the court to give a few points of handicap to the litigant with less able counsel and less adequate resources.

These symbols and metaphors are poetic devices to capture the attention of the reader or to heighten emotions. They are not useful in providing an accurate description or explaining a complicated process. The litigational process is extremely complex. It is bound by rules, regulations and principles. Metaphors and analogies becloud an understanding of the process. The basic system of litigation is very old. Many of the underlying assumptions upon which the rules are based antedate the Bible. Some practices derive from the time of Edward the Confessor. Others, like the use of computers and psychiatrists, are being grafted onto the process in a continuing effort at modernization. The major principles underlying the litigational process, however, have not been fundamentally altered for more than a thousand years. The purpose of litigation, which is perhaps as old as that misty past when our ancestors banded together to hunt wild animals, is to resolve conflicts without bloodshed and violence on a basis of accepted rules rather than naked power.

Every society has some means, other than self-help, for resolving conflicts and enforcing norms of behavior. But it is only in the United States, as De Tocqueville noted, that every issue becomes a court case, a matter to be litigated and decided in accordance with the principles and procedures of law. In the century and a half since De Tocqueville observed "Democracy in America," the amount of litigation has increased enormously, both in quantity of suits filed and in the number of basic issues presented to the courts. There can be no doubt that in absolute numbers and on a per capita basis Americans are the most litigious nation in human history. Such a rush to the courthouse has brought neither an orderly society nor a law-abiding citizenry. Since the principle of resolving conflicts by litigation is so significant a feature of the American social order, the litigational process must be examined to see what part, if any, it has played in the death of the law.

The dearth of information about the litigational process is amazing. In this computerized, statistical age, there are no accurate records on a national basis as to the numbers of cases initiated or completed. We do not know the length of trial for most cases. We do not know what it costs the litigants or the public for the trial of cases. We do not know whether the results are fair or just. We do not know whether on the whole litigants are satisfied that they have had a fair trial and justice has been done or the contrary. Apparently the pollsters have never conducted such an inquiry among the millions of people who use the courts.

Any one seeking to study the litigational or trial process as it actually operates must do his own research. Although entire libraries have been written about the nature of the judicial process,[1] few books describe the nature of the litigational process. Most scholars pay little attention to what actually happens in the trial courts of the nation. The American Assembly, a distinguished group of scholars acting under the aegis of Columbia University, met at Arden House in 1965 to study "The Courts, the Public and the Law Explosion." [2] Of the six topics, one was devoted to the "Role Analysis and Profile of the Trial Judge," another to "Judicial Selection and Tenure," and a third to "The Elimination of Appeals." The nature of the litigational process, its efficacy and its fairness were totally ignored. Even a cursory look at the titles of the articles in legal journals reveals that scholarship is concerned with specific rules of law, their logic and consistency. One looks in vain for studies of the trial process and its impact on the public attitude toward law.

All law suits are tried in the same format, regardless of the issues or the parties. Essentially there are two contending parties. In some cases third parties are drawn in. A party may be the government or a group of thousands of stockholders or thousands of consumers, or a single individual. The lawsuit must involve an actual "case or controversy," in other words, an existing dispute. One cannot go to court to ask in advance for a ruling to guide one's future conduct. Most of the time of the court will be concerned with attempting to find "the facts" of the particular case. On occasion the parties stipulate, that is, agree on the facts. This rarely happens, because a minor variation in the factual situation may change the decision on the law. Facts, of course, are not absolute, clearly defined objects; a fact is ascertained in litigation primarily through the testimony of witnesses.

Anglo-American trials are based upon faith in the solemnity of an oath. Every witness places his hand on the Bible. He is asked, "Do you swear (or affirm) to tell the truth, the whole truth and nothing but the truth, so help you God?" And he replies, "I do." In the Middle Ages, when the populace believed that divine vengeance would be visited immediately upon one who swore falsely, the taking of an oath may have ensured truthful testimony. It is impossible now, looking back at old records, to know how much perjury occurred in other ages. In 1774, an English court explained the significance of the oath:

> Nothing but the belief in God, and
> that He will reward and punish us
> according to our deserts, is necessary
> to qualify a man to take an oath.

Today, of course, nonbelievers are permitted to affirm and testify. The validity of testimonial evidence is based upon a moral responsibility to tell the truth.

A judge can only wonder if anyone tells the truth. Many lies are patent and intentional. Two witnesses take the stand. Each swears to tell the truth. Each looks the judge squarely in the eye and tells a diametrically opposite story. The judge and jury are supposed to observe the demeanor of the witnesses on the stand and determine who is telling the truth. But one can only guess.

Recently a court in California accepted a lie-detector test as evidence, although the tests are generally considered unreliable. Judge Allen Miller stated his reasons:

Perjury is prevalent and the oath taken by witnesses has little effect to deter false testimony. The principal role of the trier of fact is the search for truth and any reasonable procedure or method to assist the court in this search should be employed.

Unfortunately there is no easy litmus test for truth. Machinery is not infallible. Certainly the operators of these devices are fallible, and the validity of the test is dependent upon the operator, who must also testify in court.

Some witnesses lie unintentionally but equally dangerously. The witness is convinced that he has seen or heard certain things and so testifies. Other, more cautious, witnesses destroy the value of their testimony by truthfulness. Such a witness is asked on cross-examination if he is absolutely certain. "Well, Your Honor, it all happened so long ago. I can't be sure," he replies. This truthful testimony is of no value. Less critical and intelligent witnesses, having convinced themselves that events actually happened two or three years ago or even ten years ago as they now recall them, will declare their beliefs with absolute certainty. Such testimony is acceptable. The witness may be right. But he may be honestly mistaken. Neither the judge nor jury has any reliable means of ascertaining the truth.

Most witnesses, if they do not actually lie, tell much less than the whole truth. A distinguished law professor has argued that it is the duty of a lawyer to lie on behalf of his client. I doubt that many lawyers follow his advice. Few clients need it. A particularly artless litigant testified with respect to a document showing his title to certain property, "My lawyer told me I didn't have enough evidence, that I needed something in writing." Within days such a writing was "found."

Joe Goulden, in *The Superlawyers*,[3] describes how a lawyer avoids suborning perjury but makes clear to all but the most stupid client the evidence that either is required or that must be avoided.

"You are looking," the Washington Lawyer told me, "at one of the dumbest sons of bitches in Western civilization." He nodded across the Falstaff Room of the Sheraton-Carlton Hotel to a middle-aged man who smiled politely and then very deliberately returned his attention to another man at the table. But during the next half-hour I saw him glance back at our table, as if the Washington Lawyer was an unpleasant memory.

"This fellow," the Washington Lawyer was saying to me, with three-martini candor, "is in the . . . business in Maryland. Three, four years ago, he came to me, on recommendation of a friend of mine in Baltimore, and said he needed some help in a bad way. He had been doing some odd-ball discounting to some customers and not to others, and the way he admitted it to me, it was a clear-cut violation of the Robinson-Patman Act, because it was as discriminatory as hell. Apparently one of the unfavored customers had complained to his lawyer, who in turn had complained to the Federal Trade Commission. Trouble was coming; it was just a matter of time.

"Now, in a situation like this, the documents should tell the whole story, and I don't see any reason why a man should help the Federal government build a gallows for himself. At the same time, the bar rules are pretty simple: If I advise him to go burn everything, I can be disbarred for interfering with the processes of justice.

"So I take another route. I tell him just what I told you—without all his sales records, the FTC will have a hell of a time making a case. Oh, they could, but only by backtracking to customers. But I know the FTC is so short-handed they won't do that except in a major case. 'Do you still have any documents around that could hurt you?' I asked him. 'Some of this stuff must be getting pretty old, and most people turn over their records fairly *fast.*'

" 'Oh, no,' he said, 'I've got everything. My bookkeeper is meticulous.'

"I tried again. 'You know,' I said, 'there's no law that says how long you've got to keep stuff, so long as you have enough to substantiate your tax records. That must be quite a storage problem, maintaining all those old outdated files.'

"God, he didn't even blink. 'Oh, we have plenty of space,' he said. 'We just put it in crates and put it in the back of the warehouse. It's all right there.'

"I gave up. He was so damned dense he wasn't about to tumble to what I was saying and I didn't dare take it a step further and tell him to go home and have himself one hell of a big bonfire. I kind of like being a lawyer, you know. Just as I feared, the FTC subpoenaed enough to make a case, and it cost the poor bastard one hell of a lot of time and trouble. 'But why didn't you just tell me I should have cleaned out the files,' he kept asking me. I finally unloaded on him and gave him an informative little talk.

"He's still mad at me. He haggled over the bill, and he cussed me all over Washington and Baltimore. I don't give a damn, though; I still have my law license."

A psychiatrist whom I once retained to testify on behalf of a client asked me, "What do you want me to say?" Obviously most witnesses are not so naïve. But are their actions much different?

Few trial lawyers or judges find that truth emerges from the litigational process. On the contrary, they find that perjury and falsehood are as commonly heard from the witness stand as truth. All too often the truthful litigant loses and the liar wins.

Every day countless people commit perjury either consciously or unconsciously. Given the same data, doctors will reach diametrically opposite conclusions depending, of course, upon which party hired them to testify. The same is true of scientists, engineers, financiers, handwriting experts and even statisticians. The judge and the jury, when there is one, can at best make an uneducated guess. As one lawyer remarked, "If the client can afford it, he can always find an expert to support his cause."

Every factual issue must be proved by testimony. Even so simple and common a question as the speed at which an automobile was going can rarely be agreed upon. Occasionally the police "clock" a car and record its speed. But these devices are subject to error and must be operated properly. The driver probably did not look at the speedometer at the exact moment in question. If he did, he may not tell the truth. Other eyewitnesses may not have had adequate opportunity to observe; their estimates may be honestly mistaken; or they may lie. Hours of court time are devoted to testimony of witnesses in an effort to ascertain such a "fact" as the speed of an automobile at the time of the accident.

It has been said that if a legal right depended upon whether the sun was shining at the time of trial, no one would look out the window and see for himself. Each side would provide a witness who would testify as to the observation he had made. Undoubtedly the witnesses would disagree. Each would be cross-examined to determine his qualifications to express an opinion as to whether the sun was shining. The witness' reputation for veracity as well as the condition of his eyesight might be an issue. On that question there would also be expert opinion, probably in sharp disagreement.

Such inconclusive and unreliable testimony is the basis for deciding "facts." The judge or jury must decide on an either/or basis. In a trial one party must win and the other lose. The accused is either guilty or not, just as a girl cannot be a little pregnant. But evidence is generally inconclusive. All too often at the conclusion of a case, after days or weeks of testimony, I am no more certain of the intention of the parties in entering into a contract, or the negligence of the doctor, or the safety of the product than I was at the beginning of the trial. From the pleadings or the indictment, the judge knows what the contentions of the parties are. Their theories and a good deal of the evidence have been developed in pretrial proceedings. The trial itself often reveals nothing that was not known in advance.

The theory of litigation is that by the process of testifying, the sharp cross-examination of the witnesses by opposing counsel, observation of the manner and demeanor of the witnesses, falsehood will be revealed and winnowed out and the judge or jury will find the truth. This is another myth.

Mr. Justice Andrews ruefully admitted that "rough, average justice" was all that could be expected from the litigational process. That is scarcely enough to justify the vast amounts of learning, effort, time and expense devoted to the trial of cases. But it is unfortunately a great deal more than most people ever get.

We are still bemused by the notion that the adversary proceeding in which each side presents its evidence and the court decides on the basis of this information only, no matter how inconclusive or incomplete, is the best and fairest way of deciding every type of dispute. Often the lawyers will deliberately refrain from bringing out certain information derogatory to their clients or helpful to the other side. Except in criminal trials, where the prosecution is *supposed* to reveal exculpatory information, the choice of information to be presented is a matter of tactics and strategy.

The United States Supreme Court has declared that it will not raise trial strategy to the "dignity of a Constitutional right and say that the deprival of this defendant of that sporting chance" denied him due process of law.[4] A more appropriate question is whether the sporting trial affords *anyone* due process or a just result.

Most cases involve questions of fact: Is this defendant the man who committed the crime? Does A owe money to B? These are the "sordid matters" of which Mr. Justice Cardozo wrote. Haggling over money is not very elevating or spiritually satisfying, nor is the difficult matter of determining who is lying. But the results of these trials often profoundly and disastrously affect the lives of ordinary people. Conviction or acquittal is of the utmost importance to the accused. The denial of adequate financial recovery may destroy a family.

Mr. Justice Cardozo was convinced that from such cases shining truths emerge. One must remember that he was an appellate court judge. He did not sit through settlement conferences and trials. He did not accept guilty pleas from barely literate defendants who are represented by strange lawyers whom they see fleetingly. He did not hear barefaced lies or half-truths from countless witnesses—many stupid, others slick and clever. He only read records of those cases which involved enough money or an interesting enough question of law to reach the highest court of New York or the United States Supreme Court.

Truth, shining or tarnished, does not emerge from many trials, not because court, counsel or litigants are deliberately perverting justice but because the nature of the litigational process obscures truth. It is so complex and costly as to defeat many who are not intellectually strong and financially secure. It is heavily weighted in favor of those who can afford to retain able counsel and pay for the time needed to find evidence and to endure the delays and strain of trial.

Of all the civil lawsuits instituted fewer than half will ever come to trial. Of this number, barely 5 percent will be tried by juries. What happens to the other cases? What are the considerations that impel a litigant to withdraw a civil suit or to settle it? How long did the litigants have to wait for a hearing? And of those who did get a decision, how many actually are able to enforce it? After the plaintiff wins a verdict, more often than not, he must sue again to collect it, or compromise and accept a lesser sum. In criminal cases, we know that 90 percent of criminal convictions are obtained by plea bargaining and that fewer than 5 percent of the cases are tried by jury. In civil personal injury cases we know that it takes more than twenty-one months after suit is filed to get to trial in most jurisdictions. In many, it takes five years or more from the filing of suit to the actual trial. With painstaking effort it might be possible to study the litigational process, to compile data, to evaluate procedures, to test results for fairness, efficiency, cost and speed. No one has done so.

Time and money are real considerations, often of far more significance to the individual than the issue of law involved. A more basic inquiry is the accessibility of the litigational process. We do not know how many valid claims are never filed because of hopeless discouragement, because the cost of achieving one's just deserts far exceeds the award that will be rendered, or because the litigant simply cannot afford to use the machinery of litigation at all. Although the courts are paid for by taxes levied on everyone, including the poor, they are not free. In order to sue, one must pay a filing fee, a fee to have the defendant served with papers, a fee for a notarial seal, a fee for witnesses, a fee for a lawyer. An energetic and sophisticated person can go in to small-claims court and represent himself. Poor, semiliterate people who do not keep records and receipts have great difficulty in doing so.

At present, the poor are effectively debarred from the use of civil courts. It even costs money to file a petition to be permitted to proceed in forma pauperis, as a pauper. Surely this is a demeaning barrier to the assertion of one's rights. And such pleas are granted only as a matter of grace and often denied.

In 1970, I wrote, "I have never known anyone too rich to go through bankruptcy but I have known many people too poor to be able to be relieved of their debts." The United States Supreme Court in 1973 held that filing fees in bankruptcy do not have to be waived for the poor. "There is no Constitutional right to obtain a discharge of one's debts in bankruptcy," [5] the Court ruled. Any description of the litigational process is incomplete unless one is aware that it is closed to those who cannot afford it, perhaps one-third to one-half of the population.

In criminal prosecution, the considerations that impel an accused to plead guilty are time and money. If he cannot afford the expenses of investigation, witnesses and counsel, if he cannot raise bail, an innocent accused will plead guilty to a lesser charge and obtain his freedom more quickly, cheaply and with greater certainty than going to trial in an effort to exonerate himself.

The civil equivalent of plea bargaining is settlement. Chief Judge Fox of the Federal District of Michigan points out the not inconsiderable advantages of settlement over trial. First, it is a final disposition of the case. There is no appeal from a settlement. Second, it saves time. There is no trial. Third, it cuts down the backlog. Judge Fox also suggests that settlement may produce a fairer result if both parties agree to a figure rather than risking the vagaries of juries, uncertain witnesses, and unbending rules of law. A trial judge thus finds himself haggling over money rather than ruling on disputed points of law.

Most judges comfort themselves with the thought that settling a case instead of trying it is a victory (1) for the public, which is saved an enormous expense, (2) for the judge himself, who has improved his batting average in disposing of cases, and (3) for the plaintiff, who at least will take home some money, probably a lesser sum than if he went to trial, but at least he has something in hand now instead of two or three years later after appeals are exhausted, and (4) for the defendant, who might well have had to pay a higher award and is saved additional counsel fees and expenses. Few judges dare to ask themselves if such settlements have advanced either law or justice.

These questions—Does the litigational process provide just re-sults? Does it promote a belief in law?—we have ignored at our peril.

At trial, the search for truth and justice must be conducted along very restricted paths. Litigants, witnesses, lawyers and judges are bound by rules developed in other cases, in other generations or centuries, which have little to do with the problems presented to the court today. The trial judge has a very limited scope of discretion. He must apply the rules, though justice be thwarted at every turn.

In most jurisdictions, if a badly injured plaintiff was ever so slightly negligent and the defendant grossly negligent, the plaintiff cannot recover. If machinery malfunctions, injuring someone, the owner is not liable unless he was negligent in maintaining or inspecting the machinery.

A person injured in an accident not occurring in the course of his employment who is unable to work is entitled to recover expenses, pain and suffering, and loss of earnings. If the injured party is successful, he or she will recover that sum, perhaps four to eight or more years after the injury. He will not get interest. A factory hand earning $175 a week will recover that amount. An unemployed housewife will not be paid for loss of her time. An executive earning $100,000 a year will recover his loss of earnings. The executive probably has insurance, savings and assets to help him over the period of unemployment due to injury. The factory hand and the housewife may have no resources to help them survive an illness or injury. The law does not grant recovery on the basis of need but only upon provable monetary loss.

The rules governing the admission of evidence are like the laws of the Medes and the Persians, old and immutable. Hearsay testimony, which is what someone else told the witness, is excluded except in certain well-defined situations. It is excluded because there is no right to cross-examine the first speaker, who is not present at the trial, with respect to the truth of his statement. Often the application of the rule makes no sense. Many arrests are made because an unknown citizen stopped a police car or phoned the police to report a crime in progress. For example, a policeman is stopped by an excited civilian who says, "Go to the corner of First and Main Streets, a man with a goatee and a green jacket is robbing and beating an old woman." The policeman immediately drives a block to that location, finds a dead woman on the street and a man with a goatee and green jacket running away.

In court the policeman will testify, "I was in my patrol car No. 437, at 8:23 P.M., and driving down Main Street at the corner of Second. I was stopped by an unknown man in a car who said—"

"Objection, Your Honor."

"Sustained. Officer, do not tell us what the man said, but only what you said or did."

"As a result of information received, I proceeded to First and Main Streets where I saw the body of a woman lying on the street and a man in a goatee and green jacket running east. I pursued the man and apprehended him."

It may take an hour or more of testimony to develop what happened. It may be impossible ever to show the connection between the man in the green jacket and the dead woman.

On the other hand, when it is a question of reputation, hearsay is freely admitted and factual evidence is excluded.

"What is the reputation of Mr. Jones, among those who know him, for honesty and peaceful disposition?"

The witness testifies that Jones is known as an honest, law-abiding, peaceable citizen. But unless Jones introduces such evidence, it is not permitted to show that in fact on three previous occasions Jones embezzled money or that before this offense he had committed numerous vicious attacks on other people.

The most unreliable hearsay is presented to the judge in the form of presentence investigation reports made by faceless bureaucrats who are never brought to court to be subjected to cross-examination. If the report indicates that the defendant is steadily employed, a good family man who supports his wife and children, and the offense is not too heinous, he will probably get probation. The judge will reason that it costs the taxpayers anywhere from $4,000 to $10,000 a year to keep the man in jail and that public assistance for a wife and six small children may become astronomical. If the man is jailed for several years, on release the family relationship will in all likelihood be broken, the man will have great difficulty getting a job and the taxpayers may end up by supporting husband, wife and six children almost indefinitely. Accordingly, this man will probably be placed on probation. On the other hand, an unfavorable report based on malicious neighborhood gossip may result in a jail sentence of many years for a person no more guilty, vicious or dangerous than the man released because of a good presentence report based entirely on hearsay.

To assay the difficulties of the litigational process, let us examine a typical case, that of Mrs. Thomas. It was randomly assigned to me by the computer, one of 250 major civil cases, those allegedly involving more than $10,000. More than two-thirds of these cases were over five years old. Many were ten years old. The acts giving rise to the litigation, of course, occurred a number of years before suit was instituted.

In some of my cases in the ten-year age bracket, the defendant was clearly liable. Often the individual defendant pleaded with his insurance company to settle. But the carrier refused to do so. Time and the intervening death of the plaintiff have saved insurance companies and defendants great sums of money which would have been paid if the case had come to trial promptly. Since in a tort suit—accidents of all sorts, defective products and the like—the amount due is in dispute, there is no interest accumulating and no incentive to settle.

Mrs. Thomas' case was one of these where liability was reasonably clear—a rear-end collision. She was driving her car in the afternoon rush-hour traffic and stopped for a traffic light. Arthur Schmidt, who was driving the Robertson Corporation truck on company business, ploughed into the back of her car. Both of them stopped. Schmidt said he was sorry, but the company was insured. She needn't worry. He promptly reported the accident to his employer, who immediately notified the insurance company. Mrs.

Thomas went home and called her insurance company. By the next morning she had a splitting headache and a terrible pain in her neck. She could not raise her right arm.

Her insurance company advised her to get a lawyer. Mrs. Thomas went to a reputable doctor, who diagnosed her ailment as a tear of the ligament where the neck and shoulder join. The only remedy was surgery. Since there was but a 50 percent chance of recovery in a woman of her age, he did not recommend it. Mrs. Thomas had to give up her factory job and take occasional light employment. Fortunately she owned a house, which she sold, and with the proceeds and help from her children she managed to stay off relief for *ten* years until her case came to trial. Many others disabled in accidents survive on public assistance for years while awaiting a trial or settlement of the case. The insurance company offered Mrs. Thomas $3,500 just before the trial. She refused the offer.

Fortunately for Mrs. Thomas she had a new jury. Her case was their first one. By the end of the month, after hearing at least six cases of cervical sprain or lumbar strain, a jury will award very little for back injuries. The insurance company had had Mrs. Thomas examined by a doctor of their choice who testified that she had suffered a minor sprain which "should have healed" in three months. He suggested that she was suffering from "compensation neurosis." After all, a menopausal woman could exaggerate her aches and pains. Perhaps she didn't want to work. The judge hears this same doctor testify week in and week out. He never finds that anyone has a real injury. Even amputees had some pre-existing ailment which would have required an amputation irrespective of the accident, the good doctor finds. The jury does not know this. They do not know that there is insurance and they may not be told. Mrs. Thomas was also fortunate that Schmidt was driving the company truck so that she could sue his corporate employer. A jury knows that a company has assets and probably is insured. If the case had been simply Mrs. Thomas against Mr. Schmidt, a nice young man, who knows what the outcome would have been? Would the jury award a large sum against a young man who might have to sell his home to pay for Mrs. Thomas' injuries? The jury awarded Mrs. Thomas $18,000. The defendant (really the insurance company) appealed. Mrs. Thomas' lawyer wisely advised her to take $12,000 now instead of waiting for the outcome of the appeal and possibly a new trial. She cannot wait another three or four years. By then the doctor who treated her may have moved away or died. Where will the witnesses be? And if their testimony at the second trial varies from that given at the first trial, who will believe them?

This case took four days. A courtroom with all the personnel and a jury of twelve citizens plus two alternates were occupied for this entire time. It costs the taxpayers, depending upon the community, from $1,000 to $2,000 a day for a court and jury. Five busy doctors left their patients and came to court to testify. Each of them was paid from $100 to $700 for a courtroom appearance. The jury did not know this. In fact, the jury operates in ignorance of most of the crucial facts. And the system operates in total ignorance of how the jury comes to its decision.

Often during the course of even a short jury trial, I find the jurors are dozing, if not actually sleeping. How can they pay attention to the subtleties of a charge and remember it exactly? Even in a simple case, the legal issues may be complicated and the charge confusing.

The facts of another routine case were really not in dispute. A little girl went to an apartment building to do an errand for a friend who lived in the building. After seeing the friend, she went to take the elevator down to the first floor. She pressed the button, the elevator came, she opened the door. Somehow the automatic elevator started up and the child fell down the shaft. Common sense would dictate that, of course, the owner of the building is responsible if something goes wrong. But the law places liability upon him only if he can be found negligent. The doctrine of so-called exclusive control applies, and the legal test of responsibility is whether or not the owner did everything reasonably possible to guard against such occurrences. What the owner did, of course, was to take out insurance to pay the victims of such mishaps. This could not be revealed to the jury. Nor could the owner, who wanted to pay for the expenses of the little girl's injuries, require the insurance company to do so. Fortunately for the child, the owner who testified at the trial obviously appeared to be wealthy. The child's family was indigent. The jury returned a small verdict for the child.

This was a portion of the charge required under the law. Read it once and see if you can apply it to the facts. Remember that the jury heard it only once in a hot and stuffy courtroom, sitting on hard wooden chairs:

> In civil cases such as this the Plaintiff is required to prove his case by a fair preponderance of the evidence. What do we mean by a fair preponderance of evidence? If you will think of the scales of justice, on one side is the pan in which the Plaintiffs, Marcella and her mother, place their evidence, and on the other side is the pan in which the Defendant Company places its evidence and all the evidence in the case which favors it. In order that the Plaintiffs may recover, it is necessary that the scales tip in their favor so that there is a fair preponderance of evidence showing that the Defendant was negligent. If the scales are even there can be no recovery. If the scales tip in favor of the Plaintiffs ever so lightly that is sufficient—that is proof of a fair preponderance of the evidence.
>
> The evidence need not be eyewitness evidence. Circumstantial evidence is good evidence, and if you are persuaded by such evidence you may find for the Plaintiffs.
>
> If you find that the elevator worked improperly and that this malfunction of the elevator was the proximate cause of the accident, and that the elevator was in the exclusive control of the Defendant, and that if the Defendant had exercised due care in maintaining the elevator the accident would ordinarily not have happened, and that the evidence of the cause of the accident, that is, the malfunction of the elevator, if you so find, was not equally available to both parties but was exclusively available to and in the possession of the Defendant, and that the accident itself was unusual and the likelihood of harm to Marcella or a person of her class, a visitor or tenant of the building, could easily have been foreseen and could have been

prevented by the exercise of due care, then you will find under the law that this exclusive control of the Defendant over the elevator raises an inference of negligence on his part. This shifts to the Defendant the burden of going forward with the evidence. The burden then is upon the Defendant to prove that he used due care.

If you find that the elevator was not in the exclusive control of the Defendant, as I have outlined to you what exclusive control means, there is no inference of negligence and the burden of proof that the Defendant was negligent rests with the Plaintiffs and they must prove that the Defendant failed to exercise due care under the circumstances.

What do we mean by due care? The care which a reasonably prudent person would exercise in maintaining an elevator, bearing in mind that when he owns or is responsible for a passenger elevator, he owes the duty of highest care to the passenger.

Now I have used the term "proximate cause." In order for the Plaintiffs to recover you must find that the accident would not have occurred if the Defendant had not been negligent, and that such negligence in maintaining the elevator under the standard of highest care was a substantial factor in bringing about the Plaintiffs' harm."

Would twelve people hearing this once and being asked to repeat the substance all give the same answer?

While this case was being tried and the backlog being reduced, at least twenty more suits were instituted. No matter how many judges there are or how hard they work, they must run faster simply not to fall farther behind.

There are many relatively simple devices and procedural changes which could speed the trial process and reduce costs, delays, errors and appeals. There are obvious ways in which the litigational process could be made more accessible to the poor. Important public issues could be tried in tribunals different from the ordinary courts, so that the law would be clarified and made applicable to everyone promptly. All kinds of changes are possible if the public and the legal profession are convinced that change is required.

I do not mean to imply that mere revision of the litigational process so that it operates swiftly and fairly to all persons—rich and poor—would restore a belief in law and transform a nation of scofflaws into a nation of citizens who respect and obey the law. A number of distinguished and dedicated people have already attempted to make the law operate more fairly in certain areas; Ralph Nader's crusade for consumer protection is an obvious example. The movements to establish a "right to treatment" for the mentally ill and to obtain recognition of prisoners' rights attack notorious but limited injustices. The provision of counsel at public expense for the poor is also a well-motivated but partial effort to make the litigational process function more fairly.

One must remember that the movements for law reform and the rights of the poor did not begin in 1960. There have been countless earlier crusades that culminated in a new law or a new service. The Workmen's Compensation Acts which were passed in every state in the early part of the twentieth century were designed to take these cases out of the costly and complex court procedures and to provide a quick, cheap and easy method for employees to obtain a small but certain compensation for injuries incurred on the job. It was supposed to eliminate the need for lawyers and to provide prompt payments. Despite a wealth of experience during these decades, we do not know how much the processing of these cases through the administrative machinery costs in comparison with court litigation. We do not know whether the employees are protected adequately. The maximum payment for total permanent disability in New York, for example, is two-thirds of the average weekly wage. In California it is 65 percent of the average wage for 400 weeks and then 60 percent for the remainder of the worker's life. In Illinois the maximum death benefits if the survivors are a widow and four or more children is $34,485. Obviously, a widow with four young children could not live very long on this sum. Do such people then fill the relief rolls, being supported by the taxpayers instead of the employer's insurance coverage? We do not know how adequate or how prompt compensation payments are. We do know that many employees must retain counsel to process their claims. In the words of the late Supreme Court Justice Frank Murphy, the Workmen's Compensation Acts are "deceptively simple and litigiously prolific."

Providing free counsel for the poor has not equalized their standing before the law nor improved their substantive benefits. A study in the *Yale Law Journal* of June, 1973,[6] reveals that in landlord-tenant litigation in Connecticut, tenants represented by the legal services organization for the poor were less successful than those privately represented and that the proceedings took four times as long.

All of these reform movements have attacked specific evils through the use of the old litigational process. The results have been disappointing because the root cause of much unfairness is the litigational process itself. Currently popular panaceas to "divert" cases from the courts to other tribunals may alleviate some delays. But the underlying problems will remain. No one knows whether the new tribunals will be any fairer or more satisfactory, since they, too, are based upon the same substantive laws, the same adversary system and approximately the same procedural rules.

In the era of space flights, moon walks, computers and all manner of technological devices, we are trying cases in very much the same way that they were tried in the Middle Ages, when few people were literate, when there were no typewriters, tape recorders or videotape. We require every witness to appear and testify in court before a judge and jury, or a judge sitting alone. We proceed on the assumption that all cases will be tried before a jury and base all our rules on that assumption, when, in fact, jury trial is the exception. We assume that because a jury must hear testimony, a judge must also sit and have testimony read aloud to him.

In countless courts every day, there is the absurd practice of having a lawyer or witness read a statement aloud to a judge. A court stenographer transcribes it and then, some weeks later, the judge reads the notes of testimony. Hearings before such bodies as the Federal Power Commission consist almost exclusively of written testimony which is read aloud and then transcribed. Today most adults grasp information better from reading than from hearing because they can go back over an unclear passage. If one's attention wanders for an instant, the train of thought is not irrevocably lost. In earlier times, oral testimony was a necessity. Today it is not.

Technologically it is possible to take the testimony of witnesses on videotape. The police often do this. Testimony of expert witnesses is also often videotaped to ensure its availability at the time of trial, when the expert may be busy, ill or out of the state.

Once freed from the conceptual vise of the adversary system, it would be possible immediately after an incident to take the statements of all eyewitnesses before a judicial officer on videotape. This officer could be given power to question and cross-examine to obtain all of the information, to attempt to ascertain deficiencies in the witness' powers of observation, his biases, his untrustworthiness without regard to the interests of the parties. An entire trial can be taped in advance of presentation to a judge sitting alone or with a jury. The parties can and should have access to all this information so that they can obtain any other witnesses or data that are required. A trial that takes a week with live witnesses, delays, objections and so on could be heard in less than a day in such a manner. If the judge believed more information was needed, it could be obtained without the necessity of recalling these witnesses or the risk of losing their testimony. Trial courts could be empowered to call their own expert witnesses, who would not be engaged by either party. The actual scene of the incident could be photographed fairly, without trick shots or foreshortened angles, by a court photographer. Instead of testimony based on faulty memory or bias, inaccurate estimates of distances and other subjective and faulty descriptions, accurate and reliable photographs, tape recordings and other mechanical evidence could be used. While some of these devices can be introduced in the adversary system of trial, making it shorter and more reliable, these remedies are insufficient. We must seek a better and fairer way of resolving disputes than the adversary combat between counsel.

In centuries past, disputes were resolved by trial by ordeal. The accused was thrown into a pond. If he sank, he was guilty and the problem of penalty was obviated. History describes trial by battle or duel. The parties often hired experts to do their fighting for them. This was not too dissimilar to the adversary system of litigation in use today in which lawyers are retained (hired) to fight the battles of the clients.

It is obvious to us living in the twentieth century that battles, duels, and ordeals can decide which party is stronger or more skillful in swordplay or has more endurance. Such procedures cannot, in our view, determine which party is truthful, which party is justified in his behavior, or which party has infringed on the rights of the other. In like manner our adversary system tests the relative skills of counsel and the relative endurance—both psychological and financial—of the parties. But does it disclose the facts or reveal the truth? The entire system of trial is based on the belief that if both parties are represented by lawyers and the court requires the observance of the rules known as "due process of law," a fair and just result will be achieved. But the skills of the lawyers run the gamut from incompetent to brilliant. There is an equally wide spectrum in the resources of the parties. An indigent, semiliterate, friendless derelict may be opposed by all the forces of the government bringing a criminal prosecution against him. An impoverished widow may face a multimillion-dollar insurance company when she seeks to recover for the death of her husband, who was involved in an accident. Simple citizens who purchase merchandise that malfunctions, or who are subjected to noxious fumes, nuclear fallout and other highly sophisticated and lethal dangers are locked in battle with the wealthiest and most powerful international corporations and cartels. Often probably guilty persons are acquitted beause they are represented by highly skilled and experienced counsel and the prosecutor is an inexperienced neophyte or an aging hack. Plaintiffs in negligence cases are on occasion awarded extremely high verdicts when they are represented by able and ingenious counsel, who receives a third of the recovery, while the defendant (insurance company) is represented by a mediocre lawyer who is on retainer and paid at an hourly rate. Our litigational process is really a test of the skills of the lawyers who are engaged in a duel on behalf of parties whose strengths are rarely equally matched. Occasionally David may slay Goliath. Such a marvel is remembered in literature and in legal history. The countless occasions when might conquers irrespective of right are not celebrated in song or jurisprudence.

Although a judge charges the jury that they are present for the sole purpose of finding the truth, almost every aspect of the trial belies this purpose and frustrates it. The litigational system is indeed one of the causes of dissatisfaction with the law contributing to its death.

*. . . while man is mortal, litigation
may not be immortal.*

Ocean Ins. Co. v. Fields,
18 Fed. Cas. No. 10406
(1st Cir. 1841)

7: Ultimate Error

The decision of the trial court is only the bell signaling the end of
round one in the combat known as litigation. If the contestants
can still struggle to their feet, the fray can continue almost indefinitely. After a civil case which lasted more than two weeks
and in which a very reasonable jury verdict was returned, both
attorneys filed the customary post-trial motions. I had a conference with them. "Why don't you end this litigation now?" I
asked. "You had a fair trial. Neither of you took exceptions to my
charge. What are you complaining about?" If counsel believes
that any part of the judge's instructions to the jury on the law is
unfair, incorrectly states the law, or is prejudicial, he is required
to take an exception. Since this was not done, it was clear that
both able and experienced lawyers believed that there were no
substantial errors and, therefore, no real grounds for an appeal.
Under such circumstances, the winning party usually accepts a

155

slightly lesser sum than the trial award in compromise to avoid the expense of an appeal.

This time plaintiff's counsel adamantly refused to do so. "The worst that can happen," he remarked, "is that we will get a new trial on appeal, and next time my client may get a bigger verdict."

Defense counsel replied, "After I get the notes of testimony, I may be able to find some reversible error that I am not now aware of." He did not state the obvious, that during the appeal his client has the use of the money. The fact that this trial has already cost the taxpayers more than $20,000, that the result is substantially fair, that both sides have had adequate opportunity to present their claims is irrelevant. They will both appeal and appeal.

An old joke is repeatedly told by lawyers. Counsel wired his client at the conclusion of a trial: "Jury verdict in. Justice was done." The client wired back: "Appeal at once." All too often this is what happens. In criminal cases, unless the accused is acquitted, the number of appeals that can be taken is almost endless. An acquittal, although precluding an appeal, will not stop a determined prosecutor from continuing to pursue the defendant. Often a new indictment is brought against the defendant on other charges which could and should have been included in the first trial.

The inordinate length of time from the act giving rise to a civil law suit or criminal prosecution to the final conclusion frustrates and bewilders all who are involved in the process. In any analysis of the reasons for the death of the law, the system of time-consuming and costly appeals cannot be ignored. Courts exist for the sole purpose of providing a resolution of disputes. Instead of an answer, the parties are often faced with a lifetime of expenses and irritations as they pursue the mirage of justice through the murky corridors of innumerable courts, countless hearings, appeals and retrials.

This is not a new complaint in Anglo-American law. In the sixteenth century Shakespeare asked, ". . . who would bear . . . the law's delay?" and replied that the alternative of suicide might be preferable. Dickens, in *Bleak House,* described the presumably fictional case of *Jarndyce* v. *Jarndyce,*[1] which dragged its weary way through the courts for generations. This satire on the law's delay was published in 1853. In 1972, the United States Supreme Court in the case of *Barker* v. *Wingo*[2] on a fifth appeal sent the matter back to the lower courts to be tried a sixth time. Most litigants abandon their futile quest for justice before a sixth trial. They settle, compromise or simply give up the fight. But appeals through three courts and two trials and a second set of appeals and a third trial are by no means unusual. The court system is structured to permit and, indeed, to encourage this process of appeals and retrials.

In most states there is a four-tier set of courts: First, the local courts, which hear minor matters such as traffic violations, misdemeanors and small claims. The judges in these courts are often persons without legal training or any special qualifications. This is the common practice in England. Some of these judges, or magistrates, in America are competent and learned, others are persons of little education, limited sympathies and sensitivity to the rights and problems of the people on whom they pass judgment. They may hear as many as thirty, forty or more cases in a day. It is little wonder that mistakes are made and litigants are dissatisfied. The variations in qualifications of lower-court judges, the formality of procedures followed, and regularity of the records they keep is wide. One can only conclude that there is a similar variability in the quality of justice rendered in these courts. From the decisions of these lower courts there is some form of appeal, review or new trial for those who can afford to continue their quest for justice or vindication.

The second tier is the court of general jurisdiction, in which felonies and major civil cases are tried. From the decisions of these courts, appeals can usually be taken to an intermediate appellate court. From the decision of that court there may be an appeal or review to the highest court of the state, which is known as the court of ultimate error. This nomenclature derives from the common-law writ of error directed by a higher court to a lower court to correct its mistakes. In a colloquial sense, the highest court of the jurisdiction is a court of ultimate error because the mistakes of this court may be the ultimate or last errors to which the litigants are subjected. But not always.

After the litigants reach the highest court of the state and obtain a decision, at least one party is usually dissatisfied. If he can afford to proceed further and can raise a federal Constitutional issue, he then takes his case to the United States Supreme Court. Failing to get a hearing there, he may then begin the entire process over again in the *federal* system, with a trial in the district court, an appeal to the court of appeals, and a plea to the United States Supreme Court. Unlike the state courts ° and the intermediate federal appellate courts, which are required to pass upon all cases which meet the technical requirements of jurisdiction, the United States Supreme Court can refuse to hear all but a very limited number of cases in which the parties have an absolute right to appeal. Under its power of discretionary review the Supreme Court refuses to hear all but a fraction of the cases presented to it. If the Supreme Court chooses to hear a case, instead of deciding the question it frequently remands the matter to the lower courts for a new trial. The entire process of trial and appeals will then be repeated.

Much of the time and energies of federal judges is spent not in deciding substantive questions but in deciding whether or not they should hear the case: Does it present a question of federal law or rights under the United States Constitution?

In the law there is a tacit premise that cost/benefit considerations determine the use of the appellate process. The parties are supposed to ask these questions in determining whether or not to appeal: Was the decision legally in error? Was the result substantially unfair? What are the probabilities of success, that is, will the appellate court find that there was an error of fact or law? Is the amount involved worth the time and expense? Is the legal

---

° In many states, the highest court has discretional jurisdiction similar to the writ of certiorari in the United States Supreme Court.

issue involved sufficiently important to take the time of the litigants, lawyers and the courts?

Like the free-market theory of willing buyer and willing seller, this is also a myth. The appellate courts are cluttered with cases that present no legal issue of importance and cases that present no question of substantial injustice. Why are they there? For the same reasons that originally brought the parties into court. The factors that impel people to go to court in the first place are often irrational. Neighbors sue over an insult, a tomato hurled in a fit of rage, a tree limb overhanging the property boundary by six inches, and other trivia. Since they are not moved by reason or deterred by cost, such parties appeal and appeal. Through the process of trial and appeal, legal issues will be developed, legal error asserted and the trappings of a legal case will envelope the original episode. When one lawyer withdraws from the case in disgust, another will be found to carry on the vendetta.

Similarly, criminal prosecutions are brought for incidents that a less legally oriented society would ignore. Children are prosecuted for larceny of a candy bar. Adults are frequently criminally prosecuted for fist fights, automobile accidents and unfortunate business ventures. These episodes are through the use or misuse of the criminal process transformed into prosecutions for assault and battery, assault with intent to maim or kill, and false pretenses, embezzlement and conspiracy. Sometimes this abuse of criminal process is politically inspired. Other times it occurs simply through ineptitude or careless investigation. Underlying these human errors and excesses is the premise that the courts—both the trial courts and the appellate courts—exist for the purpose of bringing into sharp conflict and legal conclusion all of the day-to-day problems of life. Neither civil pleadings nor bills of indictment disclose the facts. A complaint in trespass may involve a serious injury arising out of a real dereliction of duty. It may, however, involve a trivial matter in which both parties acted reasonably and responsibly.

A pedestrian who is knocked down and seriously injured by a motorist may have a legitimate claim for substantial damages.

Another pedestrian who twists his ankle boarding a bus brings the same type of action, which is heard in the same time-consuming and expensive manner even though he was probably careless and his damages are small. There are procedures for the quick resolution of small claims in almost every state. However, frequently the litigant and his lawyer will magnify the injuries in an attempt to get a bigger settlement or a substantial verdict. A prosecution for robbery may be simple theft of a trivial sum or it may involve a dangerous holdup.

A prosecution for fraud and embezzlement may involve a carefully calculated scheme to fleece consumers or investors in which many people have been tricked out of substantial amounts of money. The sale of worthless roofing material advertised as "sure to stop all leaks" was a legitimate prosecution brought before me. On the other hand, some prosecutions arise because a business deal failed and an irate partner or investor who cannot recover his money persuades the prosecutor to bring criminal proceedings against the unfortunate or inept businessman. I also tried a case involving the prosecution of corporate executives who themselves lost their money in an ill-fated business adventure brought at the instigation of sophisticated investors who also lost money. This prosecution resulted in the jailing of the hapless executives who could not raise bail and an arraignment, a preliminary hearing, a hearing on a motion to quash the indictment, and a trial. All of these futile procedures cost the taxpayers thousands of dollars for the time of the prosecutors, the various courts, and the public defender. By this time the corporate executives were indigent. In this case, I acquitted the defendants. Had they been convicted, the case would have wound its way a year or two later to an appellate court, unless by that time the sentence would have expired. Counting the "back time," that is, the time served in jail prior to trial and the time between conviction and appeal, sentence is often served before the case is heard on appeal. If the defendant can afford bail, of course, he will not have been imprisoned at all and may stay out of jail two or three years or more until his conviction is sustained by an appellate court.

At the appellate level, it is easier to see the play of interests because the facts and issues have already been sharpened and pruned through the process of trial. The resolution of the conflict at this level is not determined exclusively by the merits of the contending parties. More often it depends upon their respective strengths and staying powers. These factors in turn usually depend upon the financial resources of the parties and their emotional fortitude and determination. The wealthy litigant with able and resourceful counsel has an immeasurable advantage over the average person, just as the government, with all its resources, has an incredible advantage over the average person accused of crime.

The protracted prosecutions, appeals and ultimate release of "Treetop" Turner illustrate the relatively insignificant role of the legal merits in determining the outcome of an appeal. "Treetop" Turner, an illiterate black man, was convicted of murder. His conviction was sustained by the state supreme court but set aside by the United States Supreme Court. He was tried a second time. That conviction was again appealed. The conviction was again sustained by the highest state court and again set aside by the United States Supreme Court. The process was repeated a third time. After the third reversal by the United States Supreme Court,[3] the state finally abandoned its futile effort to convict a man against whom it had insufficient evidence. Turner survived this ordeal only because he had the rare good fortune to be represented by a wealthy, able private attorney who could afford to take the time and effort and had the exceptional skill and determination to obtain justice for an indigent, friendless man.

Paul Ware, a poor black teen-ager, was arrested and interrogated for a period of more than twenty-four hours. During this entire time he was manacled to a chair in a small, windowless room. He was not advised of his Constitutional rights or provided with counsel. Ultimately he confessed to four heinous murders. His court-appointed attorney moved to have the confession suppressed and obtained a favorable ruling from the lower court. Over a period of four years, the prosecutor appealed this ruling again and again in a vain attempt to have the United States Supreme Court reverse the Miranda decision.[4]

The appellate process was manifestly abused in both these cases.

However, the actions of the prosecutor, though unwarranted, were not illegal. Neither of these accused men had any form of redress against these repeated appeals by a powerful prosecutor. The most they could hope for was ultimate vindication and release after years of imprisonment. Most defendants are not so fortunate.

Armanda Beltrante is one of perhaps tens of thousands of people—children and adults—now imprisoned in jails and mental institutions who have no access to the appellate courts. Beltrante spent twenty-two years in prison from the age of sixteen, when he allegedly broke a window. He was jailed, not for breaking a window—that offense was never proved—but because he had an I.Q. of 89 and was diagnosed as having "criminal tendencies." The Public Defender inquired into his case after twelve years, but took no action on his behalf. Ultimately he was freed as a result of efforts by the American Civil Liberties Union. This man had no statutory right of appeal. There is no mandatory provision for the judicial review of persons held in institutions who have not been convicted of crimes or who have been convicted and have served their sentences.

The indigent are disadvantaged at trial and on appeal. Oftentimes, however, people who are not paupers but have limited resources are even more seriously disadvantaged. An indigent litigant represented without charge by a publicly funded agency which provides legal services for the poor does not need to calculate the costs of appeal against the benefits to be attained. He has no costs. Consequently there is no deterrent to his taking appeals even in cases in which he is not imprisoned and has no substantial issue of legal error or prejudice. Such cases often involve convictions for a minor offense in which the penalty imposed is nonreporting probation, convictions routinely accepted by some public defenders. Nonreporting probation in itself is a farce, an expensive bookkeeping device and a semantic screen. The judge who, under the law and the facts, must convict the defendant feels that the offense does not merit imprisonment. The offender is not dangerous, and, therefore, does not need supervision by an overworked probation officer. He cannot afford to pay a fine. The rules of the game are observed by a sentence of nonreporting probation. Any person who had to pay costs and counsel fees would never consider appealing such a decision. The indigent defendant has nothing to lose by taking an appeal. The legal services agency also has nothing to lose. The client is another statistic building up the caseload and demonstrating the agency's need for more funds and staff.

The significance of the legal issue involved, its applicability to a large number of people, or its importance to the national economy, the political process, the public welfare and safety, or the freedom of the individual are not the determinative factors in whether a litigant appeals a decision of a lower court in civil and criminal cases. This is a decision made by the individual and his lawyer. It is based not on the needs of the public or the state of the law but on the interests and capabilities of the parties. Many legal agencies for the poor appeal all decisions. The nonindigent client's decision to appeal is dictated largely by his financial resources.

Except in rare cases of class action or those involving ideological issues which are undertaken by organizations dedicated to the promotion of the particular cause, the litigants are motivated by self-interest. The desires to obtain or preserve one's liberty or to retain or obtain money or property are in most cases the decisive factors in deciding to take an appeal. Appellate courts, however, should not be treated like common carriers that must provide accommodations to everyone who can pay the fees. The appellate courts might well limit their consideration of cases by asking two fundamental questions: (1) Was substantial injustice done to one of the parties? (2) Is there an issue of law which should be decided, revised or clarified in the interest of other people who may be affected? If cases were tried by competent counsel before able and fair judges, appeals would be warranted only in those cases raising a substantial and unresolved legal issue.

Appellate courts, other than the United States Supreme Court and the highest courts of some states, do not have discretionary review powers. They do not ask these questions. The reviewing tribunal instead directs its attention to this issue: Did the trial court (or administrative body) commit error? In presenting this question, the lawyer taking the appeal will comb through the notes of testimony of the trial looking for some mistake on which to make an argument to the appellate court. The point at which most legally reversible error in jury trials occurs is the judge's charge to the jury. This is delivered orally. The jury is not permitted to take notes of what the judge says. Even in a simple accident case, it requires at least a half an hour for the judge to set forth the principles of law that are to govern the jury's conclusions. In a complicated case like the conspiracy trial of the Harrisburg Seven, the charge takes several hours. One word may be too little, two may be too many. Either is fatal, and may require an entire new trial. In a recent case, when a jury could not agree and asked the trial judge for further instructions, he gave them the guidance they requested and urged them to continue their deliberations. He then added, "This case has gone on for several weeks. It cost a great deal of money. If you fail to reach a verdict, it will have to be tried again. I think I have said enough." The court of appeals, reviewing the cold print of the record, reversed the jury's verdict saying that the trial judge had said "too much." They found that he had coerced the jury.

Another recent federal case illustrates the minute attention devoted by appellate courts to the precise verbiage of the trial court. The plaintiff, a patient, was suing her ophthalmologist for negligence in treating her. The judge charged at length and then clarified the duty of the doctor by telling the jury: "Now, there was some question as to whether my statement of ordinary care might have been confusing. Of course, I am talking about ordinary care in the standard or the status of the person exercising the care. I think what counsel wants me to clarify is that the care that I might exercise or you might exercise might be different from the care that a doctor of Dr. Reichel's profession and standing would exercise. It is the care which *he* would exercise based on his ability, his background and his expertise." The decision was reversed because the appellate court decided that the trial judge should have given the following charge with respect to standard of care: "An ophthalmologist acting within his specialty owes to his patient a higher standard of skill, learning and care than a general practitioner. He is expected to exercise that degree of skill, learning and care normally possessed and exercised by the average physician who devotes special study and attention to the diagnosis and treatment of eye diseases. Due regard must, of course, be shown to the advanced state of the profession at the time of the diagnosis or treatment." [5]

The quest for verbal precision, the examination of the record for reversible error—the one word too much, the use of "may" instead of "shall," the admission or exclusion of an insignificant bit of evidence—is based on the belief that procedural regularity is the touchstone of justice. Mr. Justice Frankfurter declared, "The history of American freedom is, in no small measure, the history of procedure." [6] Like many apothegms, this is at best a half-truth. Obviously a fair hearing is a minimal requirement. But merely to observe procedural regularity is by no means to ensure fairness or justice. To make a fetish of procedure is to pervert the larger aims of the law.

This attention to detail often prevents a real consideration of important legal issues. A record of tens of thousands of pages is a barrier to appellate review. Both time and cost as well as human limits of patience are involved. In the Great Lakes Diversion case, *Illinois* v. *Michigan*,[7] which involved the very significant legal and practical problem of water rights affecting at least half of the population in the United States and the rights and duties of local governments with respect to water supply and sewage disposal, the rights of shippers on navigable waters and the power of the states, hearings were held before a special master for many months over a period of eight years. To review such a monumental record with care would impose an intolerable burden on any judge or any court. The legal issues were clearly delineated and understood by the parties *before* any hearings were held. This case involved the rights of sovereign states which, of course, could devote the manpower and money to the protracted litigation of an important public issue. How much time and attention did the appellate court reviewing the special master's findings devote to this case? Or did it simply rely on the conclusions of the one judge who heard the evidence?

In *SEC* v. *Texas Gulf Sulphur Co.*,[8] the parties were wealthy investors and a solvent multimillion-dollar corporation. The question at issue, although complicated by the mazes of Securities and Exchange Commission regulations, essentially involved the right of insiders in management to profit on the basis of information not disclosed to the public and to issue information designed to discourage others from investing. Before this question was finally resolved the Securities and Exchange Commission had passed on the case, nine federal judges and nine justices of the United States Supreme Court had reviewed the matter. Seven opinions were written which fill seventy-nine pages of fine print in two columns in the reports. The question has not been laid to rest. Like many other decisions, it provoked more questions that it answered.

Similar unduly long and excessively fine procedures obtain in routine litigation of concern only to the parties. Consider the case of Mrs. B., a wealthy widow, since remarried. She sued the manufacturer of the small plane her husband was piloting when it crashed, claiming the plane was defective. After two jury trials and two appeals, no one knows whether or not the plane was defective or unsafe. More than a half dozen aeronautical engineers testified, as well as pilots, psychologists, weather experts and accountants. On every issue there was competent expert evidence going both ways. The first trial lasted five weeks. It was reversed on appeal because the trial judge's charge to the jury contained a statement of the law on a point which had not previously been decided but which the appellate court found to be erroneous. The second trial lasted four and a half weeks. At approximately $1,400 per day, the taxpayers have financed Mrs. B's "day in court" to the sum of $53,000, not counting the time of the appellate courts. She paid costs of $15.00 for filing a complaint, $10.00 for jury fee, and $5.00 for filing an appeal. It also cost her some $7,000 for the transcript of the testimony, without which her appeal would have been virtually impossible. If she were not wealthy, she could not carry her case to the appellate courts.

After the second trial, another appeal will wend its slow way to higher courts. If upon leisurely consideration an appellate court should decide that one or more of the statements of law was erroneous and possibly affected the jury's decision, there will be a new trial. This time another judge will be faced with other, equally unclear, problems. His likelihood of being right in the eyes of the appellate court is no better than that of the first or second judge. The case may be remanded for a third trial.

If one of the litigants cannot afford to proceed, he will have to abandon the legal pursuit of his rights. The claim of equal justice under law becomes an obvious mockery at the appellate level.

There is no simple answer. Appeals and postconviction remedies, though frequently criticized as unduly delaying justice and clogging overcrowded court calendars, are not mere surplussage to be lightly discarded.[9] Almost daily, there is brought to court the chilling case of an innocent person who has spent ten or twenty years in prison for a crime he did not commit. Prior to the enactment of postconviction statutes and provision for free counsel, these innocent victims could not bring their cases to the attention of the courts.

The rights of all persons disadvantaged before the law—including nonwhites, women, children, the aged and the mentally ill—can seldom be vindicated except upon appeal. The trial judge, who is required to follow the decisions of the higher courts, cannot revise or restate the law in order to do what he conceives to be justice between the parties. The view of precedent as a straitjacket inhibiting a lower court from deciding a case reasonably was clearly enunciated in a recent case. An intermediate court, adhering to the principle of stare decisions (following precedent), held: "There is no question that a declaratory judgment proceeding would eliminate a multiplicity of suits; resolving in one action, with all the parties present, the disputed issue of fact—and give plaintiff the right to an affirmative action to resolve the matter of its obligation to defend in the trespass actions rather than to be put to costly defensive actions where it must await the choice of time and method of remedy by third parties. . . . We would readily hold that an action for declaratory judgment should be available in this case. However, we are bound by precedent. . . ." [10]

This may be considered a form of "buck passing" by the disgruntled litigants who, if they cannot afford an appeal, must abide by a decision which the judges have declared is unjust.

Many a trial judge is torn between his duty to follow the law and his duty to treat the people before him humanely and fairly. A lovable old judge used to dismiss minor criminal charges against people he thought were not dangerous and berated the prosecutor: "There are wolves roaming the streets and you bring me squirrels and chipmunks." Such an attitude is like that of the middle-aged lady who scolds the policeman for giving her a traffic ticket instead of devoting his energies to catching muggers and rapists. Both are scofflaws.

Appellate courts reviewing a case on the cold print of the record, without seeing the people involved, view the law and the functions of the judicial system differently. Time and expense, the difficulties of the litigants and the problems of administering government seldom enter their considerations. The United States Supreme Court recently declared, in *Fuentes* v. *Shevin,* "Procedural due process is not intended to promote efficiency or accommodate all possible interests: it is intended to protect the particular interests of the person whose possessions are about to be taken." [11] Similarly, Federal Judge Frank J. McGarr declared that, "The courts do not exist for the abstract determination of legal and social issues."

Those who believe in the validity of our legal system consider that the peaceful determination of legal and social issues that create conflicts among the citizenry *is* the function of the courts, and particularly of the appellate courts. Whether a judge calls an issue abstract or concrete may determine whether the court will decide the question. It does not eliminate the issue, which will be litigated again and again until a satisfactory statement of the law is obtained.

Although much litigation could be eliminated by more comprehensive and up-to-date legislation, there will always be unanswered, unanticipated questions arising even under the most carefully drawn statutes. Courts must interpret such legislative lacunae or ambiguities. How should this be done? Traditionally a court decides only on the basis of the particular facts in evidence, no matter how anomalous or unusual they may be. The legal issue, however, is usually larger and of broader application. By confining the decision to the specifics of the case in question, the courts give little guidance to others who will face a similar problem. So, unless the facts of another dispute are identical, there will be other lawsuits which could have been avoided if the court had dealt with the subject in the abstract. Mr. Justice Douglas, dissenting from this traditionally narrow view of the appellate function, has urged that appellate courts make "an authoritative pronouncement at the beginning of a controversy which saves countless days in the slow, painful, and costly litigation of separate individual law suits. . . ." [12]

Few appellate courts follow Mr. Justice Douglas' admonition to make a definitive pronouncement of the law at an early stage. The majority adhere to the doctrine of judicial abstention, under which an appellate court decides each case on the narrowest rather than the broadest issue. The court abstains from ruling on Constitutional rights of applicability to all citizens and confines itself to the singular and often anomalous facts of the particular case. In this manner, by slow and partial declarations, the courts ultimately arrive at a decision after several cases and many years of litigation and appeals. This same decision might have been made in the first instance, saving time, expense and trouble. Meanwhile, the rights of other people are being delayed, compromised and perhaps lost. The entire process of trials is slowed so that each new glimmer of intelligence from a higher court can be assimilated by trial judges, lawyers, and—in criminal cases—the police.

The immediate effect of these narrow opinions is illustrated by a series of Pennsylvania Supreme Court decisions. In 1970, the Pennsylvania Rules of Criminal Procedure were adopted providing that after arrest an accused person shall be taken "without delay" before a judicial officer where he is formally charged with a crime, advised of the charges and his right to counsel, and bail is set. Despite this rule, it was and is the invariable practice of the police to question each person arrested in the hope of getting further information with respect to the crime and a confession. In April, 1972, in *Commonwealth* v. *Futch*,[13] the Pennsylvania Supreme Court for the first time held that "without unnecessary delay" means without unnecessary delay and that any evidence obtained against the accused as a result of an unnecessary delay must be suppressed. This opinion left open myriad questions. What is a necessary delay? How long can it be? If the accused makes a confession during a period of "unnecessary delay," is it a result of the delay? Should this ruling apply to people already arrested and questioned but not yet tried, or should it apply only to those arrested after the date of the decision? The opinion was scrutinized by prosecutors, defense counsel and trial judges. All defendants who had given statements during the period between arrest and preliminary arraignment promptly filed motions to suppress these statements. Every trial judge had a different opinion. Many held that whatever the Supreme Court meant, it certainly had not intended the decision to apply to persons arrested before the decision. In due course, scores of such cases came on for trial. A year later, the Pennsylvania Supreme Court set aside the conviction of one, Tingle, which was based on a confession made before the decision in *Futch*. Confusion and pandemonium again ensued. In the *Tingle* opinion [14] the court held that the confession was "the result" of the delay. Again no guidelines as to the meaning of "result" or the length of permissible delay. Countless petitions to reopen the issue of confessions of untried defendants were filed and heard. Many were denied. Six months later the Pennsylvania Supreme Court again set aside a conviction based on a confession obtained between arrest and preliminary arraignment. Several accused persons have had three or four hearings to determine the admissibility into evidence of a confession made between arrest and preliminary arraignment. Meanwhile, prosecutors, defense counsel and trial judges try to read the enigmatic messages of the oracular high courts. The cost to the taxpayers runs into the millions. The cost in anguish and delay to the defendants is hard to measure. Many are in jail because they cannot raise bail. They may be innocent. Many are out on bail. They may be committing more crimes.

Neither the courts nor the scholars have seriously considered modifying the nature and function of the appellate courts. There is little thoughtful discussion of the role and function of appellate review.[15] Should it be narrowly restricted to the facts of the particular case, procedural errors, and a limited view of the law? Or should it declare definitively rights and procedures of broad applicability?

The appellate process could encompass both aims: to protect the particular interests of the parties whose case is before the high courts and to make an authoritative pronouncement on the law so that others will not have to litigate and appeal the same question. The present system of appellate review accomplishes neither goal. The rights of the particular litigants have usually been compromised irreparably by the delay. No court can undo six or twenty-six years of wrongful imprisonment. No court can by any award of money undo the years of deprivation and hardship while awaiting the successful appeal.

All too often the decisions of the state supreme courts and the United States Supreme Court promote confusion and litigation rather than authoritatively settle a question. A striking example, illustrating the waste of court time, the taxpayers' money, the rights and money of the litigants, and unsettling the law so that government officials must litigate again and again to find out the parameters of their rights and duties, is the treatment of pornography by the United States Supreme Court. In 1952 (before Earl Warren was appointed to the Bench) the Court held that the states could not censor movies in advance of their public exhibition.[16] In the succeeding twenty-two years, this question has been before the United States Supreme Court seventeen times. Each case represented police time in making the arrest, preliminary hearings, indictments, trial, appeals through the entire tier of state courts—three or four courts of different levels—and appeal to the United States Supreme Court. The amount of judicial time and man hours of supporting court personnel devoted to this single, relatively unimportant question is impossible to calculate. Each of these cases has wound its slow, tortuous way from legislative enactment, to arrest, trial, and countless appeals. At the same time questions of critical importance involving sources of revenue, protection of environment, racial discrimination and equal access to public facilities were refused consideration by the Supreme Court.[17]

What is important and significant will always be a matter of individual judgment. It will vary with the temper of the times. But some criteria are obvious: the number of people affected by the ruling, the irremediable nature of the action in question, the cost to the public in failing to decide. Recent appellate decisions reveal that these criteria are frequently ignored. For example, recently the United States Supreme Court refused to consider a suit filed by eighteen states seeking to force automobile manufacturers to develop pollution-free engines. The Court also refused to consider an action by the Sierra Club to prevent development of Mineral King Valley, which allegedly would be deleterious to the environment and irreversible. At the same term, the Supreme Court decided patent cases, a case involving the rights of the small Amish sect, which had previously been before the courts, and spent much time on questions involving the appropriate forum in which litigants may sue.

The recent proposal of Professor Paul Freund of Harvard Law School to add another federal court between the court of appeals and the United States Supreme Court has been warmly approved by some lawyers and judges and bitterly criticized by others. Mr. Justice Douglas says that the United States Supreme Court is not overworked and does not need another court to screen out appeals. Former Supreme Court Justice Goldberg points out that many legal issues, formerly deemed settled by firm precedent, would never reach the United States Supreme Court for reconsideration if they were strained through the sieve of a tribunal established to screen out cases. The principal vice of this proposal and others like it is that it complicates and lengthens rather than simplifies and shortens the process by which cases are decided on appeal. It does nothing to promote the resolution of issues of broad application so as to avoid further litigation. It does nothing to discourage the endless multiplicity of appeals.

The unsatisfactory functioning of so critical and visible a portion of the legal system as the appellate courts cannot be ignored in discussing the death of the law. Americans look to the appellate courts for a definitive statement of the law—a clear delineation of the rights of citizens and the limitations on government. We have been taught to expect a fair and just resolution of conflicts at the highest judicial level. Incompetence, corruption and stupidity at the lower levels of government are venial sins which the public, understanding human fallibility, can accept. But more is demanded of the higher guardians of the law. The shortcomings of the appellate courts are more disillusioning and disastrous. When rulings fluctuate from week to week, when important issues are left undecided, when neither government agencies nor the lower courts know what is lawful and what is impermissible, the public disregard for the strictures of the law is understandable. Moses went to Mount Sinai once, not every Monday.

No rational person would suggest that the Constitution has solved all problems for all time. A living institution must change and adapt to changing physical, scientific, and social conditions. It must adapt to the norms of behavior and the ethical notions of the time. But a living institution must be aware of the larger community it serves. It cannot be bemused by the elegance or symmetry or internal logic of its own discipline to the neglect of the results of its actions.

The appellate process, which is an integral part of our legal system, must bear a large share of the onus for the uncertainties and delay which characterize law in action. Moreover, the appellate courts are even less accessible to the poor and disadvantaged than the trial courts. The pyramidal, hierarchical nature of the judicial structure is both anti-egalitarian and authoritarian. The decisions of the high courts—removed as they are from the people involved in the litigation and in time from the precipitating incidents giving rise to the litigation—have assumed an oracular quality incompatible with a democratic populist nation. This growing disjunction between the problems of daily life and legal decisions as pronounced in the marble temples of the appellate courts has also contributed to the obsolescence of the creed of the law.

*So don't worry about some of these freakish
decisions that an individual judge hands
down. Even if it's your case and it's one you
wanted to win. Chances are the defendant
will be busted again before long and we'll
get another crack at him. And the judge's
decision ends right there on the bench. It's
not going to have a damn thing to do with
the next case you try.*

Joseph Wambaugh, The New Centurions

8: Cops and Courts

Any discussion of the death of the law in the United States would
be incomplete without an examination of the principal functionaries in the legal system. Our complex legal structure, like
any modern bureaucracy, is composed of administrators, clerks,
messengers and typists. Courts utilize the services of psychiatrists, accountants, computer analysts and social workers. But
aside from the legislators and government executives, the three
principal classes of participants in the legal process are police,
lawyers and judges.

The police are especially significant. They are the most numerous group. They are the most visible. In many ways, they are
the most powerful members of the legal system. Policemen are
armed with clubs and sophisticated weaponry. Policemen can
take action directly without the necessity of getting warrants,

writs and papers. Policemen are in the community. They are on the streets. They go into bars, restaurants, homes and businesses. A policeman is often the citizen's first and only contact with the law. For many an American, the only law he knows is administered with a nightstick. From that decision there is seldom an appeal. The role of the police in promoting public hostility to law cannot be ignored in any analysis of scofflawism and the death of the law in the United States. While the power and authority of courts is waning, the strength and popularity of the police is increasing, although in some segments of the community the attitude toward the police is unremitting fear and hatred. This shifting balance of public esteem has caused a growing exacerbation of relations between the police and the judiciary which is disquieting to the legal profession and disturbing to the public. Although the police and the courts are engaged in a common effort to remove criminals from the streets and to protect society, today these two agencies often see themselves in conflict.

Like many other social conflicts, this one is waged with the skills of public relations personnel, the use of the media and politicians. Almost every large police department and large court system has a public relations staff. These employees are often called "information officers" or "community coordinators," but their function is to present their respective agencies to the public in a favorable light. They have large budgets and use the well-known techniques of Madison Avenue bolstered by sociological "research," statistics and public opinion polls. To the uninitiate it may seem strange that government agencies should spend the taxpayers' money to brainwash the public. However, it is a common practice of many agencies of government. The police are not unique in their concern with public relations.

Violations of law by law-enforcement agencies pose a difficult and critical problem in a free society. The police reflect the general public attitude of scofflawism, and by their conduct they contribute to this disregard for law. The National Conference on Criminal Justice in 1973 concluded: "The unique relationship between the people and the police in America requires that the police be answerable to the public if their authority is to be respected and accepted by the people." [1] This is a general statement of policy with which everyone could agree. The implementation of that policy raises thorny questions for all of us.

One hundred years ago, Mr. Justice Holmes, then a Massachusetts judge, upheld the right of the town of New Bedford to fire a policeman for engaging in political activity. He ruled: "The petitioner may have a Constitutional right to talk politics, but he has no Constitutional right to be a policeman. There are few employments for hire in which the servant does not agree to suspend his Constitutional right to free speech, as well as of idleness, by the implied terms of his contract." [2] Today when one of every eight employees works for the government, such a cavalier disregard of a policeman's rights as a citizen probably would not be tolerated. Society is properly more sensitive to the rights of policemen. Similar sensitivity by the police to the rights of the citizens is also required. Civil liberties groups and police fraternal organizations are cognizant of these problems and working to bring about greater mutual understanding.

The duty of police departments to account to the public for expenditure of funds, detective operations, patrol duty and the countless other activities of a modern police force has been largely overlooked. Police review boards to investigate cases of alleged police brutality have been bitterly opposed by the police who fear, with reason, that such nonjudicial hearings may prejudice the rights of the individual policeman. Public accountability of the police department is a much larger and more important issue. It involves the right of the public to know what is being done with public funds and how efficient, honest and effective the police force is. Since no satisfactory mechanism for achieving this end has been developed, critics of the police have turned to the courts for information and sanctions. Neither the police nor the courts have been happy with these cases.

Bitter confrontations between the power of the police and the power of the judiciary have not contributed to respect for law. A court ordered the New York Police Department to destroy its files on a million citizens. Whether this order was actually carried out or whether the police retain this information in some other form is not known. In Philadelphia, a federal court issued an order prohibiting police from moving peaceful demonstrators away from Independence Hall during a visit by President Nixon. The police ignored the order and arrested the demonstrators. The courts under such circumstances are faced with difficult and unsatisfactory choices. They can ignore the facts and permit their orders to be flouted or they can force a further confrontation by attempting to jail the police. In such a stark test of power, the ultimate loser is the law.

I know of no instance in which a court has held a police department in contempt of court or jailed a police commissioner and the upper echelons of officers for violating a court order. Such rulings are common in labor disputes. Unions have been fined large sums and their officers have gone to jail. Officers of a teachers union, for example, have been sentenced to months in jail when the union went on strike, violating a court order. This special reluctance of the courts to impose sanctions on the police may be wise. The courts must rely upon the police to enforce their orders, to detect crime and apprehend criminals and to maintain order. A sharp conflict between the courts and any agency of government or government official, from the President to the cop on the beat, is fraught with danger to the entire system—which must rely upon voluntary compliance. When policemen are prosecuted for shooting civilians, beating them and making illegal arrests, they are rarely convicted. The sympathies of the jurors, black and white, are usually with the policeman, who is in an exposed and dangerous position even when he kills an unarmed person. Such acquittals, following a due process trial in which the judge may have acted with perfect propriety, exacerbate the tensions between courts and police and between the citizenry and the entire criminal justice system. Those who believe that the evidence of police misconduct was overwhelming are inclined to blame the judges rather than the anonymous miscellany of citizens composing the jury. It is easy to infer, though often wrongly, collusion between the courts and the police. The police, on the other hand, often believe that judges and lawyers are hostile to them and ignorant of the risks to which they are subjected.

Public confidence in the rule of law is badly shaken by such incidents and such cases. The continuing conflict between the police and the courts is submerged beneath daily routine activities, but it permeates American society, which has lost its belief in the efficacy of law and the importance of obedience to judicial orders. The old Roman question: "Quis custodies custodiet?"—Who guards the guardians of the law?—cannot be answered in the United States today. The police, who should be the guardians, in many instances have placed themselves above the law. By so doing they contribute, as we shall see, to the death of the law they have sworn to uphold.

The real disagreements between the police and the judiciary have been exploited by politicians. President Nixon, aided and abetted by his Attorney General, John Mitchell, ran for office on a tough law-and-order platform. Judges were denounced as "coddling criminals." President Nixon explicitly declared his intention to remake the United States Supreme Court which, he stated, had been overly solicitous of the rights of the accused.[3] Mayor Rizzo of Philadelphia and John Marchi of New York as well as countless congressmen and senators campaigned on this issue, inflaming public opinion. What began as legitimate differences of opinion has through these influences developed into outright hostility, creating a potentially dangerous situation. The results of this conflict have shaken the confidence of the public in both the police and the courts. These two agencies established by a democratic society to safeguard the individual and maintain the peace are both suspect. Distrust of the agencies of law enforcement naturally leads to distrust of the law.

The police occupy a unique position in a democratic society. They are in a legal sense civilians—citizens with all the rights, privileges and immunities of citizens, protected by the Constitution. Policemen, however, unlike the rest of the citizenry, are legally armed with all the might of an old-fashioned shillelagh plus the most sophisticated technological weaponry, including guns, mace, walkie-talkie radios, armored vehicles, helicopters and other devices. Policemen are of the people but set apart from them by the symbolic power of the uniform, the actual power of weapons, and the legal power to deprive people of their liberty. In making an arrest a policeman acts as spy, militia, judge and jury. In most cases, he must act quickly, under pressure of real danger to himself, to others and fear that the suspected criminal will escape. The policeman also has awesome powers to grant clemency. He can look the other way, he can stop a suspect and let him go. He can apprehend him and then not book him. All this is done on his own. No record is made. He is not held to standards of proof, evidence and procedural regularity. There is no written record. The integrity and judgment of the individual police officer are the only safeguards against abuses of such enormous powers.

Like the army, the police have an esprit de corps. They face dangers together. They must rely on each other for safety, often for their lives. Naturally, criticism of one policeman is resented by others. Like the regular army—not the draftees—policemen are a self-selected group. The educational qualifications are not high. It is a career opportunity for those who cannot afford a college education or advanced vocational training. The rookie policeman does not need the approval of a political leader or a trade union official to get a job. Until the 1960s a job on the police force was respected. The ethnic composition of police departments reflected to a great extent the immigration and upward-mobility patterns of the nation. When the Irish fled from the potato famine and arrived here penniless, without urban skills, the young men joined police forces. Later waves of immigration from eastern and southern Europe brought Poles and Italians to the police departments. With the northern migration of blacks and the push for racial equality, police departments today offer a great opportunity for advancement to blacks. Today in large urban police departments and in many state police departments are found every race and nationality. There are orientals, Mexicans, Puerto Ricans, blacks, Jews, Italians, Wasps. For many of the European ethnic groups it is a family tradition. For others it is a step up into the mainstream of

American middle-class life. The pay is good and steady. The fringe benefits—sick leave, vacations and retirement—better than in private industry. Now, in many police departments, there is an opportunity to attend college on the job at public expense and to advance into a semiprofessional or professional status as an urban sociologist, a computer specialist, a statistician, or an operator of one of the many technological devices such as lie detectors, voiceprints, breathalysers, urinalysis and the like.

The numbers of policemen have increased enormously in recent years. Compare the numbers of police per hundred thousand in the following large cities in 1950 and 1972:

	1950	1972
New York	18,236	30,828
Philadelphia	4,889	8,183
Chicago	6,961	13,125
Detroit	4,313	5,555
Los Angeles	4,124	7,083
Houston	605	2,077 [4]

These figures do not include the nonuniformed police who do undercover work, clerical work, technological work and other activities of which the public is largely unaware.

The members of the jury panel in a criminal case are asked whether they are related to any person working for a law-enforcement agency. At least a fourth of the people randomly chosen for jury duty have one or more relatives on the police force. In Washington, D.C., there are, in the picturesque phrase of a government official, "wall-to-wall" policemen. The influence of the police on public opinion is incalculable.

Policemen are viewed by many as their friend and protector against the omnipresent and threatening criminals. Others, particularly the nonwhite, the young and the dissident, view the police as an enemy. There is substantial evidence to support both views.

The courts and especially the judiciary stem from a different tradition. Law is a learned profession. A lawyer must today have graduated from college and from law school. Simply to obtain post high school education for six or seven years requires either money or exceptional ability in order to receive scholarships and financial help. Judges are selected from among the fairly exclusive group of members of the bar. They are chosen as a result of political influence or ability, or a combination of these qualities. The professional life of a lawyer or a judge is fairly sedentary, removed from the dangers of the street. Physical strength is not a qualification for the bar or the judiciary. Although the bench in recent years includes large numbers of minority groups, it is still considered at least an upper-middle-class calling.

The two groups—diverse in background, training and experience—meet on a daily basis. It is in a court of law that accusations of wrongdoing, corruption, brutality or simple overreaching and overzealousness are made against the police. It is the judge who must decide between the claims of police and civilians.

Conflict between the police and the courts is inevitable and increasing because the average person is becoming more resentful of the exercise of government authority over him. The so-called law-abiding citizen often refuses to submit to a routine check of his automobile. With 6 million arrests a year, a sizable number of citizens testify in court as to the impropriety of police conduct. The accused citizen is protected by a presumption of innocence. The police officer, unless he is a defendant in a criminal case, is not so protected. Occasionally, I have refused to permit a policeman to testify unless he was represented by counsel. As a result of the policeman's testimony as to the circumstances of the arrest, the force used to subdue the suspect, the scope of the search, the policeman might subject himself not only to a civil suit for damages by the accused but also to charges of violation of departmental regulations which could result in loss of employment and pension rights and benefits.

The exercise of brute physical force by the police is revealed in many routine, insignificant cases which are seldom reported by the media. James Robinson, a Negro, was accused of numbers writing. Robinson's wife testified that the doorbell rang. Before she could go downstairs and open the door, two policemen had broken in the front door with a sledgehammer; other policemen surrounded the house. Mr. and Mrs. Robinson were ordered to sit in the living room under the guard of an armed policeman while other policemen ransacked their house. Three numbers slips were found. The defendant denied they were his and accused the police of "planting" them in his bureau drawer.

The policemen testified that they rang the doorbell and the defendant looked out of the window; then they heard the sound of toilets flushing (obvious destruction of the evidence); that after waiting a reasonable interval they broke in the door. The police had a valid search-and-seizure warrant. The police further testified that two numbers slips were found on the floor under a bureau and one slip was found in the defendant's pants pocket.

Seven police officers involved in the case were in court. They resented the sharp questioning by defense counsel, the imputation that they were lying and harassing the defendant. It was undisputed that the police had broken down his front door.

Robinson was acquitted because it could not be proved that the two slips allegedly found under the bureau belonged to him. Three other adults lived in the house. The one slip in his pants pocket contained only seventeen numbers and could have been the slip of a player, not a writer. But Robinson was charged with being a numbers writer. Under the law he was presumed to be innocent. He could be convicted only by proof beyond a reasonable doubt. If two inferences could be drawn from the evidence, namely, that the slips under the bureau belonged to Robinson, and that the slips belonged to another occupant of the house, the court is required to accept the inference favorable to the defendant. After the trial, in the corridor outside the courtroom, Robinson and a white policeman almost came to blows as accusations of lying were exchanged. The policemen who saw their case discharged were obviously resentful. They believed, probably with good reason, that the defendant was a big numbers writer involved in vice, payoffs, and other crimes. They had spent a great deal of time and effort to convict him and they had failed. When

Robinson surreptitiously made an obscene gesture as he left the courtroom, this was too much for the police. They let their anger out on Robinson, but the real resentment was against the court.

The hostility of the police to the courts is reciprocated by the irritation of judges with illegal and stupid actions by policemen which require the courts to acquit possibly guilty defendants.

Rodriguez, a suspected drug pusher, was arrested when the police saw him talking to an informer. They thought he was making a sale. Rodriguez was immediately taken to the police station, where he demanded his lawyer and refused to talk. Meanwhile other members of the vice squad rushed to Rodriguez' apartment and seized a huge quantity of heroin. There was no reason why the police did not get a search-and-seizure warrant. There was ample probable cause and a judge would have issued such a warrant without question. Before the trial, a motion to suppress the heroin seized in Rodriguez' home was granted. The judge really had no choice. The search was not incident to the arrest, having occurred several miles from the scene of the arrest. At trial, the informer failed to appear. The arresting police officers could only say that they saw Rodriquez put his hand palm to palm with the informer. Since a bag of heroin is not much bigger than a postage stamp, the police could not see the transfer of the heroin. In the mazes of bureaucracy the bag had inexplicably been lost. Rodriguez walked out of court a free man. Had the police taken the trouble to get a search-and-seizure warrant the $10,000 worth of heroin seized at his home would have been in evidence, and inevitably a sure conviction with a stiff sentence would have followed.

Powell was charged with armed robbery. He had held up a series of laundromats. One of the owners had an alarm button under the counter and pressed it when he saw Powell pull a gun. The police arrested Powell as he was running down the street. This laundromat owner could not identify him, except by his clothing, which was bluejeans and an army jacket. He had been too frightened to look at the robber's face. He could not even estimate height, weight or age. The police were sure they had the right man. So they took his picture, put it in a group with seven or eight other pictures, and brought them around to Mr. Cercone, another laundromat owner, who had been robbed the day before. Cercone immediately identified Powell. The police did not keep a record of the pictures. Counsel for Powell moved to suppress Cercone's identification because there was no showing that the selection of photos was fair. Powell had a beard. If the other pictures had shown men who were cleanshaven, obviously Cercone would have selected Powell. To get around this difficulty, six months later, just before the trial, the police held a proper line-up. They went to Cercone's house and took him out to the detention center—a ride of almost an hour. Cercone is an elderly man. He had worked all day. It was after ten in the evening when he was finally taken into the room to view the line-up. Confronted with seven bearded young men, all of whom looked somewhat alike, Cercone became confused and identified someone other than Powell. Cercone testified at the trial and stated under oath that he was positively certain that Powell was the man who robbed him. He would never forget that face. On cross-examination he admitted that he had identified "the wrong man" at the line-up. The jury acquitted Powell. Of course, they did not know that Powell had a long record of convictions for armed robbery. Had the police kept the photos, the time-consuming, expensive line-up would have been unnecessary. The judge, looking at the photos, could have determined whether or not it was a fair array. The day after the holdup, Cercone certainly could recognize the man who had robbed him. Six months later, he could not be sure.

Bradshaw was arrested at 9:10 P.M. with a warrant. He was wanted for a series of burglaries. The police were sure they had the right man. He had been seized with some of the fruits of his labors on him—a monogrammed watch, an imported sweater, an expensive camera. The detectives believed that Bradshaw was part of a ring. So instead of arraigning him promptly, which they are required to do under the law, Bradshaw was put in a cell for interrogation. He was handcuffed to a chair and left in this small windowless room until 3:00 A.M. It was an exceptionally busy night and no one had time to talk to Bradshaw. A signed statement confessing to more than a dozen robberies was obtained from him in the early afternoon of the next day, some eighteen hours later. This confession had to be suppressed. There was no evidence, other than the confession, that Bradshaw had stolen the goods. At trial he was convicted of receiving stolen goods but acquitted on the burglary charges. He was back on the street within a year. Had he been arraigned and then questioned, the confession would have been admissible.

Every trial judge sees cases like these day after day. It is frustrating. Often a judge may be torn between his desire to get dangerous armed criminals off the street and the strictures of the law. Those who "bend the law" in the interests of "justice" are themselves scofflaws. Not only is a judge who himself violates the law an anathema, he is also a very dangerous and expensive public servant.

A trial judge has no business reading inadmissible evidence or looking at the criminal record of the defendant before pronouncing the verdict. A judge, who presumably answers to a "higher" interest than the law, is no different from the Watergate burglars, who claim they were acting from super-patriotism and loyalty to the President. Such judges are costly to the taxpayers because their decisions are frequently reversed on appeal and a new trial is granted. The public must pay for two prosecutions instead of one. By the time of the second trial, most of the witnesses will have disappeared and a guilty defendant will be acquitted, thanks to the first overzealous judge. The original defect, which cannot be remedied by the courts, is these police errors.

The National Conference on Criminal Justice convened in 1973 by President Nixon surveyed the cases in the District of Columbia which had been dropped after arrest and found that about half of these prosecutions had been discontinued because of "defects attributable to the police." The *New York Times*, in July, 1973, after making a careful investigation of narcotics arrests around the country, reported:

Innocent Americans around the country have been subjected to dozens of mistaken, violent and often illegal police raids by local, state and narcotics agents in search of illicit drugs and their dealers. . . .

Such incidents have resulted in at least four deaths, including one policeman slain when a terror-stricken innocent woman shot through her bedroom door as it burst open. In California one innocent father was shot through the head as he sat in a living room cradling his infant son.

Details of each raid vary, but generally they involve heavily armed policemen, arriving at night, often unshaven and in slovenly "undercover" attire, bashing down the doors to a private home or apartment and holding the innocent residents at gunpoint while they ransack the house.

Police lawlessness cannot be dismissed as mere "overzealousness" or bureaucratic ineptitude. Policemen differ markedly from other public employees who also commit blunders and are corrupt, lazy or overzealous. A policeman, unlike other public officials, is armed with authority to deprive a citizen of his liberty forthwith. The most corrupt tax collector cannot jail a citizen on his own authority or by exercising force. A stupid or corrupt building inspector can make a great deal of trouble for a landlord and cause him a great deal of expense, but he cannot haul him off to jail. A lazy welfare department employee can cause infinite hardship and suffering to a needy family, but he cannot beat them over the head with a nightstick, handcuff them and drag them to the police station.

It must also be remembered that the policeman is the citizen's first line of defense against the many perils that beset everyone in contemporary society. The policeman is or should be the citizen's protector against the mugger, the robber and the thief. He is the woman's protector against the husband or paramour who beats her. He is the child's protector against the older or bigger children and the adults who threaten and abuse him. In most communities, only the police will respond to a call to take injured or stricken people to the hospital, to rescue those caught by flood, accident or other peril. In countless situations, the policeman is the on-the-spot mediator who reconciles battling spouses, irate neighbors, shopkeepers and customers, and parties involved in the countless accidents and minor disputes that are characteristic of life today.

The policeman who finds himself in the midst of a dispute is called upon to act. He can be the accuser, the witness, judge and jailer. His decision is made on the spot, with no guidance but a police training course and his sense and feelings. Weeks or months later his actions may be judged by a court that has the benefit of legal training, lawyers, witnesses and an orderly procedure.

Many times the police are wrong. Some policemen shoot first and ask questions later. But many policemen exercise remarkably good judgment. In some cities, the police dismiss charges against half the children they apprehend. They conciliate countless cases of irate adults and drop or fail to press charges. Were it not for this common sense and humane conduct of the police, the courts would be even more overloaded with trivial cases.

The police see themselves as the upholders of law and order, the only bulwark between the law-abiding citizenry and total anarchy. They see the courts as protecting the guilty and making the job of the police even more difficult than it is. The courts see evidence that the police violate the law, that they make illegal arrests and conduct illegal interrogations and complain that the courts are required to free possibly guilty suspects because of the lawlessness or ineptitude of the police. There is a measure of truth in both these charges.

Policemen, however, believe that they are disadvantaged in the continuing public debate between those who see police overstepping the legal bounds and interfering with the rights of citizens and those who see the police unduly hampered by legal restrictions. Police Chief O. W. Wilson of Chicago writes: "These misunderstandings continue unabated because the police are not a vocal, scholarly group that devotes much time to presenting, in a favorable light, the facts that bear on the problem. The literature in consequence is principally devoted to the case against the police, little has been written in their defense." [5]

This is an ingenuous statement depicting the police as inarticulate, silent victims of a campaign against them by the intellectuals. In fact, policemen are the new heroes of society. They have supplanted the clever lawyer, the noble doctor and the scientific genius as the heroes of popular literature, movies and even comic strips. This may be a singularly telling example of the "bluing" of America, the political ascendancy of blue collar or middle America which has been so assiduously courted by politicians and suddenly discovered by sociologists and demographers. Policemen are appealing folk heroes of the seventies. After the turbulent sixties, characterized by disenchantment with colleges and universities, dethronement of the Eastern establishment and the intelligentsia, the hardworking, beer-drinking family man is a refreshing literary figure. He is a welcome change from Rabbit Redux and Portnoy.

Although the policeman folk hero bears some resemblance to Archie Bunker, one should not be misled into thinking that his only concerns are his family and his paycheck. The police force of America has become politicized in recent years. Like students, teachers, farmers, blacks, Chicanos, women and the aged, the police are exercising political power as a group. In many communities they are a power to be reckoned with. Professor Herbert Reid of Howard University, who directed a study by a Commission of Inquiry into clashes between the police and the Black Panther Party, noted the growth of police departments as independent political powers.[6] Like priests and military officers, policemen no longer consider their calling one which keeps them aloof from partisan political struggles or prevents them from running for political office. Often the very fact that a man is a policeman lends him charisma and a belief, often shared by the electorate, that he is particularly well equipped for public office. More and more policemen are running for political office and getting elected. Public opinion polls of policemen are taken measuring their attitudes with respect to the courts as well as to public issues and political candidates. The increased numbers of policemen, their strong fraternal orders, the militant organizations of police wives, and the outspoken criticism of the courts by the police pose an unprecedented problem of law enforcement in the United States.

Dictatorships have always relied upon the power of the military for public support as well as for the brute force necessary to effect a coup or takeover and to maintain power over an apathetic or unwilling populace. In the United States, the military has been under civilian control. President Truman did not hesitate to recall General MacArthur when he exceeded the limits of his authority. To date no national confrontation between the police and courts as representing opposing powers within the government has occurred. In any number of local communities, however, the police have been a decisive bloc in the election of mayors, judges and other public officials. The police have openly exerted pressure on charities not to support agencies which supply legal services to clients who sue the police. In many more subtle ways the political force of the police has been felt.

The budget of the police, like that of the military, is often considered sacrosanct. Few public officials ask for an accounting of how the police budget is spent, whether the money is used wisely and efficiently or even whether it is used legally. The amounts involved are not trivial. The National Conference on Criminal Justice reports that $3.5 billion was spent for police protection in the United States in 1960. For the year ending June 30, 1971, the amount spent for police protection exceeded $10 billion. On a per capita basis for local police only, citizens were paying these amounts in 1970:

New York	$76.54
Detroit	66.65
Chicago	57.44
Philadelphia	48.03
Los Angeles	39.60
Houston	21.33

Each year the sums increase. In New York City, for example, the police department submitted a request for $36.4 million in the 1973–74 capital budget for weapons, horses and other equipment. In addition, large sums are spent by the Law Enforcement Assistance Administration and foundations studying or supporting programs to reduce crime. Of the $860 million spent by LEAA in 1971, $370 million was devoted to police services and hardware for the police departments.

What has all this money accomplished? Very little. For example, although the New York City police force has increased by 55 percent, the number of police on the street remains constant. A New York policeman spends on the average of nine hours and forty-five minutes after the arrest of each arrestee in what has been described as "byzantine" legal procedures.

Despite the expenditure of these large sums and the use of sophisticated equipment, 80 percent of those who commit crimes are not caught. A success rate of only 20 percent would put most enterprises out of business. The primary business of the police is to maintain order, deter crime and apprehend criminals. The success rate is appreciably lower than 20 percent if one includes unreported crimes. Many victims of crime do not report these crimes because they feel it is a futile, time-consuming and empty ritual. The police, in failing to apprehend criminals, are also failing in their deterrent function. No individual who plans and calculates risks would be deterred by a 20 percent chance of his failure. For the professional criminal, the probabilty of arrest is slight. Police inefficiency might even be said to contribute to this form of crime. Even impulsive street criminals, who do not plan or calculate risks, might might be deterred by a very high probability of arrest. We do not know, because no American police department in a large city has achieved even a 50 percent arrest rate. Those departments which claim a very high arrest rate (40 percent) include such crimes as drunkenness, which are reported only when an arrest is made. If one examines only the arrest rate of serious crimes in which there is a victim, it would be appreciably lower.

Some thoughtful citizens and sociologists are beginning to question the efficiency of the police. A recent Kansas City study indicates that police patrolling has little, if any, effect on the crime rate.[7] Significantly, there was no appreciable change in the crime rate in New York City when the entire police force was on strike for six days in January 1971. These facts should cause a careful scrutiny of the entire spectrum of police operations, which have always been considered a matter of professional, internal judgment for police officials to make. Obviously some outside scrutiny of the deployment of personnel and equipment, functions such as surveillance, data banks, auto patrolling, vice squads and the like is needed to discover why the police are not more successful in apprehending criminals and preventing crime. The nexus between police ineffectiveness and disrespect for law, though not subject to quantified proof, appears to be clear.

Another factor contributing to the death of the law in America is lawlessness by law-enforcement officials. This lawlessness runs the gamut from brutality by individual policemen to organized and calculated manufacture of false evidence. Many varieties of police misconduct are revealed only in court when a defendant with an able attorney exposes the illegal and prejudicial actions of the police. Such cases polarize the courts and the cops.

In a routine robbery case which did not involve any political ideology such as Black Panthers, hippies, or demonstrators, the following testimony was elicited.

Defense counsel questioned the arresting policeman:

Q. "Did you have any physical contact with him [the defendant]?"

A. "No."

Q. "You didn't strike him?"

A. "No, I didn't. If I would have struck him—"

Q. "Just answer the question."

A. "—it would have been at the street."

Q. "Officer, now, you have been going on and on and you know what the problem is here?"

A. "I realize that."

Q. "Just answer the question."

A. I didn't touch him *inside* the detective bureau." [Emphasis added.]

The defendant then testified:

Q. "And then what happened?"

A. "They took me to a friend, they started taking me out of the bar and started beating on me."

Q. "Who beat on you?"

A. "The two arresting officers."

Q. "The men that testified here today?"

A. "Yes."

Q. "How did they beat you?"

A. "They stomped me in the back of the patrol wagon."

Q. "How did they do that; did they punch you, kick you?"

A. "They both punched me and kicked me."

On redirect examination of the two officers this was not denied.

The public is justifiably outraged and concerned when a policeman is killed while on duty. Unfortunately, this is not an unusual occurrence. In 1971, 126 policemen were killed on duty in the United States. In New York City alone 10 policemen were killed and 333 injured. There is no doubt that a policeman's lot is neither a happy nor safe one. Frightened men are not always careful. They may misread the factual situation and shoot unnecessarily. It is difficult without a long and exacerbating fact-finding commission or criminal trial to ascertain the true situation and the "probable cause" the policeman had for acting as he did. Was it fear, bad judgment, recklessness or malevolence? The public seldom knows.

While one cannot and should not weigh one life against another, certain facts raise questions. Ten New York policemen were, as we have noted, killed on duty in 1971, but ninety-three civilians were killed by the police during the same period. Many of them were described in the official reports as "perpetrators" of crimes. No one knows if, in fact, these "perpetrators" were really dangerous criminals or whether the police acted with propriety. Since they are dead, the facts will never be discovered. The shooting of Fred Hampton, the Black Panther leader, by Cook County, Illinois, policemen is but one of many instances in which police are accused of poor judgment, mistake or malevolence. Kenyon Franklin Ballen of Montgomery County, Maryland, was paralyzed as a result of a bullet wound when police and treasury agents raided his apartment on June 7, 1971. A Philadelphia policeman shot and killed Indian Leroy Shenandoah in a brawl on March 2, 1972. By chance, the incident was filmed by a movie company which happened to be on the scene; the film proved that the policeman acted without provocation. A Brooklyn policeman shot to death James Parris, a vagrant suffering from brain disease, on May 1, 1970. The list of such killings is long and dismaying.

Few citizens are in a position to evaluate the propriety of police conduct. Could the police have used tear gas or mace instead of deadly bullets? Could the officer have aimed at the legs instead of the heart or head? There are fierce partisans who believe that the police can do no wrong and those who believe with equal conviction that policemen are wantonly brutal and have no respect for the rights of citizens, particularly those who are black, poor, hippies, or dissidents. Countless incidents can be found to support both views. Significantly, the Governor's Justice Commission of Pennsylvania, after conducting public hearings into the operation of the Norristown police department, reported:

> A sizable portion of the Norristown community believes that a few officers of the Norristown police department will resort to violence or brutality in the performance of their duties. Numerous witnesses testified about the use of excessive force against themselves or about having observed a similar use of force against others. Although Mayor Caida presented evidence that tended to refute one allegation of police brutality, the large number of such complaints cannot easily be dismissed. Significantly, the Commission found that this violence appears to have been directed indiscriminately at blacks, whites, the poor, and the well-to-do.[8]

A judge who listens to the testimony of the police and their accusers finds some instances of inexcusable brutality and some instances of deliberate provocation by citizens, but more often misperceptions of fact by both parties. Police are called in situations of turmoil and emergency. Many policemen are young and nervous. Probably even the most experienced policeman feels apprehensive when he gets an emergency call. Under such circumstances some police may overreact.

Much unnecessary police violence occurs because of administrative errors, incomplete or misleading information transmitted to the police on the beat or on patrol. Consider these cases which I heard in one week:

§A dozen citizens with no prior criminal involvement were charged with aggravated assault and battery on police officers. The evidence disclosed that a phone call was received at police headquarters reporting a fight in the backyard of a small house in a congested street which is the border between two hostile ethnic neighborhoods. One patrol car was dispatched. Those policemen found a family party in progress. Some of the guests had had a little too much to drink. The officers broke up the fight in minutes and were preparing to leave without making an arrest. These are routine occurrences. Meanwhile, another neighbor had also phoned the police. A bus load of riot control policemen and several patrol cars were instantly sent to the scene. It was night. Without checking with the first car load of police, all of whom were equipped with walkie-talkie phones, more than a hundred policemen swarmed into this tiny house, guns drawn and night sticks flailing. In the melee, several policemen and civilians were seriously injured.

§A young drug addict, shouting obscenities, attempted to cross a six-lane highway during rush hour. He was hauled to safety by the traffic cop. A few moments later, several patrol cars arrived, and, without stopping to talk to the officer on duty, four policemen, in the patrol cars, beat and severely injured the young man who was, at that time, safely on the sidewalk and in handcuffs.

§A car was reported stolen, license number given and the direction in which the thief was going. Two patrol cars sighted him and gave chase, sirens blaring. It was 3:30 in the afternoon and the cars sped through narrow slum streets teeming with children on their way home from school. One six-year-old, who did not move quickly enough, was run over and killed.

§On another crowded street, a young boy snatched a few dollars from an ice-cream vendor. A police car happened to be driving past and observed the crime. An officer jumped out of the car and shot the fleeing boy, paralyzing him for life.

In none of these cases were the police officers charged with assault, murder or even misconduct. The facts were revealed in the course of the prosecution of the civilians. The drunken family brawlers were accused of assault and battery on a policeman. The drug addict was accused of resisting arrest. The car thief was on trial for larceny of auto. And the ice-cream thief was accused of armed robbery, larceny and conspiracy because he was with a friend who had a knife in his pocket. No action was taken against any of the police officers involved in these incidents.

The manufacture of evidence by the police is revealed only in rare cases when the accused has persistent counsel. Such episodes occur most frequently when there are no eye witnesses to the crime. In these cases, the proof of the accused's guilt may depend upon analysis of paint, blood, hair, clothing or other physical objects. These bits of evidence are routinely examined by crime laboratories which are part of the police department. Customarily the technicians are informed of the crime being investigated and are fully aware of the type of evidence needed to convict. Often the testimony of so-called scientific experts is the most dangerous because it has an aura of impartiality and infallability. Frequently, that is not the case.

Testimony identifying hair on the accused's clothing as being that of the victim is routinely admitted in evidence, although it is scientifically impossible to identify an individual by a few hairs. Once, when I was defending a man accused of murder, an expert witness offered to testify as to the impossibility of making such identification. This testimony would simply corroborate a multitude of studies on the subject. But in researching the law, I discovered that this very expert had testified in another case for the prosecution and made a positive identification of another defendant on the basis of four hairs found on the victim's body.

When confronted with this prior testimony, the expert stated by way of extenuation, "But that was a heinous crime."

Occasionally a case which reaches the appellate courts reveals a chilling glimpse of the "scientific" validity of such evidence. Lloyd Eldon Pate was convicted of the murder of an eight-year-old girl who died as a result of a brutal sexual attack. A sentence of death was imposed. There were no eyewitnesses to the crime. The most important piece of evidence was a pair of men's undershorts covered with large, dark-reddish stains which had been found three days after the murder about a mile from the scene of the crime. A chemist for the State Bureau of Crime Identification was duly qualified as one who had made more than a thousand blood-typing analyses. He testified that the spots on the underwear were human blood, type A. The defendant's blood type was O. The victim's blood was type A. Of course, approximately one-fourth of all the people in the world have blood type A. The judgment of conviction was sustained by the Supreme Court of Illinois. On a habeas corpus proceeding in the federal court, the defendant obtained permission to have the shorts chemically examined by an impartial expert. It was then revealed that the stains were not blood but paint. The state did not dispute this fact. The United States Supreme Court reversed the conviction.[9] The case had been before the trial court, the Supreme Court of Illinois, a federal district court twice, a court of appeals, and the United States Supreme Court before the conviction of this innocent man was set aside. In the meantime, the real murderer was free. It is doubtful that after a lapse of almost a decade he will ever be found. But, on the police statistics, the case was marked "cleared by arrest." One cannot help wondering about the validity of that expert's testimony in a thousand prior cases in which he had testified.[10] And what is or was the attitude of these thousand convicted persons sent to jail, or perhaps to the electric chair, on the basis of such false, police-inspired evidence? What must be the attitude of their friends and relatives toward law and the administration of justice? These questions are seldom asked by the proponents of law and order. But they cannot be ignored in a nation in which the crime rate is so high. Unfairness and injustice naturally engender hostility in the affected civilian populations. Obviously, more just and efficient operations by the innumerable police departments in this nation are desirable and a goal that must be achieved. But this is not a complete answer to the role of the police in the death of the law.

The lawlessness and violence of the public are, as we have seen, mirrored by the lawlessness and violence of the police. A citizen militia, which is essentially what local and state police and the national guard are, inevitably shares the prejudices, hostilities and attitudes of the general citizenry. Policemen, on the whole, reflect the anti-intellectual, antidissident attitudes of the blue-collar environments from which most of them have come. This is equally true of black and Puerto Rican policemen and policewomen as of white police officers. Jewish policemen share the attitudes of the police force at large and are just as hostile to student demonstrations as Irish or Italian policemen. Changing the racial composition of the police force, which is so often recommended, may be desirable simply as an end in itself to eliminate discrimination in this important area of public employment. But more minority members on the police force will not reduce violence and brutality. Nor will courses in intergroup relations, raising salaries, and upgrading educational requirements.

Public accountability for the budget, the deployment of forces, the use of deadly weapons, and the efficiency of the police administration, of course, are desirable reforms. What is the cost/benefit ratio of our constantly growing police forces? Can they be reduced without further endangering public safety? These are questions the public should ask.

Underlying these problems of police management and functions is a much deeper question. Are the police—our most numerous and visible members of the law-enforcement branch of government—a positive or negative factor in the lawlessness of our society? Have they contributed to the death of the law by their own lawlessness and ineffectiveness?

All Americans have been dismayed by the revelation of illegality and disregard for law and truth in high places. This has been well publicized. The illegality and overreaching by the police is not often front-page news. But in every community the people see policemen "cooping" (sleeping on the job), accepting free meals and other small favors, turning a blind eye and a deaf ear to flagrant violations of the law. If any teen-ager in the ghetto knows where to get dope, where to fence stolen goods, where to buy liquor and guns illegally, then they also know that these illegal enterprises flourish with the tacit consent of the police. The poor, who are most often the victims of crime, know that there is little police protection for them. Their children are beaten, robbed and molested on the way to school. They see vandalism all about them. The middle class walks in fear through the city streets. They have no assurance that the police will protect their persons or their property. The increase of patrolmen, the use of sophisticated weaponry, the marvelous communications system of walkie-talkies, radio cars and compu-terized data machinery have all been tried at enormous cost. But they have been largely ineffective. The police cannot impose obedience to law on a lawless society. This is an impossible task. The problems of lawlessness and violence by law-enforcement agencies cannot be separated from the same problems in the larger community. We ignore them at our peril. We have placed our reliance for security and order in the police and made them almost a paramilitary elite. But the police forces are composed of ordinary men and women, members of the community who share the general attitudes of the citizenry. The police take what they can get, legally or illegally, because that is what they see all around them. Policemen are particularly vulnerable to graft and bribery because of their daily contact with crime. For every policeman who takes a bribe there is a civilian who gave the bribe. Movies like *Serpico* reveal the problems of the honest cop in a dishonest society. The role of the police in contributing to the death of the law is one of reaction and interaction with the public, a double helix of spiraling violence and lawlessness. Meaningful change in illegal conduct by the police can be wrought only by corresponding attitudinal changes in both the police and the public.

Why is there always a secret singing
when a lawyer cashes in?
Why does a hearse horse snicker
Hauling a lawyer away?

Carl Sandburg, "The Lawyers
Know Too Much"

"I don't like lawyers, nannie."
"No one likes lawyers, little boy."

J. P. Donleavy

High were those headlands, the eagles promised
Life without lawyers. . . .

W. H. Auden, "The Age of Anxiety"

9: The Hated Hessians

Law without lawyers is a concept difficult for Americans to imagine. In some areas of the world, simple tribesmen live in accordance with their legal principles quite happily without the presence of lawyers. But in the United States everyone who gets into difficulties, from the President to a drunken derelict or a small child, needs and is entitled to the services of a lawyer. Since 1963, representation by counsel has been raised to the status of a Constitutional right. The entire legal structure of the nation depends upon the competent, zealous and ethical activities of lawyers. One must, therefore, consider the role which lawyers have played—wittingly or unwittingly—in the death of the law.

It is all too easy to blame lawyers for all of the misdeeds of their clients, the miscarriages of justice and the public disregard of law. A facile editorial writer declared: "Watergate and its aftermath were created by lawyers. It is now up to the rest of us to find the remedy." [1] A podiatrist proudly asserted that none of his profession was involved in the national or local scandals. Neither were carpenters, steamfitters, school teachers or members of countless other occupations. It is the function of lawyers to represent people who are in trouble, people accused of violating the law. It is the function of lawyers to advise and represent those who make the laws and administer them. Inevitably, every real and alleged misdeed by a private citizen, a great corporation, or a government official becomes the business of lawyers. Whether they must share the responsibilities for their clients' actions and whether the lawyers' activities have promoted or contributed to the endemic lawlessness of the United States are the questions this chapter will consider.

Distrust and hatred of lawyers have long been old characteristic themes of English and American life and cannot be blamed on Watergate. The habit of blaming lawyers for the troubles of society is an ancient one. In 1381, during the ill-fated rebellion of Wat Tyler, many lawyers were killed by the angry public because they were the visible instruments of law-enforcing policies that were bitterly hated. This is still the role of many lawyers who evict tenants, repossess goods purchased on time, and resist payment of claims for injuries, defective merchandise, and the like. Lawyers were the visible agents of the English upper classes, who demanded the closing of the commons, thus forcing the poor farmers into the city slums to become the factory hands on whose labor the Industrial Revolution was built. In the 1930s in the United States lawyers were the agents who foreclosed the mortgages on the farms of the Okies and Arkies, who then became the migrant workers in the factories in the fields. Lawyers as agents for wealthy corporations and individuals devise the tax laws and interpret loopholes that permit accumulations of great fortunes and special privileges. Lawyers are also the visible agents of the enemies of society—alleged criminals, communists, anarchists and perpetrators of violence. When lawyers succeed in freeing these clients, public wrath is vented on the lawyer as well as the client. Legal technicalities or niceties are scorned by people who resent the results of laws and litigation. Lawyers are, with some justification, held responsible for the outcome of these cases which are so widely criticized.

Lawyers, as an integral component of the entire legal system, share not only the blame but also in a real sense a part of the responsibility for the failure of the law to provide an orderly society. The role of the lawyer must also be analyzed to understand why this elaborate system of government, including laws, litigation, and appeals, fails to provide just results for a large segment of society.

In order to understand the pervasive role of the lawyer in American life, a few statistics and comparisons are helpful. The United States, as we have seen, has more laws regulating the conduct of the citizen than any other nation and more procedures to contest the validity and administration of these laws. We have more courts and more quasi-judicial bodies than any other nation. We also have more lawyers. There are some 350,000 lawyers in the United States, or one attorney for approximately 532 people. There are only 348,000 doctors and 118,000 dentists to serve the same population. In England there are approximately 25,000 lawyers (both barristers and solicitors) or one for every 2,000 persons. It is reported that in China there are only 30,000 lawyers for a population of 800 million. Despite the inaccuracy of statistics and the difficulties of comparing the practice of law in countries with different legal systems and different standards of individual rights, it is clear that both absolutely and on a per capita basis there are more lawyers in America than in any other nation.

What do these lawyers do? Only two-thirds of them are engaged in the private practice of law. Of the other third many are in business and other unrelated occupations. Many heads of large corporations, charitable foundations, and universities are lawyers. There are at least 40,000 lawyers employed by agencies of government. In 1972, 2,000 were employed by the Office of Economic Opportunity to represent the poor. And 2,500 to 3,000 by Legal Aid and Defender offices. Large numbers are on the legal staffs of corporations and insurance companies. More than 2,500 persons teach full time in the nation's approximately 125 accredited law schools. At least 10,000 lawyers are employed as full-time judges.

Lawyers play an exceedingly important role in the political life of the country and have from its inception. Of the 52 signers of the Declaration of Independence, 25 were lawyers; 31 members of the 56 member Continental Congress were lawyers; 24 of our 37 Presidents were lawyers. Significantly, perhaps, the nonlawyers include Washington, Truman, and Kennedy.

Despite the strenuous efforts to elect more blacks, more women and more young people to the legislature in recent years, the Congress remains largely a body of white, middle-aged, middle-class male lawyers. This is also true of the fifty state legislatures and the countless local law making bodies. Of the 100 United States Senators at this writing, 67 are white, male attorneys. A majority of the members of the House of Representatives are also lawyers. The five women members of Congress, newly elected in 1972, are lawyers. Mayors, schoolboard members, and members of government regulative bodies and authorities are predominantly lawyers. There are no national statistics on the occupations of ward leaders and committeemen. The preponderance of these people, who constitute both the workers and the policy makers of the political parties, are also lawyers.

The word politician has a pejorative connotation. The *Random House Dictionary of the English Language* defines politician as "a seeker or holder of public office, who is more concerned about winning favor or retaining power than about maintaining principles." Since so many lawyers are politicians and government officials, this symbiosis of law and politics cannot be ignored.

Although many lawyers never set foot in a courtroom and really act as advisors or counselors to their clients in the management of their businesses and their private lives, the role of the lawyer is essentially a public one, for the promulgation of laws and enforcement of laws cannot be delegated to the private sector. Although many disputes are settled by mediation, conciliation and arbitration—essentially private agreements to agree—when these fail, the public force of law is required. And in all of these operations the participation of lawyers is necessary.

Today the legal profession is in a state of turmoil, assailed from without and bitterly attacked from within. It is accused of being unethical. It is charged with failing to represent the poor and the middle class. Lawyers are accused of being tools of the vested interests, agents of corruption, pawns of politicians, and the cause of the delays and failures of the legal system. In my introductory indoctrination lesson as a new judge, an older colleague declared, "The first thing you must do is to learn to hate all lawyers." Shakespeare was more direct. Dick the butcher, an honest fellow says, "The first thing we do, let's kill all the lawyers."

With such a bad image, one might wonder why 350,000 Americans have chosen to be lawyers. There were in 1973 more than 100,000 students attending law school with the intention of becoming lawyers. Thousands more have applied for admission to law school but have been rejected. It is not an occupation one undertakes lightly or easily. Today most attorneys in the United States are both college graduates and graduates of a three-year law school. The cost in out-of-pocket expenses and lost earnings may range from $50,000 to $200,000. Tuition at many universities and law schools is more than $2,000 a year. There are living expenses and books. Most law schools accept only those who pass a rigorous aptitude test. Obviously these young men and women could earn at a minimum $7,000 a year in some other job if they were not attending law school.

What are the attractions and rewards that impel so many able and intelligent people to want to become lawyers? For a fortunate 5 or 10 percent, there is lucrative practice in a few large law firms. For a much smaller group there is the glamour of a glittering trial practice. For some, government service with its siren lure of power—for good or ill—appeals. For others, law is a new children's crusade to right the nation's wrongs, to bring justice to the poor and disadvantaged, and to enforce the ideals of liberty and justice for all.

The practice of law for most lawyers, however, fulfills none of these goals. Instead it is an occupation of unending work, and considerable monotony and drudgery. On the whole it is an ill-paid profession when compared with medicine. It provides few, if any, fringe benefits. In 1970, the average lawyer earned less than $12,000 per year.[2] The average income for all wage earners, the majority of whom do not have college degrees, was $7,000. If more refined statistics were available, it is likely they would show that nonlawyers with seven years post high school education earn on the average considerably more than lawyers who have spent an equal amount of time in college and law school. Lawyers in large firms earn an average of more than $30,000—many earn in excess of $100,000—but fewer than one-fourth of the private practitioners are members or associates of such firms. Most lawyers, unless they are government employees or associates of a large firm, have no paid vacations, no sick leave, and no pension other than self-employed social security and private insurance. Lawyers are subject to the surveillance of the organized bar through various boards of censors who have the power to deprive an attorney of his license and the right to earn his living by the practice of law. A lawyer is restricted to the state in which he is licensed to practice. He is subject to criticism not only by the press but also by his clients who, when dissatisfied, can make complaints to the Bar Associations, charges which he must answer at peril of losing his license to practice law. In addition, a lawyer is subject to the contempt power of the judges before whom he appears. If he is late to court, if he fails to appear when summoned, if he represents his client too zealously or too indifferently he may be fined and imprisoned.

By comparison, a college graduate with no additional training and no certification as to character can become licensed to teach in the public schools. In New York City, for example, the entering salary in 1970 was $8,000. A teacher has tenure, paid vacations, paid sick leave and after twenty-five years will receive a pension. A policeman with no education beyond a high school diploma (and often even that is not required) had a starting salary in New York of $10,699 in 1972. In Philadelphia, his entering salary in 1973 was

$10,896. A policeman is protected by civil service, a strong organization (Fraternal Order of Police), and can retire with a good pension after only twenty years of service in New York City. He can retire at age 50 in Philadelphia. Four plumbers who work for the San Francisco Water Department earn $35,000 a year, more than a city lawyer.

Both young and old are bemused by the mystique of the law, fostered by history, literature and the mass media. Young people entering law school are beguiled by an astigmatic vision of the lawyer's life as a combination of J. P. Morgan and Don Quixote. Anthony Lewis, the newspaper columnist, described the ideal role of the lawyer: "The lawyer's obligation is to the open mind. He must eternally try to square the moral necessity for equality with the experienced need for diversity, our craving for ordered tranquility with our irrepressible desire for freedom. It is no accident that those are the themes of American constitutionalism. In this society I believe there is no higher calling than that of the lawyer." [3]

Although Anthony Lewis attended Harvard Law School for a year, he is not a lawyer. He observes, from a distance, the headline cases, not the run-of-the-mill litigation on which lawyers depend for their livelihood. He sees the singular and the exceptional, not the daily operations of the legal system which could not function without the work of lawyers.

Taking his premises as a proper goal for the legal profession, one must ask why lawyers have not seen their function to be the promotion and reconcilement of ordered tranquility with freedom, and equality with diversity. One must also ask other searching questions. Do lawyers contribute to the improvement of the nature and quality of life in the community? Should we, as a nation, need this number of lawyers? What types of legal services are required and in what numbers? How many lawyers are needed for the rich, for the people of modest means, and for the poor? What kind of skills do these various classes of lawyers need? Who will pay for their services? Are the law schools of the United States adequately training their students for the actual functions which they will perform? Are the students being trained for the functions they should perform? In fact, do we know what lawyers really do and do we have a clear image of what the lawyer's functions should be?

None of these questions can be answered without understanding the role of the lawyer vis-à-vis his client. As an individual and in his private dealings, a lawyer, like every person, is expected to maintain a standard of truth and morality. When representing a client, however, a lawyer is subject to an entirely different standard of ethics and conduct. The role of the lawyer is anomalous. He is supposed to represent the interest of his client with utmost fidelity. Communications between lawyer and client are privileged, like those of priest and penitent. At the same time, the lawyer is an officer of the court sworn to uphold the public interest. Obviously the interest of the client is often at odds with that of society.

In fact, it is precisely at these points of conflict that the services of a lawyer are needed. The client accused of crime wants to be acquitted. The interest of society, at a minimum, is in stopping his illegal conduct and incarcerating him so that he cannot continue his antisocial behavior. The public may also demand vengeance and punishment. The interest of the corporate client or individual entrepreneur is to make money. The interests of society are to have better and safer products at lower prices. Within the corporate structure, the interests of management are an aggrandizement of power and wealth. The interests of the stockholders are larger dividends and a greater return on their investments.

Charitable foundations under the law exist for the promotion of science, education, the arts and the relief of the public burden. But as an institution, a charitable foundation has an interest opposed to that of the public at large. The foundation wants to grow, to avoid paying taxes, and to develop the programs that appeal to management. The public interest may lie in taxing these billions rather than in financing retired politicians, poets and research scientists. The foundation may be interested in exploring patterns of genetic differences, social role-playing, psychological personality changes, global power struggles, and other problems that raise issues the public does not wish to consider.

Government agencies often find themselves in conflict not only with citizens but also with each other. The Department of Transportation wants to build a highway. The Environmental Protection Agency wants to preserve the landscape. Every agency wants a larger share of the tax dollar.

In each instance, the individual, the corporation, the foundation and the government agency calls upon a lawyer to represent this special interest against the claims of all other interests and those of the public as a whole.

Lawyers are scrupulous in avoiding a conflict of interest when representing clients. If there is any possibility that two or more of his clients may take different positions, that their interests are not completely congruent and compatible in all respects, the lawyer will withdraw from representing one or more of these clients so that he can devote himself completely, without any countervailing considerations, to the interest of the other client. The rules on conflict of interest between clients are strict. They have been developed with searching attention to all details and possibilities. A whole body of law and ethics exists on this subject. But the legal profession has never acknowledged the inherent conflict of interest that exists in almost every case between the lawyer's duty of fidelity to his client and his duty to the public as an officer of the court.

A lawyer is licensed by the government and is under a sworn duty to uphold and defend the laws and the Constitution of the United States. Despite the license and the oath, the role of the lawyer is, by definition and by law, amoral. The lawyer is required to represent and to defend the guilty as well as the innocent. He must press the position of his client even though it is contrary to the public good, popular opinion, and widely accepted standards of behavior. Canon 7 of the Code of Professional Responsibility promulgated by the American Bar Association declares:

> The duty of a lawyer, both to his client and to the legal system, is to represent his client zealously within the bounds of the law. . . . In our government of laws and not of men, each

member of society is entitled to have his conduct judged and regulated in accordance with the law, to seek any lawful objective through legally permissible means, and to present for adjudication any lawful claim, issue or defense. . . . The advocate may urge any permissible construction of the law favorable to his client without regard to his professional opinion as to the likelihood that the construction will ultimately prevail. . . .

In other words, the skilled judgment of the lawyer that his client's case is spurious or without merit is irrelevant. The lawyer must, therefore, be a Hessian, a mercenary, available for hire to do the bidding of whoever pays him.

In criminal cases, the duty to represent the client zealously, regardless of the lawyer's judgment as to guilt or innocence, raises many questions which have not been adequately explored. The lawyer's duty is most often misunderstood when he defends a person believed to be guilty of a heinous crime or of holding unpopular opinions. When the lawyer succeeds in getting the client acquitted, in the public view, he has cheated "justice" by means of technicalities.

The fact is that many times only the client knows whether he is guilty or innocent before the trial. All too often *after* the trial no one is sure. For the lawyer to prejudge his client and decide the matter of guilt or innocence himself would make a mockery of the entire system of trial. Lawyers can be just as mistaken or prejudiced as anyone else. No client should first have to convince his lawyer of his innocence, virtue, and honor before he can get representation. Under such a system, the lawyer would, in effect, vouch for the client and be responsible for his veracity. The lawyer would be chargeable with the guilt of his client. This would place intolerable burdens on both lawyer and client and effectively debar the persons most in need of representation from obtaining the services of a lawyer.

The principle of confidentiality between lawyer and client is extremely important and well established in the law. Information obtained in the lawyer-client relationship is sacrosanct and its revelation cannot be compelled. This, too, is essential. Otherwise, a client would confide in his lawyer at his peril. The only time a lawyer can "inform" on his client within the canons of ethics is when the client reveals that he *intends* to commit a crime, not that he has already committed a crime. Two lawyers representing Robert Garrow, accused of murder, did not reveal that they had seen the bodies of two other people whom their client had killed. It was only after Garrow, while testifying, indicated that he was involved in four murders that the lawyers felt free to divulge what they knew. This is a dramatic and unusual example of the moral dilemma of counsel, who are bound, under the Canons of Ethics, to respect the confidential information received from a client and also are duty bound not to hide physical evidence of crimes.

A lawyer, knowing that his client is guilty, must nonetheless defend him zealously and utilize every legal position and argument available if the client does not wish to plead guilty. No one knows how many guilty people are acquitted, just as no one knows how many innocent persons have been convicted. The annals of the law are replete with cases of persons whose innocence was uncovered after the convict had served years in prison or had been executed. It is more unusual to learn of the guilt of an acquitted person. One interesting case widely reported in the press involved the accused slayer of Candy Mossler's husband. This young man had been represented by the great defense lawyer Percy Foreman. According to the report, after the trial the young man threatened Mr. Foreman saying, "I killed one old man and I wouldn't mind killing another." Foreman is said to have replied, "But who would defend you this time?"

Many less dramatic examples abound of counsel taking positions which the Canons of Ethics require but which the lawyer knows are factually unjustified. In civil cases, frequently a lawyer will advise his client that under the facts and the law he has no legitimate defense to the claim against him or that he has no valid claim against the person he wishes to sue. Often clients will accept the judgment of the lawyer and pay debts which are legitimately owing, refrain from bringing unjustified suits, and make reasonable settlements of claims where there is a valid dispute as to the facts or the law. Frequently, however, clients will not accept the advice of counsel.

If the client wishes to sue or to contest a claim, the lawyer must either zealously pursue his client's interest or withdraw from the case. If lawyer A withdraws, lawyer B will accept the case and the fee. After trial, both lawyers may be convinced that the judgment is legally sound and fundamentally fair. But if the loser wishes to appeal, counsel can always find some questionable point in the proceedings on which to base an appeal. Often a lawyer will say to me, "It was a fair trial, Judge. The verdict is not unreasonable. But my client refuses to pay. He insists that I take an appeal." And so the lawyer must scan the trial record to find some point of error to raise in order to satisfy his client. As long as the client can afford to litigate, the lawyer will, and under the Canons of Ethics is expected to, continue to represent him.

The role of the lawyer as a hireling doing the bidding of his client must be contrasted with that of a doctor. Both lawyer and doctor are skilled professionals advising a lay person who is ignorant of many critical facts. The patient knows his symptoms but cannot diagnose his ailment. Few doctors can speak with absolute certainty. But most can advise as to the prognosis, the likelihood of successful recovery from surgery, and the likelihood of more serious illness if surgery is not performed. Under the law, the patient must give his informed consent to the treatment prescribed by the doctor. Few reputable doctors will undertake surgery or treatment at the patient's dictation if it is contrary to the doctor's medical judgment.

The client, like the patient, knows some of the facts involved in his situation. But he is not aware of his legal rights and liabilities. He cannot intelligently estimate the likelihood of success or failure in litigation. For these critical opinions, he must rely on his lawyer. But the lawyer must follow the bidding of the client even when he believes the likelihood of success is nonexistent and that both the facts and the law dictate a contrary course of action. The lawyer whose advice is rejected has only two options: represent the client in accordance with the client's wishes or withdraw from the case. In criminal cases, the lawyer is not free to withdraw without obtaining leave of court. If his withdrawal will unduly delay litigation, leave will be denied. If the lawyer is employed by an agency for the poor he cannot withdraw, because no other lawyer will be available for the client. And thus day after day lawyers who are required to take unreasonable positions, defend or prosecute claims without merit, and take appeals from decisions which are right and fair.

A paying client is often dissuaded from taking unjustifiable positions because the cost of doing so far outweighs the likelihood of success. It is simply not worth the investment in costs and lawyers' fees. But an extremely wealthy or an extremely unreasonable client may get sufficient psychic satisfaction from persisting in litigation despite the costs. The courts are cluttered with cases of neighbors' feuds, family vendettas, and contract claims arising out of personal spite, pique, or hostility. A judge usually suggests to the parties and counsel that they try to reconcile their differences, pointing out the possible penalties that might be incurred. Frequently attorneys representing both factions will say, "Judge, we have pleaded with them to withdraw charges [or pay damages, etc.], but neither side will listen to reason." Counsel as Hessian must act in ways that are contrary to his own judgment.

Indigent clients, of course, are not deterred by a calculus of cost/benefit, since they do not pay counsel fees. Consequently an indigent client will appeal a justifiable conviction even though the likelihood of success is minimal and the penalty only nominal. Again, counsel must carry out the client's wishes no matter how unreasonable or lacking in merit they may be.

This amoral abnegation of judgment on the part of lawyers required by the adversary theory of law permits the legal system to operate in a mindless fashion unrestrained by the values, calculations and considerations which operate in most areas of life. This is a problem which the establishment lawyers of the bar association, the poverty lawyers, and the counter-culture lawyers have failed to probe. It is certainly one of the factors to be considered in the etiology of the death of the law.

Accepting the present role of the lawyer, which is to represent his client zealously without regard to the lawyer's own professional opinion, one must ask whether the clients and the public on the whole have been well served. There are no surveys or studies that seek to answer these questions. With respect to the clients, one can only draw tentative conclusions from the complaints made by former clients, many of whom are simply disgruntled or want to avoid paying the lawyer's fees. Others have legitimate complaints that counsel failed to appear when the case was called, that the lawyer used the client's funds for his own purposes, and simply that he was incompetent.

Many trial judges complain that lawyers are unprepared, that they are rude and captious. Of course, lawyers complain that judges don't know the law, are rude, lazy and temperamental. I have seen lawyers and judges who fit these descriptions. Unfortunately, many assistant prosecutors and public defenders are novices. They are frequently overworked and have inadequate time to prepare their cases. Private counsel also have the same failings. Good trial lawyers are usually overworked. Those who represent poor but not indigent people receive modest fees which do not permit them to spend enough time in preparation for trial. Briefs are often sloppy, misspelled and with inaccurate citations. Good secretaries are expensive. No one individual can pass judgment on the competence of an entire profession, but it is not ungenerous to say that many lawyers do not give their clients skilled, well-prepared and well thought out representation. This is the opinion of many trial judges who regularly see the trial bar in action.

What are the skills, judgment, wisdom and ethics of the much larger proportion of the bar who are not trial lawyers? This is almost impossible to ascertain. When counsel advises clients not to litigate and they follow his advice, no one can know whether it was based on sound judgment and an adequate knowledge of the law. Some people with justifiable claims have not pursued them because they were incorrectly advised by counsel that they had no legal rights. The mistakes of nontrial lawyers are often revealed in will contests which could have been avoided had the lawyers who drafted the will done so skillfully and with proper understanding of the law. The deceased client and the intended beneficiaries of his estate can do nothing to rectify the mistakes of counsel. At this writing, malpractice suits against lawyers are still a rarity. Understandably one lawyer does not wish to file charges against another member of the bar, just as doctors are most reluctant to testify against other doctors. In fact, no one knows the level of competence or ethics of the bar.

It is extremely unusual when a wealthy client makes a complaint to a bar association or the courts with respect to the incompetence or unethical conduct of his counsel. Such clients, who pay fees at the rate of $100 per hour or more, have little difficulty in finding other counsel if they are dissatisfied with their first lawyer. Usually these clients are worldly and sophisticated people who cannot be duped, cheated or otherwise taken advantage of by counsel. Wealthy clients are also aware of their needs and the obstacles which they face in court and out of court. For such clients, a lawyer can be simply a draftsman doing the tedious work necessary to carry out the great plan of the architect-client. More often the lawyer assumes a much larger role. He advises on legal matters and other problems. Often he slips almost imperceptibly into a managerial role, a member of the board of directors, the executive committee and ultimately becomes an investor or owner with a stake in the success of the enterprise. Such lawyer-client relationships on occasion end in an unhappy rupture. More often, the identity of interests creates close and permanent ties between lawyer and client, a relationship of mutuality, equality, and even friendship.

The indigent client has an entirely different relationship with his lawyer. They are strangers who have one brief, perfunctory contact, part, and return to their separate worlds. Often the client does not know the name of the lawyer provided for him by a poverty agency, public defender or the courts. Certainly the lawyer seldom knows his client. I cannot forget the case of Richard Watkins, who was accused of armed robbery. He was brought from the prison in handcuffs and taken to a detention cell like all other defendants in custody awaiting trial. As each case is called, a deputy sheriff goes to the cell block, calls out the name of the defendant and escorts him into the courtroom, where he has a brief whispered colloquy with his lawyer. In the case of Richard Watkins, the defender moved to suppress the evidence on the grounds that it was illegally obtained. Two policemen testified that they had a body warrant for Richard Watkins, that they went to his home, served it on him and in plain sight in the living room saw some of the goods allegedly stolen in the robbery. Watkins then took the stand. According to the defender's file, Watkins claimed that he had come to the door and surrendered, that the stolen goods were in a back room in a closet, and that the police had illegally searched the premises.

Watkins was called to the stand and asked by *his* lawyer where he was when he was arrested. He replied: "In a bar."

His attorney then asked, "Did the police officers take you back to your apartment?"

"No," said Watkins. "They put the cuffs on me and took me down to the precinct."

Many defendants are disoriented, drug addicts or emotionally disturbed. Was this one? Since his counsel sat in silent amazement, I questioned the defendant.

"Mr. Watkins, do you know where you are?"

"Sure. In court."

"Sir, do you know that you are accused of an armed robbery that allegedly occurred on the fifth of May at the corner of . . . ?"

"No, I ain't. I'm accused of arson," he said.

We had spent forty minutes taking testimony in the case of the wrong Richard Watkins. His attorney had never seen him before.

Obviously he had not discussed the case with him. This Richard Watkins was returned to the cell block and fifteen minutes later another Richard Watkins was brought to the courtroom.

A trial judge sees many instances of incompetent, inadequate representation of poor clients. Robert M., charged with possession of narcotics, was a typical "flying bag" case. The arresting officers testified that as they slowly patrolled a street in a high-crime area in a police car, they saw Robert and a companion standing on the corner. As the police car came to the corner they observed Robert drop something on the ground. The policemen stopped the car. One seized Robert, who made no effort to flee. The other retrieved a crumpled Kool cigarette pack on the ground about three feet from Robert. Inside were four bags of heroin. This was the entire case.

Counsel did not put Robert on the stand. Probably he had a long prior record. Counsel did not present any evidence on behalf of his client. In cross-examining the arresting officers, defense counsel failed to question them about the condition of the street, the presence of other debris, the fact that known drug addicts frequented the area. Defense counsel could have called as a witness anyone from the neighborhood to testify that the streets are always littered with debris. He could have had the spot photographed. He could have called the streets department for a report as to the day and hour of the week in question that the streets were cleaned. He could also have asked the policemen the street value of four bags of heroin, which was about a total of $20. He did none of these things. Robert M. was found guilty by a jury, really convicted by the incompetence of his lawyer. The jurors thought that four bags of heroin were worth a thousand dollars, that Robert was a dangerous pusher instead of a poor junkie. They were never given information which would raise a doubt in their minds as to whether the crumpled cigarette pack had in fact been dropped by Robert or whether it had been lying on the sidewalk before the police appeared.

Thousands of postconviction hearing applications are filed each year by people like Robert, alleging that they have not had adequate representation. Rarely does such a prisoner succeed in proving through another strange lawyer appointed for him by a judge who has never seen him before that he has not had adequate representation even though the courts are well aware of the type of legal services that indigent clients receive.

Federal Judge Edward R. Becker, in a public speech, stated, "A client is better served by a private practitioner than by an employee of a corporation such as the public defender or community legal services." [4] A study by the Center for Studies in Criminal Justice, The Law School, The University of Chicago, of the administration of justice during the April 1968 Chicago disorders, reveals many disquieting aspects of the justice system. With respect to legal representation, the study reports: "The Public Defender assumed the representation of almost all of the defendants at bail hearings—even the nonindigent—and also represented the great majority of defendants at later stages of the criminal proceedings, particularly those with less serious charges. But the mere presence of the Public Defender by no means assumed effective representation for defendants. On the contrary, at many bail hearings the Public Defender was not responsive to the defendant's interest." [5]

An obvious way of making the lawyer responsive to the client is to permit the client to choose his own lawyer. If the indigent client, like the affluent client, had the right to hire and fire his lawyer, no matter from what source that lawyer received his fee, the lawyer would be responsive to the wishes and needs of the client.

The National Council on Criminal Justice in 1973 made many recommendations for improving legal services for the poor, but it did not suggest that the poor litigant have a right to select his own counsel. When questioned about this singular omission, members of the staff replied that such an idea had not occurred to the Council or staff.

Legal representation for poor people, despite Lyndon Johnson's war on poverty and the enthusiasm and dedication of many lawyers, still follows the pattern established in the 1920s. In 1919, Reginald Heber Smith published his seminal and shocking book

Justice and the Poor,[6] in which he challenged the organized bar to provide counsel for the nation's poor. At that time there were fewer legal problems besetting all Americans. Poor people were then, as now, disproportionately accused of crime. But there was no legal requirement that they be represented by counsel.

Legal services were provided, in the custom of the times, as a charity for the deserving poor, much like Christmas baskets distributed by well-meaning, comfortable members of the middle class.

The legal profession could have assumed the burden of representing the indigent on an individual basis. But it was cheaper and easier to establish separate law offices for the poor under the guidance and control of boards of directors self-selected from among the wealthy. For sixty years, legal-aid and defender offices operated on such a charity basis. In some communities public defenders were provided for those accused of serious crimes. At no time did the indigent client have the right to choose his lawyer or even to refuse the services of the lawyer provided for him. Nor does he now in most jurisdictions.

There are no overall studies of the adequacy of legal representation for the poor. Those who observe the courts know that all too frequently the lawyer for the poor is inexperienced and tries to compensate for lack of skill by self-righteousness. The serious and conscientious lawyer employed by such agencies is seldom given adequate training and guidance. Indeed, the functioning of most law offices for the poor prevents adequate representation even when able counsel is available. Many of these offices function on an assembly-line principle. One lawyer interviews all the prisoners in jail at stated intervals. If a prisoner arrives just after the interview, he waits without remedy until time for the next interview. Another person prepares the file. A third individual argues the pretrial motions. And a fourth lawyer, whom the client has never seen before, actually tries the cases or, in most instances, pleads the client guilty. In Boston, as in many communities, the defender uses untrained college students to interview prisoners. The interviewer is given a questionnaire to follow. Paragraph

Two, "Arrest," lists twelve questions, but it does not include the crucial "Was he arrested with a warrant?" On such inadequate data the defendant's case is prepared and tried.

The case of James Lightbourne, who refused to plead guilty at the behest of his court-appointed counsel and spent more than two years in prison in New York City Tombs, awaiting trial, unfortunately is not unusual.[7] One day after I had accidentally learned that an indigent man had been in jail over six weeks on a twenty-four-hour detainer, without having been seen by a lawyer, I requested the defender to file a petition for an immediate hearing. "Your Honor," the abashed young lawyer replied, "motions are filed by another branch of the office." Some three thousand lawyers work for such bureaucracies, and represent more than 50 percent of all adults accused of crime, 90 percent of all juveniles accused of delinquency and perhaps 20 percent of small civil claims and domestic problems. Surely such representation of the majority of defendants is a major cause of disenchantment with the law and cynicism toward a system which promises equal justice under law and provides neither equal treatment nor justice.

The middle-income client is the forgotten man in the legal system. Counsel fees and costs for such a person who is sued in a civil action or criminally prosecuted can be catastrophic. The minimum fees allowed to court-appointed counsel for an indigent client accused of a felony are seldom less than $1,000. In addition, investigative expenses of $200 are allowed in routine cases. Homicide cases, political cases, and cases involving serious Constitutional questions require much more time and consequently much greater expenses. Defense of civil claims is equally costly. The winning party in a civil action may recover costs and counsel fees. More often he does not. A person accused of crime who is acquitted has in most instances no legal means to recoup the costs of his defense. He may under restricted circumstances sue for malicious prosecution. But this is again an expensive proceeding which has little likelihood of success.

Prosecution of some civil claims can be undertaken on a contingent fee basis. Counsel is paid a percentage of the recovery. If the case is unsuccessful, he is not paid. Most accident claims are prosecuted under contingent fee agreements. Insurance companies and law offices which represent them oppose the contingent fee. Negligence lawyers are frequently subject to censure for ambulance chasing, questionable arrangements with doctors, and other aspects of this type of practice. For some attorneys it is extremely lucrative. For many it is not. A lawyer may spend several weeks of preparation, three or four weeks of trial, defend post-trial motions and an appeal, write a brief, argue in the appellate court, and ultimately lose. His investment of two or three months' work is gone irrevocably. Often a client cannot afford to wait and will settle for a small sum. Some lawyers will finance a client who has a substantial claim for several years. This practice is of extremely dubious propriety. But it is safe to say that without the contingent fee few middle-income people could afford to use the courts to recover for the multitude of injuries and harms done to them in our highly mechanized society.

Several bar associations advocate insurance for legal fees. Large businesses, wealthy individuals, doctors, lawyers and other persons who in their daily activities risk the likelihood of being sued now carry extremely costly insurance. Most middle-income people are employees. They do not anticipate that they will need legal counsel. They hope that they will not be accused of crimes or sued for breach of contract, assault and battery or other unusual occurrences. They, of course, carry insurance for automobile accidents, accidents occurring in their homes or business premises. These are foreseeable dangers which prudent people guard against. But the cost of legal insurance, for example, to recover the value of a coat lost or damaged by a dry cleaners, or the costs of recovering for defective merchandise over a period of years might far exceed the benefits received. The average citizen is well advised to forgo his legal rights rather than incur the expense of asserting them. Few people who receive traffic tickets, even though they believe the charge is not justified, will defend themselves. The time and trouble exceed the cost of the fine. Certainly, counsel fees would be more than the fine. For all of these people with meritorious defenses and good small claims, the judicial system is a cruel hoax with its promise of equal justice under law. For them there is no practical legal remedy.

Neither the courts nor the organized bar have honestly faced the problem of providing equal and adequate legal services for the indigent and for persons of moderate income who cannot afford the crushing costs of litigation. With the decrease in federal funding for legal services for the poor, the legal profession and the public will have to make difficult decisions with respect to financing the costs of legal representation for indigent people accused of crime in those situations in which they have a Constitutional right to counsel. Financing of legal services for poor people in the many circumstances in which they need a lawyer but do not have a Constitutional right to free counsel cannot be ignored. Sooner or later the courts will declare that such services must be provided at public expense. It is obvious, for example, that children who may be removed from their homes because of emotional or other problems need a lawyer just as much as children accused of delinquency. Adults alleged to be mentally ill, emotionally disturbed, or incompetent also need a lawyer, for they may be institutionalized permanently in a legal proceeding with fewer Constitutional and procedural safeguards than the adult accused of crime. There are many civil actions which have serious consequences—mortgage foreclosure, eviction, repossession of goods purchased on the installment plan, denial of public assistance, medicaid, pensions, social security and other benefits. The poor, the semiliterate, the unsophisticated all need a lawyer in such circumstances. Where will they obtain competent counsel? Who will pay the costs of such representation?

There are no easy answers to these questions. Each question in turn raises more questions. How can society provide competent lawyers, responsible and responsive to their clients regardless of the financial status of the client? *The "rule of law" under our system actually protects only those who have competent counsel.* It is an indisputable fact that private individuals cannot secure justice without the aid of a special professional order to represent and to advise them. This is true of all people in our complex overregulated society. It is especially true for the poor, who are less sophisticated and less well educated than the non-poor.

It is evident that graduation from an accredited law school and admission to the bar, despite the time and expense involved, do not equip the fledgling lawyer with the skills necessary to provide adequate representation for a client. Howard James' book *Crisis in the Courts* was based on his observation of trial courts throughout the nation. He described the lawyers he saw as learning on a "do-it-yourself" basis at the expense of their clients. This is true of defense lawyers for the poor as well as prosecutors, who presumably represent the public. Many a guilty person goes free because of the ineptitude of the prosecuting attorney. Often the prosecutor, like the defender, has never spoken to the witnesses before he sees them in the courtroom. Sometimes he does not know how to ask a question. Often neither prosecutor nor defender knows the community well enough to make an intelligent selection of the jury. They do not know how to cross-examine a hostile witness. All too often, neither the prosecutor nor the defender takes notes during the trial and cannot on cross-examination or re-direct examination bring out the inconsistencies, weaknesses, ambiguities and outright lies implicit in the testimony of the witnesses. If the guilty person is convicted and the innocent acquitted, it will be a matter of chance or luck rather than an intelligent decision based on the facts and the law.

Lawyers and judges have known for the better part of this century that the law schools are not training students to practice law. As Professors Herbert Packer and Thomas Ehrlich admit, "the law school graduate generally is not competent to do *anything* very well." [8] A distinguished practicing lawyer in Michigan wrote me as follows:

My personal experience has demonstrated the truth of your criticism of legal education. I scarcely knew where the courthouse was located, and had little idea of what to do when I found it. My law school experience (in a first-rate law school) in drafting pleadings consisted of drafting one negligence declaration and my court experience consisted of a half day listening to uncontested divorce cases and lunch with the presiding judge.

A more recent graduate of an excellent law school describes his own ineptitude and lack of training in a scathing attack on the law. This is a sorry situation for the neophyte lawyer and an even worse one for his client. Law students are in revolt. They have demanded practical courses. They have insisted on going out into the courts and seeing for themselves what is happening. Reluctantly, the law schools have acceded to these demands by adding a few "clinical" courses. But the goals and teaching methods of the law schools have not changed. In order to understand the strange schism between legal education and the practice of law, it is necessary briefly to look at the history of the law school movement, a development unique to twentieth century United States.

For centuries the lawyer learned the tools of his trade through the time-honored apprenticeship system. He "read law" in the office of an older lawyer. This custom still prevails in England. The monopolization of law training and legal education by law schools had its inception in a 1920 Resolution of the American Bar Association. The transfer of legal professional training to academia followed the trend toward formal and extended schooling in all fields of activity. Today journalists, musicians, poets and artists as well as doctors and lawyers are trained in universities.

The gap between town and gown, between practicing lawyers and professors, has been steadily widening. In the 1920s, '30s, and even '40s, many professors at the leading law schools were or had been distinguished practicing lawyers and judges. Today the standards for accreditation of the Association of American Law Schools restrict the number of part-time practicing lawyers on the faculty. Many of today's law professors have never actually practiced law. At most they have spent a year or two as law clerks to appellate judges. Since these professors have tenure, teach generally a maximum of nine hours a week, and consult on the side, they have little incentive to change the system or to adopt a curriculum which many of them would be incompetent to teach.

The practicing bar is aware of the need for change. Robert W. Meserve, former president of the American Bar Association, stated the obvious: "We are faced with the challenge of modifying and modernizing our process of legal education so that legal study becomes more relevant to current legal practice." It is interesting to observe very similar comments thirty years ago when Professor Jerome Hall noted "serious defects in legal education." [9] The Council on Legal Education of Professional Responsibility, Inc., financed by the Ford Foundation, partly in response to the demands of action-oriented students and students who are increasingly aware of the deficiencies of their education, has recently recommended "clinical" programs to take up the malaise of the second and third years of law school, which all too many students find boring and unproductive. Harvard Law School, aware of the government's requirement for affirmative action in hiring women on the faculty and the students' insistence on practical courses, accomplished both ends, without interfering with the existing faculty and curriculum, by hiring a young woman lawyer barely two years out of law school, to teach a "clinical" course.[10] One can only speculate on her qualifications.

The Carnegie Committee recommended cutting law school to two years. That proposal has the virtue of reducing the boredom by half and the cost by one-third. However, the questions as to what lawyers should learn in law school, how they should be taught, who shall teach, and how long such training should take, have been sloughed aside.

Justice E. Harris Drew of the Supreme Court of Florida wrote in 1961: "I am sure the time will come when we will give more attention to preparing the law student for the tasks that he will actually face in the practice of law rather than dealing almost wholly with theory and philosophy as is the case at the present time. Moreover, I feel that the end product would be infinitely better by a four- or five-year course in the law schools." [11]

A leading Philadelphia lawyer, who graduated from the University of Pennsylvania Law School in 1909, wrote to me a few years ago stating, "Most of [the law schools] do not want practicing lawyers on the faculty. When I was in the Law School, [Senator] George Wharton Pepper, Owen J. Roberts [later Justice of the United States Supreme Court and a distinguished practicing lawyer] and Reynolds D. Brown, were on the faculty and we never cut *their* classes."

The gap between schooling and practice has to a minor extent been filled by the large law offices which spend several years training their young associates. The alumni of the leading law schools who are members of large firms have dominated the schools, which consciously or unconsciously have designed their curricula to fit the needs of such law firms and have imbued their students with the belief that an association with such a firm is the highest goal of the most able students. Unfortunately, it has left the less academically talented graduates and those who have entered practice for themselves, joined smaller firms, or accepted employment with the new poverty and public interest firms totally without necessary training in legal skills.

Time after time a trial judge must sustain objections to questions ineptly and improperly put by such inexperienced lawyers. A poverty lawyer whom I gently reminded not to ask his witness leading questions, responded: "But, Your Honor, if I don't ask leading questions, how can I get the answer I want?" The court must, on occasion, in order to prevent disaster, interpose its own objections to questions asked by opposition counsel who often represents the state or the establishment. Ralph Nader himself has bitterly denounced his alma mater, the Harvard Law School, for training students primarily to practice in the large Wall Street firms and their equivalents in other communities.

The increased numbers of women, blacks and poor people accepted as law students have not materially changed the goals, structure or pedagogical methods of the law schools. Most of them still follow the "case method" of teaching law instituted by Dean Christopher Columbus Langdell. He believed that law was a science, to be learned by analyzing data and deducing general principles therefrom. The data were the written opinions of the appellate courts. Thurman Arnold forthrightly concluded, "No more time-wasting system of studying law has ever been devised." [12] Scarcely a lawyer practicing in the United States today was not taught by some variant of this method.

The case method was badly misnamed. No student ever examined a case from its inception to its conclusion. A case begins with an act which, it is claimed, deprives someone of a right or damages him or violates a law. The client visits the lawyer who takes this raw information, investigates and verifies it, and then casts it into the mold of a recognized cause of action by filing a paper—a pleading, summons, statement of claim or other formal document—with the court. The opposing party consults counsel, who files another paper—answer, preliminary objections, an appearance de bene esse or some other pleading—denying the charges, interposing a defense or resisting the jurisdiction of the court. Papers and cross papers accumulate. Additional information is obtained through other formal papers such as interrogatories and depositions. Later motions to dismiss, to grant judgment on the pleadings, or other means to avoid the ordeal of trial are filed, argued and decided. From a year to ten years or more after the event allegedly occurred, the case may actually come to trial. It is decided by a judge alone or judge and jury. If it is appealed, an opinion will be written by the trial court but seldom reported. If the decision is appealed, an appellate court will hear argument, read the briefs of counsel, and then write an opinion.

It is this appellate court opinion that forms the basic datum of the case method. Many lawyers have spent three years in law school without ever seeing any of the papers preceding the opinion of an appellate court. Nor have they much understanding of the lengthy and elaborate post-trial procedures that may postpone actual payment of a judgment or verdict until years after the trial.

Later jurisprudentialists like Parker and Ehrlich, abandoning Langdell's theory, declare: "Law . . . is not a science but an art, a craft." This change in philosophy has not been translated into pedagogy. Law students still spend the major part of their time in medieval disputation over the language and theories embodied in appellate opinions, ignoring most of the legal actions preceding the appeal. Conservatively, I estimate that less than 10 percent of the time of less than 10 percent of lawyers is spent in writing appellate briefs and arguing appeals. But the appellate opinion constitutes the primary teaching tool of most law schools.

When I taught law, I used to tell my abashed students that law is a trade. I maintained that a lawyer, like a plumber, must know the techniques and skills of his calling. It does little good for a plumber to be able to discuss learnedly the theories of recycling water if he cannot stop a leaking faucet. Similarly, a lawyer must know how to get a client released from jail, how to stop a sheriff's sale of the client's furniture, how to protect a corporation from raids by insiders, and a multitude of other essential techniques. A lawyer should also have a background of information which includes economic, social and political history, accounting, corporate finance, Constitutional theory, jurisprudence, philosophy, ethics, anthropology, sociology and psychiatry. A lawyer should be trained in the precise use of language. He should have a sensitivity to the subtle nuances of words to catch and to convey shades of meaning. For words are a lawyer's principal tool. Many students can spend three years in law school without ever writing any paper except an examination.

The members of the bar, the faculties of the law schools, and the state boards of law examiners must decide what core of common knowledge is required of all lawyers as members of a learned profession and what practical skills are essential for those who will be licensed to practice law, so that a license is a certification that the lawyer can adequately represent his clients.

Today every adult in the United States is entitled as a Constitutional right to have "the guiding hand of counsel beside him" every step of the way in any proceeding in which he may be subject to a penalty of six months or more in jail. If he cannot afford to retain counsel, the state must provide a lawyer for him at the expense of the taxpayers. Obviously the need for lawyers to prosecute and defend the 6 million people arrested each year is great and pressing. But few law school graduates are competent to perform these services without much more training. As we have seen, there are many situations in which one can be more severely disadvantaged by civil actions and civil commitments. The need for lawyers to represent poor and moderate-income people in these matters is also pressing. But few law school graduates know how to perform these services.

Some tentative discussions have been held on the education and training of lawyers who will represent poor and low-income people. There is some recognition of the problem of compensating these lawyers. But the method by which such clients will retain their lawyers has not been explored adequately.

Nor has the most important question even been formulated, that is, how the legal system can be drastically simplified to reduce the need for legal representation without diminishing or infringing upon the rights of the individual—rich, moderate income and poor. Simplification of the legal process is not a new idea but it runs against the grain of Anglo-American legal history which has been one of increasing formalism and complexity. In sixteenth-century England the disjunction between law and justice was so extreme as to require the creation of a new separate series of courts where people could turn for relief from the harshness of legal doctrine. Significantly, it was easier to establish new courts than to modify the rigidities of the existing laws and courts. Therefore, the courts of chancery were created. For centuries, both in England and the United States, these two judicial fora existed side by side. In the late nineteenth and early twentieth centuries in the United States law and equity (chancery) were merged and law judges given the powers of chancellors and courts of equity.

In time the rules and procedures of equity became rigid and inequitable. Reforms such as code pleading and pretrial discovery were introduced in an effort to modernize and simplify the law.

Pretrial discovery has not appreciably saved time or made the system fairer. It has provided additional steps and barriers to speedy trial and a final disposition of a dispute.

Administrative law was also supposed to provide a cheap, simple forum for resolution of certain classes of conflicts without the need for professional legal counsel.

Each of these improvements or innovations was based on the existing legal structure and soon developed its rigidities, its delays and, of course, the need for lawyers. We have not succeeded in simplifying legal process because the problem has been entrusted primarily to lawyers. They have, on the whole, great difficulty in envisioning a structure different from what they have learned, or a procedure in which lawyers are not needed. Most lawyers are convinced that their services are essential to provide just and orderly procedures. Under our present complex system this is true, especially for the ignorant and unsophisticated. But must it necessarily be so? We have not really attempted an alternative.

Professor Victor HiLi of Columbia Law School states that China does not have a modern complex legal system because government is based on the faith that the masses can perceive what is good. He points out that "the 'rule of law' gives only partial protection to the individual and society." [13] Such protection in the United States is, as we have seen, available only to those who can obtain competent counsel.

Faith in the goodness of the masses can be as delusory and misplaced as faith in the wisdom and integrity of the holders of high office. The greatest protection against abuse of power by the powerful and mistreatment of the powerless lies in a system which limits power and which guarantees rights. Neither the Constitutional checks and balances nor the right to counsel have prevented widespread abuses and injustices. These failures of the legal system are in great part due to the excessive complication of procedures which prevent the poor, ignorant and powerless from successfully asserting their legal rights. These same complexities also permit the clever and powerful to use the law to obscure their misconduct and to obtain unfair advantages.

Lawyers have been too preoccupied with their daily tasks to consider their role in society. Law schools have been too busy accommodating the hosts of applicants to consider the content of the curriculum and the qualifications of their graduates to perform the services which they will be called upon to do. Few members of the profession have undertaken the painful and difficult task of examining the moral responsibilities of the lawyer to client and public or the justice and efficiency of the adversary system in a society in which persons of every age, class, economic and mental condition may be required to utilize the processes of the law. All of these deficiencies have influenced the clients and potential clients who are scofflaws. Sadly, one must conclude that lawyers, like policemen, are in part responsible for the death of the law and the attrition of the legal system to which they have devoted their lives.

Surrounded by her soldiers, she took
her seat on the high throne under the temple
porch, and there she laid down judgments and
laws for man, invoking abstract justice or
throwing dice in knotty cases.

The Tragedy of Dido and Aeneas

The law is the true embodiment
of everything that's excellent.
It has no kind of fault or flaw
And I, milords, embody the law.

W. S. Gilbert,
"Chancellor's Song," *Iolanthe*

10: The Dying Priesthood

Judges, even more than lawyers and policemen, represent the law in the minds of the American public. Judges embody the law, with all its virtues and its many shortcomings. The public looks to the courts for the resolution of disputes, a statement of the law, and finally for a declaration of the validity of the statutes enacted by the legislature and the actions taken by the executive. Judges in almost all societies are required to decide disputes and to interpret the meaning of laws, but it is only in the United States that a judge has the authority to countermand the enactments of the legislature and the orders of the head of state.

Since John Marshall's seminal decision in *Marbury* vs. *Madison* in 1803,[1] the development of the jurisdiction of the courts to declare laws and executive actions unconstitutional has been traced by many scholars. There are those who consider it a usurpation of powers never envisioned by the Founding Fathers. Others see this function as the great bulwark guarding the individual against encroachment by a popular majority, expressed by the legislature, by a power-seeking executive, and by local customs and prejudices. They see the power of the courts to declare statutes and executive orders unconstitutional as the final protection of the basic rights of the individual and the preservation of our form of government.

There have been few serious challenges to this jurisdiction of the courts in the past century. Although many judicial decisions have been criticized and disobeyed, the function of the courts and the judiciary has been accepted without question as an integral component of the American system. Both the public at large and most government officials have accepted the tacit premise that the answers to all the wide-ranging problems of American life for the past two hundred years and for the unforeseeable future can be found in law, specifically in the Constitution, a document of 316 lines plus 23 short amendments. It is also unthinkingly assumed that the interpretation of this oracular document is rightly entrusted exclusively to the judiciary.

In addition to this power to declare acts of the legislature null and void, American judges also have extraordinary powers over individuals. They can deprive a citizen of his life,[2] liberty and property. Judges can remove children from their parents, compel husbands to support their wives and jail them if they fail to do so. Judges can commit people to mental institutions and prisons and impose fines on them. Many problems such as family disputes, drunkenness, drug addiction and vagrancy which in other countries are handled by the family or church and ignored by government are in the United States entrusted to the judiciary. The role of the judge in the United States is, therefore, of greater significance than in other nations. The failings of the judiciary are also more dangerous to the stability of society and the belief in law.

American belief in the power of law bears a strong similarity to religious faith. In many ways law in secular America has fulfilled the function of a state religion. It has provided a unifying belief in a heterogeneous society. It has also furnished a national ritual through the celebration of such holidays as Flag Day, Law Day, Fourth of July, and Thanksgiving Day. In addition, law provides national rites: the pledge of allegiance to the flag and the oath to preserve and defend the government and its sacred scripture, the Constitution. In this faith, judges constitute a priesthood. They are set apart, like the clergy, by special robes of office. They are addressed by special titles. They have the outward trappings of a special class. If the law has become an obsolete faith, then the judiciary must be viewed as a dying priesthood.

The death of the law in the United States and the decline of the judiciary as a respected if not venerated calling have occurred almost simultaneously. The causes of these phenomena are many and interacting. There is no single act that one can isolate as the deadly germ and then seek an antidote. The singular powers of the judiciary, the exercise of these powers, the training and character of judges, and the public attitude toward judges will be discussed in this chapter.

At the outset it must be recognized that although American courts have this broad jurisdiction, they have no power to enforce their orders on an unwilling public. Like religious functionaries, judges must rely upon the faith of the citizenry. Judges cannot command the police or the military. They must have the cooperation of the executive and the consent of the public. They must rely on the legislature to respect their edicts and not undermine them by enacting contrary laws.

From the inception of this nation, the singular weakness of the judiciary under the Constitution was noted. Alexander Hamilton observed that ". . . the judiciary, from the nature of its functions, will always be the least dangerous to the political rights of the Constitution; because it will be least in a capacity to annoy or injure them. The executive not only dispenses the honors but holds the sword of the community. The legislature not only commands the purse but prescribes the rules by which the rights and duties of every citizen are to be regulated. The judiciary, on the contrary, has no influence over either the sword or the purse; no direction either of the strength or of the wealth of the society, and can take no active resolution whatever. It may truly be said to have neither *Force* nor *Will* but merely judgment; and must ultimately depend upon the aid of the executive arm even for the efficacy of its judgments." The weakness of the judiciary was feared by John Jay, the first Chief Justice of the United States Supreme Court, who resigned from office convinced that the Court could not attain its proper role.

Judges must indeed depend upon the President, the governors, the police and the military to obey their decisions and also to compel 200 million citizens to observe court orders, if necessary by force of arms. The militia is the last line of defense. It is used only in extreme cases of overt defiance, such as the refusal by Governor Faubus to obey a court order compelling integration of the public schools. The countless routine, daily decisions of thousands of courts cannot be enforced by military might; it is a practical impossibility. Moreover, the use of arms against the citizens of a democracy is psychically scarring and dangerous. For if such force fails, the entire legal system fails. The courts, in their daily functions, must, in essence, rely on the habit of obedience of the people and their belief in the law itself. Compliance with judicial orders is a celebration of belief in law. This is indeed a mass act of faith in an age of disbelief.

The conflict between President Nixon and the courts has been seen by some as a vindication of the power of the law, with Judge Sirica as an aging David defeating Goliath, the mighty President. Others rightly fear these confrontations between the executive and the judiciary as breaking, perhaps irreparably, the fragile web of self-restraint and faith in law that has harnessed this troika of executive, judiciary and legislative and enabled them to pull together for two centuries.

Is this faith in the rule of law illusory? Especially in recent years, the courts have spoken, but their mandates have been openly flouted. Every time a policeman knowingly makes an illegal arrest, every time a public official acts contrary to the decisions of the courts, every time a lower court refuses to follow the law as enunciated by the appellate courts, that faith is progressively eroded. Warrantless arrests, illegal wiretapping, prosecution of citizens for failing to salute the flag,[3] dragnet searches on the highways when no serious crime has been committed are common occurrences authorized and carried out by public officials in open defiance of clear and unambiguous decisions of the United States Supreme Court. Each such act evidences a disregard for law and contempt for the judiciary.

The public manifests the same attitudes not only in widespread violations of law but in the common disparagement of judges. The widely supported movement to impeach Earl Warren cannot be dismissed as the work of a small group of extremists, or hostility to a particular individual and the views attributed to him. Rather, it is an example of the prevalent notion that judges, in their interpretations of the law, should yield to popular attitudes and political pressures. The judge is viewed in the same light as a ward leader or a local legislator. He is considered a political figure who should express the will and follow the sentiments of his constituents. This may sound like a populist democratic principle, but law, if it is to have stability and if it is to express principles of liberty and justice, cannot yield to transient notions and prejudices. Judicial rulings cannot be determined by a plebiscite.

When Peter Finley Dunne's Mr. Dooley remarked that "the Supreme Court follows the election returns," he was expressing the mordant wit of a great political satirist, not the philosophy of the nation. Like all satirists, Dunne was at heart a purist demanding a higher standard of conduct on the part of the courts. President Roosevelt's court-packing plan was a crude effort to remake the Supreme Court in the mold of his own philosophy. Significantly, our most popular President suffered his most stinging defeat in this futile effort. The public, though chafing under many decisions of the Supreme Court which time has shown to be unwise and unnecessary, believed that the judiciary should be beyond the control of the executive and immune to political pressures.

President Nixon's success in "packing" the court with four justices explicitly chosen for their social and political views is indicative of the great change in popular attitudes toward the institution of courts and the function of the judiciary. Even the Senate, which confirmed the Nixon nominees, tacitly subscribed to the President's openly expressed views that the appropriate test of judicial fitness is one of political and social philosophy.

The defeat of the nominations of Judge Carswell and Judge Haynesworth for appointment to the United States Supreme Court may be interpreted by some as evidence of public and Senatorial respect for the institution of the courts. However, the attack on these nominees was led by the legal profession. It was supported by a wealth of evidence as to the professional short-comings of the particular individuals. Ultimately, the nominations were defeated by a Senate composed largely of lawyers who had a professional pride in maintaining standards of competence.

In the past, other nominations to the Supreme Court provoked outrage, but with few exceptions the nominees were pre-eminent in the law and they were confirmed. Louis D. Brandeis and Hugo Black were bitterly denounced by conservatives and liberals, re-spectively. The institution of the courts and the integrity of the judiciary survived the attacks on them and many other criticisms.

The attitude toward judges today is significantly different. Crit-icisms are not directed primarily against individuals and partic-ular decisions. They evidence contempt for all judges. Congress-man Bob Jones of Alabama publicly declared that the federal judges are a "bunch of ignoramuses." He was not rebuked or refuted by government officials, by the bar associations, or by an outraged public. Some of my colleagues on the bench refer to the United States Supreme Court as "the nine nincompoops."

In the 1930s, the Court was bitterly called "the nine old men." There is a subtle but significant difference in the terminology.

Referring to "nine old men" indicates they are obstructionists, a legacy from another era, but at least they are human beings. In our society old people are treated with impatience, the tacit wish that they move on and permit the younger generation to assume control. The phrase "nine nincompoops" shows an utter lack of respect for the institution of the Court as well as the incumbent judges.

Despite the exceptional and far-reaching powers of the judiciary, judges rank low in public esteem. The relative position of the judiciary on the scale of American respect can, perhaps simplistically, be plotted by comparative salary schedules. In the United States, it is axiomatic that the more important members of the community are compensated more highly. The day laborer, the subsistence farmer, the factory worker, and the domestic servant, like the peasants of earlier times, form the basis of society, and without them there could be no titans of industry and no scientific or cultural centers. But the material rewards are not bestowed on them. For millennia, the priesthood, the king (emperor, tribal chief, or dictator) and the army constituted the triumvirate of power. To their leadership went respect, reverence and wealth.

Today leaders of industry, popular athletes, entertainers and advertising executives are recompensed far in excess of the President of the United States. But if one compares judicial compensation with that of other public employees, the figures are revealing. Consider, for example, the following salaries for public and quasi-public officials:

The administrative judge of the Family Court of New York City is paid $30,000. The Community Superintendent of School District 16 of New York City is paid $35,000. The New York Police Commissioner is paid a salary of $41,000, and the heads of various police units are paid more than $31,000. A professor of history at City University receives a salary of $31,275, and the Commissioner of the Agency for Child Development is paid $35,000. The City Corporation Counsel receives a salary of $41,000; the Chairman of the City Commission on Human Rights $35,000.

Federal District Judges are paid $40,000, as is the Administrative Judge of the New York Supreme Court. But the New York State Superintendent of Banks and the State Conservation Commission members are paid $42,475. In Philadelphia, the district attorney and his first assistant, the Administrative Director of the City Hospital (not a doctor), the Director of Finance, the City Controller, the City Solicitor and the Water Commissioner and a host of other public employees were paid more than judges. Medical personnel employed by government are paid substantially higher salaries than lawyers and judges.

The National Commission on Criminal Justice in 1973 recommended that prosecutors, public defenders and judges all be paid the same salaries. Obviously there is little recognition that a judge has extraordinary powers and responsibilities. The office is considered one of relatively low value and significance.

The judge himself is treated like a cypher, a cog in the slowly grinding machinery of justice. The operation of the courts is confided to what Djilas appropriately calls the new managerial class. These are administrators, equipped with graphs, charts and computers.°

The ubiquitous computer prints out the assignments for the judges. The computer rates the judiciary. In my court, as in many large judicial systems, the computer keeps track of how many cases each judge has "disposed of." The judges are then given batting averages, like ball players. Of course, the computer cannot

---

° The following instructions were sent to judges of the Court of Common Pleas of Philadelphia and other court personnel:

The taxpayer you're talking to is your boss. Smile!
Public service with a smile.
Smile! You're in public service.
Help brighten City Hall. Smile!
Make City Hall a nice place to visit. Smile!
Through these portals walk the most important citizens
    in the world. Smile when you see them.
It doesn't cost the taxpayers a penny to see you smile.
Public service is courteous service.
This is a Court of Common Please.
You are democracy in action. Smile!

tell whether the judge's decision was proper, whether he gave the litigants a fair hearing or used his enormous power to force a settlement on unwilling and dissatisfied parties. Like ball players whose batting averages are low and are traded to other teams, the judge with a low score will be given the less desirable assignments. Such are the problems of judges in big cities.

In small communities and rural areas where there is only one judge (or two or three), an individual judge can wield tyrannical powers. Every case must come before this judge. His moods, his biases and his predilections assume enormous importance. Unless a litigant can obtain an order removing the judge from sitting on his case because of prejudice, or have his case removed to a different district, he is subject to this sole personification of the courts.

Arbitrary exercise of power by judges is neither new nor unusual. Lord Jeffreys of the Bloody Assizes is remembered for the more than three hundred people he ordered executed while he was sitting as a judge in seventeenth-century England. The name of Judge Lynch of Virginia has become part of the American language.

The common-law system of Great Britain and the United States has survived to the present despite the despotism, inhumanity and capriciousness of individual judges. Obviously in any institution where individuals have great power, some people will abuse their trust and some will be incompetent. American judges today on the whole are not more arbitrary, venal, lazy or incompetent than their predecessors in this country and in England. What has changed is the character, intensity and prevalence of the criticism of the courts. Why is the judiciary, which was only a generation ago considered sacrosanct, now subject to scathing criticism, contempt and abuse?

Perhaps the opening of the judiciary, to a limited extent, to blacks, women and persons of lower socioeconomic status and foreign backgrounds has removed the insulation of class and wealth which surrounded the bench for centuries. It may be that judges are simply a visible target for the profound dissatisfaction with the law and the operation of the courts. It is also true that the communications media have made the public more aware of injustices under law. Certainly we are living in an era in which the public is more outspoken in its criticism of all institutions and all office holders, including judges.

Although more Americans are rushing to the courthouse than ever before to assert alleged rights and demand redress for alleged wrongs, it is clear that they have little faith in the law or respect for the judges who administer it.

The public attitude toward the judiciary is one manifestation of the general dissatisfaction with the law. But the shortcomings of the judges themselves are also an important factor. For decades judges have removed themselves from the social and economic problems of the community. Insulated by the robe of office and the strictures against political activity—often surreptitiously ignored °—judges have performed their traditional role of simply deciding the cases brought before them without a real concern for, or understanding of, the matrix of life out of which the litigation has arisen, and often they are heedless of the effects of their decisions on the lives of the people involved.

For example, it is only in the past few years that the judiciary as a whole has recognized an obligation to know something about the institutions to which they commit people. With great fanfare and foundation grants, judges have recently begun to visit prisons, mental hospitals and institutions for children. Often they have

---

° Mr. Justice Fortas is the most conspicuous example of a judge who continued to exercise political power after appointment to the bench. All judges, whether elected or appointed, must have political sponsorship in order to attain the bench. Some of them continue to maintain these ties to the political party or politicians who sponsored them. Some judges perform favors—large or small—in return for this support. Judges also have patronage power. They can appoint special masters and receivers and counsel to represent defendants. They can also exercise influence with respect to the hiring of personnel in the enormous bureaucracy of the courts, probation departments and prisons. Judges handling estates must appoint banks, accountants and guardians to carry out necessary functions. All of these appointments and jobs involve the payment of money and are covetously sought. Little thought has been given to removing these powers from the judiciary and thus eliminating a continuing political power and influence from the judiciary.

been appalled by the conditions they have seen. One can only wonder why they did not investigate these institutions years ago, before they took the awesome step of ordering a man, woman or child to be confined there. The judges of the Family Court of New York City made a much publicized tour of Brooklyn to see what the lives of children who come before them are like. Surely juvenile court judges should know and understand not only the law but also the homes, the streets and the schools from which the children come whose lives they intervene in with enormous and often catastrophic effects.

There is little followup by judges on the persons they have committed to various institutions. One kindly juvenile court judge made it a practice to visit children she placed in foster homes, shelters, and with families for adoption. But very few judges follow her example. I was astounded to learn after I sent a young interne to prison to visit the people I had sentenced that no other judge in my jurisdiction had done this simple thing. I, of course, wanted to know whether the drug addicts were getting the detoxification treatment I had ordered, whether the functional illiterates were being taught to read, and whether the emotionally disturbed were receiving psychiatric care. It seems to me that the judge's responsibility does not end with the imposition of sentence. But the judiciary as a whole has not acknowledged an obligation to understand the conditions of life which bring people before the courts or a duty to those litigants after pronouncing sentence or rendering a verdict.

A probation officer may be the most important individual in a convict's life. The P.O. can charge him with violation of conditions of probation and have him committed to jail. Some probation officers shake down their probationers, demanding substantial sums of money not to report them. Others are genuinely helpful, obtaining employment, housing and education for the probationer and counseling and advising him. The judge who has committed a defendant to the broad and relatively unsupervised care of a probation officer seldom checks up to see what is happening.

When a judge hears from a probation officer or prison official with respect to a defendant, he is often astounded. I received the following letter from prison in response to a query as to the educational progress of a semiliterate convict for whom I had ordered remedial education. I reproduce the letter, including the spelling and grammar:

February 28, 1974

Your Honor:

    This letter is on behalf of Mr. _____ who is a student in my English 100-101 class located at _____ Prison for the Community College of _____.

    Mr. _____ has shown in many ways that he is determined to better himself, his interest in class is outstanding, I beleive that Mr. _____'s interest in learning is very sincere, he has a problem in reading, but trys to the best of his ability, it is my person opinion that Mr. _____ will benefit more from outside schooling rather than incarceration, I thank Your Honor for taking the time to read this breif message, I only hope that in some way this will help Mr. _____, for he is surley trying to help himself.

Thank you again
Sincerely
T.F.H.

At first, I thought the letter was written by the prisoner. But a call to the prison confirmed that the letter had indeed been written by the "college" teacher at the prison. Few judges take the time or trouble to know the probation officers. When a judge finds that one is inadequate, there is little he can do in the face of civil service and a powerful bureaucracy. But does that absolve the judiciary?

Many judges do not comprehend the stark realities of the lives of litigants who appear before them. I have heard more than one judge remark to a woman charging her husband with beating her, "Why don't you leave him?" They do not realize that a woman with six children and no money has no place to go, that if she walks out alone her children will be abused, that if she leaves another woman will move in. Likewise many judges do not understand that small shopkeepers in certain neighborhoods must have a gun handy at all times, that they dare not leave the gun in the store when they go home. It is often simplistically believed that judges who are black or Puerto Rican will be more understanding of minority litigants. This is a fallacy. Most of them are members of the middle class, upwardly striving, who either know nothing of the ghettos or wish to put behind them unpleasant memories.

Many judges, black and white, do not understand street argot. One middle-aged black woman, the victim of a street rape, was testifying before me. She stopped in confusion when trying to describe what had happened to her. "I don't know what you call it," she said. "Well, just tell me what *you* call it," I replied. We had no difficulties after that.

In civil and criminal litigation, the judiciary as a whole has not taken necessary steps to make the courts more accessible to the poor and the middle class by initiating reforms to speed the process and reduce the costs. Judges have complained about the backlog, demanded an increase in the number of judges, raises in salary, and additional supporting court personnel. They have not forcefully addressed the problem of making litigation quicker, cheaper and fairer.

Judges who daily try cases that are more than ten years old should have led reform movements to speed the litigation process. They have not done so. Instead, they have set rules and time limits on criminal prosecutions which are difficult, if not impossible, to meet. In civil cases, they have simply moved whole areas of litigation out of the courts and into other forms of remedy, such as compulsory arbitration of small claims, appointment of masters to hear divorces, will contests and other matters. Judges who have seen poor people languishing in jail for want of bail money took little action until outside agencies, such as the Vera Foundation, established bail projects. The judiciary has still not grasped the nettle of pretrial incarceration, enunciating the accepted doctrine that bail is required only to ensure the appearance of the accused at trial. In fact, some individuals are apparently so violent and dangerous that they should not be released under any circumstances. Nonetheless, they are released on reasonable bail, as mandated by judicial interpretation of the Constitution, and commit other murders and serious felonies while on bail.

Every judge knows that the cost of litigation is astronomical. Expert witnesses insist on fees from $250 to $1,000 or more a day to testify. Record custodians of hospitals, businesses and government agencies are required to appear in court and testify that the documents they bring (which they have never read and often cannot understand) are authentic records kept in the usual course of business. This is an unnecessary expense and waste of time. A letter certifying the document should be sufficient. Policemen who have made an arrest or investigated an accident or done any routine police work are required to appear in person and testify in court. Honest policemen will say frankly that they cannot remember the event at all after two to ten years. In the intervening time they have been involved in hundreds or thousands of similar incidents. They read from their reports. The court rules require the fiction that the officer-witness "refresh his recollection" by reading the document and then testify. It is an enormous waste of the taxpayers' money to have policemen in court day after day when the report could simply be placed in evidence.

On appeal, in most jurisdictions, the parties are required to *print* the record. This costs thousands of dollars. Today other inexpensive forms of duplicating papers are readily available. But few courts have changed the rules.

The judiciary has been content to leave the amendment of procedural rules and changes in substantive laws to academics who have little understanding of the day-to-day routine problems of litigation. Judges have not been a dynamic force for change in the old, unsatisfactory ways which cause so much delay, hardship and disillusion with the promise of equal justice through law.

In addition to the routine cases of crime, accidents, contracts, wills and family difficulties, many questions of unusual scope are brought before judges. Because every intractable problem in American life finds its way to the courts, judges are required to pass upon a mixed bag of questions covering an extraordinary range of issues involving nuclear physics, chemistry, agronomy, ecology, psychology and the entire realm of human knowledge. A judge who cannot change a spark plug in his own car is required to decide whether an underground nuclear explosion will have deleterious effects upon the earth, the seas, the air or the inhabitants of the planet. A judge who may never have had a course in economics cannot refuse to hear a case involving the far-reaching effects of a bank merger.

Judges are called upon to determine what tests policemen should take, what movies the public should see, and what countries a citizen may visit. Judges are also expected to understand and rule upon the far-reaching economic effects of antitrust actions, acquisitions by conglomerates and a host of financial and economic questions. Judges are also expected to understand the ecological consequences of off-shore oil drilling, location of highways, and power plants. These significant problems which may affect the future viability of the planet are entrusted to judges who have little, if any, understanding of the technical problems involved. Nor are they equipped by training or restrained by public accountability in making policy decisions.

As we have seen, there is little in the professional training of a lawyer that prepares him or her to decide these issues. And judges are simply lawyers who have been placed on the bench.

Neither the President nor the members of Congress are equipped by education or experience to act intelligently upon such problems either. However, the chief executive and the United States Congress do have staffs of experts to research problems, to gather data and to advise these officials. A judge is supplied with one or possibly two law clerks,[4] usually recent law school graduates. These young lawyers can and do find legal precedents—previously decided cases in which the facts are closely similar. But such reliance upon the findings of other judges, equally ignorant of nonlegal matters, simply perpetuates judgments which may have been erroneous when rendered and very likely are obsolete in relation to changed scientific, social and political conditions.

Judges, like state legislators, need a great deal more assistance and advice with respect to many problems which come before the courts. Many other matters that are litigated are simply not susceptible of a satisfactory solution by a court. The problems of battling spouses, schools that do not teach, tenements that are unfit for habitation, and nonconforming individuals cannot be resolved by an order of a court—no matter how wise, compassionate, honest and nonpolitical the individual judge may be. The judiciary must recognize that the burdens placed on the courts, both in numbers and in the far-reaching nature of the issues, cannot be resolved under present procedures and practices.

Those who recognize the incapacity of American courts to deal with day-to-day conflicts are prone to blame the judiciary. The New York Citizens Conference on the Courts, a broadly based civic group of high-minded, knowledgeable people, declared that "better judges" [5] are the answer to the problems of the courts. Much time has been devoted to the method of selection of judges. Complicated plans to remove the judiciary from the political process of election or appointment by having judicial candidates screened by panels of leading lawyers and citizens are urged upon the electorate with tedious frequency. It is sobering to recall that Judges Carswell and Haynesworth had been screened and approved as qualified by the prestigious judiciary committee of the American Bar Association. Federal Judges Manton, Kerner, Watson and Johnson, appointed by the President for life and approved by the United States Senate, are but a few of the federal judges who have been found guilty of crimes and either removed from office or permitted to resign. Many elected judges have also been found to be guilty of crimes or grossly incompetent. As the late Judge Jerome Frank observed, if men were angels we would not need law courts and we would not have to worry about judicial selection. Since the population of the United States is not composed of angels but of fallible men and women and refractory children, courts and judges—and their selection—will be a part of our government for the foreseeable future.

The role of the courts and the judiciary, however, is not immutable. Nor are the practices in the United States followed in many other advanced and civilized nations. In England the judiciary is chosen from the small, highly select group of barristers. One must bear in mind that there are only 25,000 lawyers in England. Many fewer cases are litigated in England. Moreover, the judiciary does not exercise the power to declare acts of Parliament or orders of the Prime Minister unconstitutional. In the stratified class society of England, lawyers and judges hold a relatively high position. The opportunities for advanced education, including law, are more sharply limited in England than in the United States. In Italy, judges are more like civil servants. They study for the judiciary, pass examinations and are duly appointed. Italian judges, like their fellows in other civil law countries, have a more limited role than the judiciary in the United States.

Who shall be a judge and how shall he or she be selected? These questions occupy much of the time of the organized bar and interested reform citizens' groups. But they should be examined in the context of the duties of a judge. Solomon in all his wisdom could not decide twenty or thirty cases a day involving domestic problems, police power, contracts, welfare rights and issues of civil liberties. As we have seen, this is what is expected of a trial judge, who must hear evidence, make findings of fact and conclusions of law on such a variety of problems every day. These are routine questions, routinely decided in some 19,000 trial courts in the United States every day.

We should be asking more basic and difficult questions. What are the qualifications—including education, in its broadest sense, experience and human values—needed by a judge? What special training should a judge have *before* assuming the bench? At present, the system is to learn through practice, at the expense of the public. Many excellent courses are provided for judges *after* they are on the bench. Some take advantage of these programs. Others do not.

What means of removal should there be? A judge cannot be removed from office for legal errors, stupidity or incompetence except in the most extraordinary circumstances. The public may rail, the press condemn, but the judge continues in office. Unless a judge is convicted of a crime [6] or becomes mentally deranged, there is no practical way to remove him. Since in our complex society even the wisest person cannot be an authority on all subjects, what assistance in the many areas of science, medicine, economics, public policy and philosophy should a judge have? At a minimum, I believe he should have access to expert opinion when he wants it, regardless of whether the litigants have produced their own expert testimony or whether they are willing to pay for an impartial expert. At present, this is not possible in most jurisdictions.

Gross incompetence and corruption are recognized very quickly. A judge who does not know the law, who rules incorrectly on points of evidence and gives erroneous charges is an expensive menace. His cases must be retried, provided the litigants can afford it. The public, of course, is paying for unnecessary trials. Such ignorance undermines faith in the system. But more than simply avoiding error is required of a judge. Trying every case in accordance with the rules is insufficient. Some cases should not be tried, because a decision either way will be unacceptable to the litigants and the community. It will exacerbate tensions and cause further erosion of respect for law. In these difficult situations, understanding as well as knowledge of the law are needed.

Wise trial judges in civil cases often avoid an explicit ruling, declaring that one party is completely in the right and that the other party must pay the entire losses or damages. Although the law requires such a finding, in fact, few cases present such a clear picture of rights and obligations. As in most human activity, there are usually mitigating circumstances and ambiguities. Jury verdicts often reflect such a compromise. A judicial decision rarely can. If the judge knows that his order will either be disobeyed or appealed in delaying actions which will take years until a final decision is obtained, he will attempt to effect a voluntary compromise, a result that both parties can live with. An understanding court will not enter an order which the judge knows will not be obeyed unless forced by the contumacy or unreasonableness of the parties. Instead he will seek a median position that takes into account the realities of the situation as well as the law.

A judicial decision can inflame hostilities or reconcile opposing parties. All too often, a judge simply follows the rules and tries a case rather than seeking a reconciliation of parties and positions. Many intelligent resolutions of conflicts made by wise judges do not result in the reported opinions that are the grist of the legal-academic mills. For example, in the aftermath of a teen-age race riot in a small town, the police maced a half-dozen black boys. Many citizens were outraged. Suit was brought under the Civil Rights Act for damages against the policemen, the municipality and the mayor and for an injunction to prohibit the police from using mace. A long trial with testimony by the police, the boys and their parents would have inflamed the community. The federal trial judge brought in counsel and the mayor and worked out a consent decree spelling out with particularity the circumstances which would justify the use of mace by the police and retaining jurisdiction so that if the decree was violated the parties could return to him without initiating a new law suit. The black community was satisfied that the police would not run wild in the future. The police and the mayor were satisfied because they had not been stigmatized as guilty of police brutality. More than four years have passed without further incident.

In a case that came before me, a neighborhood group sought to prevent the university from razing a large home which it owned but did not need. The community resented the fact that the university was encroaching on residential areas, erecting huge buildings without considering the wishes of the local people. The university took an adamant position that as owner of real estate it was entitled under the law to tear down or build as it wished so long as zoning was not violated. It refused to acknowledge that the residents had any legal standing. The citizens, angered by this attitude, camped on the property. Women came with their children, babies in carriages and older children, and simply stayed on the premises so that the demolition could not take place. The police stood by to prevent violence. The university came to court seeking an injunction restraining the residents from interfering with the razing of the building. Scores of angry people crowded the courtroom. It was clear that if an injunction was granted they would not obey the order of the court and mothers would inevitably be jailed. The situation would worsen. In conference with counsel and the leaders of the group, I suggested a delay of one week for the two parties to confer and for the residents to devise a plan for utilizing the building and financing it. The residents consulted architects and planners and reluctantly concluded that they could not feasibly adapt the building to their needs. I proposed that after the building was razed and until a new building was erected that the lot be made a neighborhood park, with the citizens planting flowers and doing the gardening. This obvious solution was hailed with relief by both sides. Each considered the result a victory. A full-scale hearing would have lasted three or four days. In the end the decision would have been to grant or to deny the injunction. A trial rarely permits the median position and sensible solution.

Although such extralegal results are quietly obtained by many trial judges, and sharp conflicts blunted or avoided, the judiciary as a whole continues routinely to process cases through the prescribed steps of pretrial, trial, decision, post-trial motions and appeals, without considering other possibilities for resolving conflicts.

The ignorance and limited perspective of some judges and the inability of all judges adequately to decide under present conditions of trial all of the difficult questions presented to them causes public disenchantment with the judiciary. In addition, the public is dismayed by judicial inaction—refusal to decide controversial, pressing and significant questions presented to them.

Courts continue to play their traditional role: namely, to decide one case at a time and to treat each as a disparate problem involving only the litigants before them. In fact, many cases involve issues which affect large numbers of people who have similar problems and who will be bound by the law enunciated in the particular case.

The courts, and especially the United States Supreme Court, fail to come to grips with the vital divisive issues of the day, preferring to decide each case on narrow grounds. Judicial activism has been highly criticized. The courts have indeed moved into areas in which they have little expertise and assumed roles which they cannot adequately fill, but in large measure, as we have seen, they have acted because the legislature has failed to act. Thus, the courts have, for example, entered the thorny fields of reapportionment, desegregation and criminal procedure. They have attempted to provide rules and regulations on the basis of one case. They have assumed responsibility for the operations of railroads, hospitals and schools. Some of these decisions have created more problems than they have solved. But more disquieting than activism is judicial inaction.

Because the critical conflicts in society, under our system, as de Tocqueville observed, become court cases, the courts become the arena for all these hostilities and struggles. The losing party in a contest often yells, "Throw out the umpire." So it is with judges. But at least an umpire or referee decides on the spot whether it is a fair ball or a foul. He cannot refuse to decide or wait for a more propitious time.

Judicial intervention is sought at the friction points between individuals, between enterprises, and between the individual or the enterprise and the government. As healthy people seldom consult physicians, so litigants do not go to court unless a dispute cannot be resolved in any other way. There must be an awareness of the problem, and it must have reached a point of exacerbation that impels those involved to undertake the long and expensive path of litigation. Some injustices may be quietly endured for decades or centuries until the level of awareness and hostility has reached the point when the oppressed demand action. One has only to look at the great movements for freedom—not only of slaves and serfs but the contemporary demands for liberation of blacks, women, the American Indians, and the poor—to realize that litigation in the United States is a barometer of the mood of the people.

The cases heard by the United States Supreme Court measure to some extent both the friction points and the temper of society. It is a distorted reflection for several reasons: First, because only those cases which the litigants can afford to appeal are presented. Second, because the light is passed through the prismatic lens of the discretional review lodged in the court. The United States Supreme Court holds the most awesome powers, but, as we have noted, it is powerless to enforce its decrees. Therefore, the court is in the position of a general on a forced march: If he moves too fast he will lose his troops, yet if he moves too slowly he will be leading from the rear. Thus, the cases acted upon by the Court are those which the Justices themselves perceive to be worthy of their consideration and which for political or other reasons they are willing to hear and rule upon.

Many important and troublesome problems are ignored or side-stepped by the courts. When the courts do not act, problems remain unresolved, generating confusion, discontent and hostility. Similarly situated parties do not know what their rights and obligations are. They must act, but at the peril of subsequently being found to be in violation of law. By examining the United States Supreme Court dockets, one can gain some idea of the problems left unanswered, to fester and exacerbate uncertainty and discontent.

In 1925, the Judiciary Act was passed, removing from the mandatory jurisdiction of the United States Supreme Court many appeals which presented rather routine matters, most of which were affirmed by the Court without an opinion. The cases heard by the Court after the effective date of the Judiciary Act indicate, to some extent, the issues the Court chose to decide. These cases reveal the issues which the justices deemed to be sufficiently important for their consideration and which they were willing to act upon.

The new era began with the 1927 term of Court. In that year, 844 cases came before the United States Supreme Court; 517 cases were disposed of without a decision on the merits. The clear inference is that the Court did not consider the issues in those cases of sufficient importance to merit extended consideration. Of the 327 cases decided, only 8 involved the Bill of Rights or the liberties of the individual citizen. None was concerned with denial of individual rights in criminal matters. Twenty-six cases dealt with court practice, procedure or jurisdiction; 43 with taxation. The balance of the cases were primarily concerned with matters of property rights and government regulation of industry.

In 1927, criminal defendants were routinely tried without lawyers. Confessions were coerced with clubs and other forms of violence. Women died from illegal abortions by the thousands. Poor, troublesome children were quickly ordered into juvenile jails in closed hearings without lawyers, or even knowledge of what they were accused of. Blacks and religious and ethnic minorities were denied employment and educational opportunities. When employed, they, like women, were paid lower wages. None of these problems was addressed by the United States Supreme Court.

Compare 1970. At the outset one must note the extraordinary increase in the business of the Court, almost 400 percent. The population of the United States in 1930 was 123,203,000; in 1970, it was 203,212,000. The amount of litigation in the lower courts also increased disproportionately during this period. In the 1970 term, the United States Supreme Court disposed of 3,318 cases, 341 of which were decided on the merits. However, 200 of them were decided by brief unanimous decisions. In only 141 cases were full opinions written. Freedom of speech and press, voting rights, juvenile rights, equal protection and other individual constitutional rights were involved in 46 cases. Thirty-four cases were concerned with the rights of individuals in criminal matters and habeas corpus.

The issues which the Supreme Court ruled on were not new. Exclusion of Negroes from juries, denial of the right to counsel, coerced guilty pleas, admission of illegally obtained evidence, and statutes prohibiting abortion were all old laws and practices enshrined in custom and sanctified by time. The presence of such questions on the United States Supreme Court docket and the Court's willingness to review the questions indicate the rising dissatisfaction with these conditions and public willingness to accept change.

The Court's refusal to decide issues of great public controversy is at least as important as its decisions. The public demands a judicial decision on every important issue. Significantly, a public opinion poll in 1972 revealed that 72.4 percent of the people questioned believed that the courts should rule on the legality of the war in Vietnam. The Supreme Court has consistently avoided this issue, although the legal questions raised by the many lawsuits challenging the war are substantial. Constitutional rights of individuals in the military service or subject to the draft have been directly jeopardized. The lawfulness of the expenditure of public funds is involved. The power of the executive, the legislature and the judiciary are all at stake in questions arising out of the alleged illegality of military actions. These legal issues are also implicit in litigation involving nuclear explosions, the Canadian pipeline, and many other pressing problems which are brought before the courts and upon which the Supreme Court has refused to decide, while it deals again and again with such insignificant questions as regulation of pornography and the precise warnings to be given arrestees.

Legal journals discuss in minute detail the phraseology of judicial opinions, the shades of difference between the majority and the concurring opinions. Those concerned with the viability of legal institutions might well study whether the courts can by ruling on highly controversial questions risk judicial brinkmanship. If the orders of courts are disobeyed or ignored with impunity, the entire stability of the tripartite system of government is endangered. Or is it more dangerous to refuse to decide these questions and leave them to fester? To decide or not to decide is a more fundamental question than any specific issue which is before the high court. To borrow a popular ecological term, it appears that judges in the United States are an endangered species. As such they must protect themselves and be protected from unnecessary dangers.

In the past a relatively small but significant number of decisions of the Supreme Court have gone against the grain of history, logic and precedent. But faith in law survived even the most unpopular and unwise rulings. For example, nothing in the language of the Supreme Court specifically prohibited the imposition of a graduated-income tax. Nonetheless in 1895,[7] the court declared that such a law was unconstitutional. It was trenchantly pointed out at the time that the Constitution did not embody the economic philosophy of Herbert Spencer. Eighteen years later, the Constitution was amended to permit the enactment of such a tax.[8] Today Pennsylvania does not have a much needed graduated-income tax because the Supreme Court of that Commonwealth has held that such a law violates the State Constitution requiring that taxes be "uniform." [9] Obviously, the conclusions of courts on this question are far from ineluctible. The Dred Scott [10] decision in upholding the right of slave owners to compel the return of runaway slaves from free states was a particularly disastrous decision. No specific language in the Constitution or precedent required such a conclusion. Nonetheless, the courts and the judges survived these decisions relatively unscathed despite the suffering of countless people. As late as 1923, the Supreme Court held that protective legislation for women and children was unconstitutional. Fourteen years later the court reversed itself.[11]

Such reversals of decisions and the many decisions by divided courts are not new. They reflect the sharp divergences of opinion on social and political issues in the nation. It is historically interesting to recall that in the early years of the Supreme Court each Justice wrote his own opinion. The Court was not expected to act monolithically. Today there is a desire for certainty in law, a certainty that has never existed. All of us subconsciously wish for clarity, uniformity and an absolutism in the law that brooks no dissent. A unanimous opinion lends support to the notion that there

is only one proper, legally and morally right answer. A multiplication of opinions by a divided Court forces us to realize that the
quest for certainty and finality on difficult public questions is
illusory.

Judges who acknowledge their own fallibility and the rapid
tempo of change which prevents any judgment from long enduring
and who also recognize the fragility of their power to enforce
unpopular decrees might well question the appropriate ambit of
judicial authority. The United States Supreme Court has in recent
years explicitly expressed its view that the role of the courts is a
limited one. The Court declared: "We do not denigrate the importance of decent, safe, and sanitary housing. But the Constitution
does not provide judicial remedies for every social and economic
ill. We are unable to perceive in that document any constitutional
guarantee of access to dwellings of a particular quality or any
recognition of the right of a tenant to occupy the real property of
his landlord beyond the term of his lease, without the payment of
rent or otherwise contrary to the terms of the relevant agreement.
Absent constitutional mandate, the assurance of adequate housing
and the definition of landlord-tenant relationships are legislative,
not judicial functions." [12]

This is harsh doctrine for many who have rushed to court in an
effort to remake society and to force more equitable and humane
laws through litigation. It runs counter to the burgeoning public-
interest law firms composed of dedicated lawyers who seek to
litigate every problem and to find the answer to all of America's ills
in judicial orders and decrees. The emergence of Ralph Nader as a
folk hero has also contributed to the myth that all wrongs can be
righted in the courts.

Reliance upon the courts and the wisdom of judges almost to the
exclusion of other avenues of redress is evidenced by the multiplicity of lawsuits brought by industry, conversationists, pacifists, and
other idealogues, the rich, the middle class, and agencies for the
poor. It has also been explicitly articulated. The American Foundation for Negro Affairs in a Black American Position Paper (1973)

declared: "The judiciary seems to be the last outpost and hope for justice under the law, especially for minorities." This statement occasioned little comment. No doubting Thomases pointed out the manifest failure of the judiciary to abolish segregated schools, to provide equality of job opportunities or education or to bring the majority of black people within the mainstream of middle-class America. There has been no public repudiation of this faith in the courts despite more than a century of failure to bring black Americans minimal legal rights and social justice through the legal process.

Despite the decisions of the Warren court, the discrepancy between the education of blacks and whites has widened. Those who could flee from the nominally integrated schools of the cities moved to the wholly segregated suburbs. Public lawyers have been hired for the indigent accused, but coerced guilty pleas follow exactly as before. The mentally ill now know that they are entitled to treatment, but the courts have not provided psychiatrists for them or the money to hire doctors and therapists. Courts have ordered that prison conditions be changed, but they remain the same and the prisoners are not released. The Welfare Rights Organizations have sued to obtain a declaration that welfare is an entitlement, not a privilege which government may grant or withhold. But only a few years' experience has shown the futility of such suits. Some thoughtful and perceptive observers have noted that landmark cases have been victories for lawyers, not litigants, that change has been nominal rather than actual. Professor George Hoshino of the University of Pennsylvania states: "In spite of some dramatic successes it is now clear that the judicial process has limited capacity to fundamentally change the illegalities and inequities of public assistance policy and administration." The Center for the Study of Democratic Institutions, in a recent issue of its magazine, comments: "What is remarkable is that the forces of law and order, sophisticated and formidable or even hypertrophized though they may be, are increasingly less capable of coping with these internal-disintegrative movements, just as, externally, they

are impotent in the face of even weak and undeveloped antago-
nists, as in Vietnam." [13]

These are minority voices expressing an unpopular, indeed,
unthinkable thought. Both the liberal humanist view and the
conservative law-and-order position are based on the belief that
law will and must provide answers to our problems. The Humanist
Manifesto II promulgated by a group of leading intellectuals from
all disciplines declares: "Thus we look to the development of a
system of world law and world order based upon transnational
federal government." [14] When the forces of law cannot cope with
the problems of daily life at the local level, it is an extraordinary act
of wishful thinking or blind faith to expect that law can control and
solve global problems.

Law should not be a growth industry. The gross national product
of the legal system in the United States, whether measured in
numbers of cases, courts, judges, supporting personnel or statutes
and treatises, has increased dramatically each year. This efflorescence of laws, litigation and the necessary facilities of police,
lawyers, and courts is matched by the growth of scofflawism.

The tendency of bureaucracies to grow and expand is evident in
the courts. But it can be controlled. Courts do not need to decide
every question. By specifically refusing to enter certain areas, the
courts can place the responsibility for action on the legislature and
the executive, who are better able to deal comprehensively with
many issues and are also better able to carry out their decisions.
Judges should recognize that there are limits both to their authority
and their wisdom. This is a harsh message to a group of public
officials who have been invested with the trappings of power and
the role of seers. S. Dillon Ripley, secretary of the Smithsonian
Institution, addressing the scientific community, warned them to
"avoid the spectacle of elder statesmen of science—latter-day
gurus, former specialists in chemistry or physics—becoming instant
experts on geopolitics or the Earth's doomsday. . . . Scientists can
be people, not always experts. . . ." [15] Similarly, judges have a
narrow specialized training. They are ill-equipped to decide every
sociopolitical, economic and human problem and conflict. They

should and must decide those conflicts for which there is no other available solution and which involve infringement of individual liberty. But they should lead in the search for other methods of resolving conflicts, for rationalizing and simplifying the litigational process, and for appropriate training, qualification and removal of judges. Unless drastic changes are made in the methods of litigation and the jurisdiction of the courts, dissatisfaction with the law in general and the judiciary in particular will continue to increase. Judges will survive, if at all, only as a black-robed priesthood celebrating the rites of a dead faith.

PART III

The results of law, law enforcement and litigation are not the discrete cases, the myriad decisions, or the actions of tens of thousands of policemen, but the nature of the society that is shaped by the legal process in all of its manifestations. This part of the book examines the role and attitudes of Americans under our laws and government. It questions the principles upon which we posit this huge structure and probes the nature and meaning of justice. Finally, the scope of law and the limitations on its role in a free society are explored. These basic questions so often overlooked in legal discussions of specific laws and rules of evidence, in studies by criminologists and in legislative debates are raised because the purpose of law is to provide a just resolution of conflicts and an orderly society. In the United States, under our Constitutional form of government, law must promote not only order but also individual liberty. Unless the entire machinery of the legal system promotes these ends and the results of law in operation are acceptable to the people, neither freedom nor order will survive.

America: Love it or Leave it

Bumper sticker

A. *A violent order is disorder; and*
B. *A great disorder is an order.*

Wallace Stevens, "Connoisseur of Chaos"

11: We Do Not Consent

The most important and critical element in the legal system in the United States is the average citizen. Analogizing the law to the economy, one might say that the legal system is producing a product, loosely known as law and justice, for consumption by the American people. The purpose of law and the entire structure of government—including the police, lawyers, judges, supporting personnel, and ancillary institutions—is to provide a just society and fair treatment for the public. But if the people as consumers of law will not accept the product, we have reached a crisis. It is not simply that the United States is a nation of scofflaws, a people who routinely ignore and violate the law. Scofflawism is a symptom of an underlying, though rarely articulated, consensus. The American people, I find, no longer consent to the exercise of jurisdiction by government officials under the rule of law. Government officials and the leaders of the bar have exhorted, pleaded and, with all the skills of Madison Avenue, have attempted to "sell" the public the virtues of law, order and justice. But the people are simply not "buying" a product they find grossly unsatisfactory.

In previous chapters, the functions and failures of the legislature, the police, the courts (both trial and appellate), the lawyers and the judges have been examined. Many lawyers and social critics acknowledge some, if not all, of these failings which have been described. Both research and reform have been directed to specific defects in the various elements of the legal structure. It is assumed that if these defects in the legal system were corrected —if the courts were more prompt and efficient, if the police were properly trained and adequately equipped with modern technological devices, if the judges were wise, learned and nonpolitical, and if the lawyers provided adequate representation for every American—rich, middle income and poor—then we would have a just and ordered society.

But the critics and reformers in their myriad programs fail to take into account the attitude of the vast majority of the population. Disillusionment with the law undoubtedly was caused in large part by these defects, by the obvious failure of the system to fulfill its promise of equal justice under law for everyone. If by some miracle of law reform and social engineering the legal system could achieve these goals at once, would most Americans be transformed from scofflaws to law-abiding citizens? I seriously doubt it. The root causes of scofflawism are deeper than dismay over the malfunctioning of the legal system. It is possible that after two or three generations of satisfactory experience with the administration of law, the public disregard for law might change. Unfortunately, we do not have a lead time or margin of fifty years. We must deal with the present. This chapter will therefore explore common attitudes of Americans toward the law and the legal system.

Many people profess to see a renewed vitality in the law and an ability of the system to provide just results. Some point to the extraordinary series of jury verdicts acquitting Dr. Spock, Angela Davis, the Harrisburg Seven, the Camden Eight, and the

Gainesville Eight. They extol the courage of Judge Sirica, the tenacity of the Ervin Committee, the integrity of former Special Prosecutor Archibald Cox, and the decisions of the United States Supreme Court. The President and many police officials note with satisfaction that crime statistics for 1972 and 1973 show a slower rate of increase for the first time in many years. There is a flattening of the curve. They note the sharp decline in riots and disorders during the past few years. From these facts, they conclude that the legal system is able to cope with the problem of crime in a democratic society. But crime in the streets, organized crime, political crimes, and general lawlessness persist. There has been no decrease in the number or seriousness of violations of law. The cases relied on to justify the fairness of the legal process are exceptional. They involve matters that have aroused great public interest and the passions of powerful people. They have required extraordinary efforts by highly motivated and unusually able people who have utilized political power and the mass media to compel the legal system to function, though haltingly. They are showcase spectacles of American law which have little to do with the average run-of-the-mill cases. The average litigant has not found speedy or efficient justice. Despite heroic efforts by the Congress to cope with important and pressing issues, the laws affecting most Americans in their daily lives have not been changed or updated. Neither the police nor the legal profession have substantially changed their methods and procedures.

The viability of the American legal system depends not upon how it treats a President, a former attorney general and other powerful people and how they accept its rulings, but upon the attitude and acceptance of more than 200 million Americans. Twenty-five hundred years ago Aristotle wrote: "The law has no power to command obedience except that of habit." Today Americans have abandoned and deliberately rejected the habit of obedience to law. No series of legal actions, regardless of dramatic effect or essential fairness or propriety, can resurrect and revitalize a faith in law which has died through attrition, erosion and disillusionment over a long period of time.

Countless Americans have rejected the idea of law as a meaningful concept for conducting their own lives and affairs. They refuse to accept legal authority. Every day people in the streets turn their backs when a crime is committed. Every day eyewitnesses refuse to appear in court and testify despite subpoenas and orders commanding them to come. Every day average Americans, by refusing to cooperate with their government, evidence their rejection of the entire legal system. They act instinctively or by habit. Few of these average citizens have consciously adopted a philosophical position. Many Americans, however, after painful soul-searching, study and discussion, have knowingly and willfully chosen not to obey certain laws as a matter of principle. Countless young men refused to register for the draft, preferring jail or exile. Others have refused to pay taxes. These people deliberately reject a system in which they have no confidence.

Every trial judge sees countless people who refuse to pay their debts, who refuse to accept court summons, who refuse to testify in court. All of them could be jailed for contempt. Most of them know it. They seldom articulate their beliefs. But their actions clearly show that they have no respect for the legal system. An extraordinary example of refusal to cooperate with the law was presented by a college student—a poor, young black man, who for some unexplained reason failed to pay his bus fare. John B. was arrested, arraigned, stood mute and was jailed. He refused to speak with the public defender or the court psychiatrists. After several months of silence, during which time he had been raped and abused in other ways in prison, a petition was filed seeking John's commitment in an institution for the criminally insane. I had him brought to court where I questioned him. John understood what had happened to him. He knew what was going on in court. He did not explain his unusual behavior. The court psychiatrist, however, stated that John B. "refused to cooperate with the system."

The psychiatrist's solution was to commit him to a mental institution indefinitely, a suggestion uncomfortably reminiscent of recent treatment of dissenters in the Soviet Union. John B. ap-

peared to me to be a nonviolent individual who constituted no
threat to the public peace. He had no criminal record. I asked the
prosecutor to drop all charges, which he was happy to do. John B.
was promptly released. At this writing more than a year later, he
has had no further contact with the law.

Refusal to cooperate with the law and to recognize its validity is
characteristic not only of radicals, students, and "hippies," it is
apparent in the behavior of citizens in all levels of society. The
poor will not permit themselves to be counted in the census.
School children refuse to stand for the pledge of allegiance to the
flag. Parents refuse to come to school on "parents' night." Business
people in more sophisticated ways avoid filling out forms, paying
taxes, and conforming to regulations. Subconsciously they, too,
are rejecting the legal system. As Hannah Arendt points out,
"defiance of established authority, religious and secular, social and
political as a worldwide phenomenon may well be accounted the
outstanding event of the decade." [1] Since law in the United States
is the epitome and expression of authority, Americans express their
defiance of authority by ignoring and refusing to cooperate with
the law.

Many Catholics refuse to accept the infallibility of the pope.
Many Russians openly defy the "approved" political doctrine. It is
easy to dismiss those acts of defiance as expressions of liberty and
freedom of the individual spirit. Or one can simply agree with
Arendt that this behavior is part of the Zeitgeist. But when the
masses of average American citizens reject a legal system based
upon the rights of the individual, freedom of conscience, freedom
of speech and due process of law, such facile explanations are
unsatisfactory.

Defiance of law in the United States has many causes. The
failures of the legal system, already outlined, cannot be discounted
as a significant factor. Essentially the law is perceived to be an
instrument of government in which injustice is not anomalous. Its
injustices cannot be dismissed simply as either human error or
systemic malfunctioning. Injustice, unequal treatment of people,
and failure to provide protection and redress for masses of people

are the evident results of the operation of the system. Therefore, the thoughtful citizen must question his duty to submit to an unjust system. Does one have a duty to obey unjust laws? This is a question being asked by more and more Americans. The number who refuse to submit to the domination of the law has for the first time in American history reached a critical point. I do not suggest that the majority of citizens have consciously resolved not to obey the police and the courts as a matter of intellectual principle, but a sufficient number of people of all ages and many strata of society have taken this position that they have affected or influenced the unarticulated, uncalculated responses of many, many more individuals. Beneath the common scofflawism of everyday life is an inchoate belief that the government per se has no right to command the loyalty and obedience of the entire citizenry. It must establish the fairness and justice of its position *before* the citizen has a duty to obey. Although there is no acknowledged exponent of the theoretical view that the citizen's duty is to obey only just laws and to cooperate only with authorities administering a socially and economically just society, this is a widespread attitude which must be recognized by anyone seeking the root causes of American scofflawism and the death of the law.

Lawyers express this attitude in different language. The late Pennsylvania Supreme Court Justice Thomas D. McBride, when he was a state attorney general, stated that it was his duty to uphold only those laws which were Constitutional. Accordingly, he refused to defend a state wiretapping statute which had been duly enacted by the state legislature. In like fashion, private citizens have refused to obey censorship statutes, State Department restrictions on travel to certain countries, and court orders requiring busing of school children out of their neighborhoods. Whether or not these laws or orders are ultimately sustained as legitimate exercises of governmental power, it is clear that affected citizens determine for themselves that such laws and orders infringe their rights and do not wait for a resolution of the dispute by the courts.

The conflicting claims of the individual conscience as opposed to the state, which demands obedience to an unjust law or an unjust legal system, is not a new issue. Western philosophers have wrestled with the problem for more than 2,500 years. This conflict between the rights of the state and the individual conscience of the citizen presents difficult questions for jurisprudentialists studying every form of government and legal structure. In the United States it poses peculiarly sensitive and critical questions because our law claims to protect these very rights of the individual which, it is asserted with much justification, are routinely and almost inevitably violated by the forces of law.

The framers of the Constitution did not address the problem of concurrently maintaining the viability of the state and protecting the rights of individual conscience, because in the context of the times the conflict did not arise over military or political power. In eighteenth-century England, confrontation between the individual conscience and the power of the state arose on the battleground of religion. The Founding Fathers unequivocally cast their vote in favor of the individual by specifically withdrawing from the government jurisdiction over religion. This is one of the great freedoms protected from government action by the First Amendment to the Constitution. The individual conscience in this critical area was thus thought to be guaranteed predominance over and protection from the state. It is important to recall that William Penn refused to remove his hat as a matter of religious principle. This small gesture was so significant to him that it was one of the factors impelling him to emigrate from England and found Pennsylvania. To us this may seem a trivial matter. But as recently as the 1940s children belonging to Jehovah's Witnesses were prosecuted for refusing to salute the flag.[2] The United States Supreme Court first upheld the power of the state to compel this gesture. The Court three years later reversed itself on the ground that the First Amendment protected the individual's religious freedom.[3] Jehovah's Witnesses are a small sect composed primarily of poor and powerless people who pose no threat to the peace or order of the nation. It was not difficult for a court faced with this small number of recalcitrant school children, whose refusal to salute the flag constituted no clear and present or even a vague and future danger to the nation, to uphold their Constitutional rights.

Today large numbers of people—young and old, rich and

poor—defy the government, asserting claims of conscience. In our secular age, the claim is not limited to a "religious" belief. People demand a freedom of conscience not bound by theology, adherence to a church, or obedience to established doctrine. When faced with the nonreligious claims of conscientious objectors to the war in Vietnam, the United States Supreme Court held that a belief entitled to Constitutional protection need not be stated in terms of a recognized theological doctrine.[4] The concession was made grudgingly and limited by the necessity of proving that the claimed beliefs were deeply and sincerely held.

Under contemporary American law, one is not required to prove the sincerity or truth of his belief by the ordeals of fire and water which were the conventional methods of proof in the Middle Ages. Following the accepted modes of court procedures, today one proves the strength and honesty of his belief by presenting the testimony of expert witnesses, usually ministers, priests and rabbis. But this ostensible recognition of the claims of secular conscience by the courts is a sleight-of-hand trick in which the courts have taken jurisdiction of the claim. They have exercised the power of the state over the conscience of the individual. These decisions, framed in the old mold of the First Amendment, have been sharply limited. They failed to meet the issue of the duty—irrespective of First Amendment rights—to obey unjust laws.

Philosophers and historians deplore religious wars and racial persecutions. Safely remote in time from these conflicts, they express judgments which favor the rights of the individual. But political leaders, faced with the practical problem of maintaining a functioning government while large numbers of citizens assert claims of individual liberty and conscience, have with rare exception upheld the power of the state. Military conscription, gas chambers, concentration camps, forcible relocation of populations, commitment to mental hospitals, and the old-fashioned firing squad have been used many times to maintain the power of the state over dissident peoples.

Discussions of the competing claims of individual conscience and the power of the state are most often framed as philosophical rather than legal problems. Countless scholarly volumes have been written about Thoreau's bravely spending a single night in the pleasant rural jail of Concord, Massachusetts. It is easy to discuss the moral rectitude of an eccentric who is safely dead and securely recognized as a great and original thinker. Henry David Thoreau in 1846 had no followers. The issue which provoked his resistance to authority was the imposition of a poll tax by a government that countenanced slavery. Whether or not Thoreau paid this pittance posed no threat to the stability of Concord, of the Commonwealth of Massachusetts, or of the United States. But the power of the state prevailed. Significantly, Thoreau's claim was not litigated. In the mid-nineteenth century lawyers and courts rarely recognized that the fundamental Constitutional issues could or should be framed as cases to be decided by the courts. Certainly, they did not press for a decision from the United States Supreme Court. In fact, Thoreau's tax was paid by his aunt. The question he sought to raise was not resolved as a legal issue but was relegated to philosophical discussion in books that were largely ignored by Thoreau's contemporaries.

More than a century later, the problem has assumed the dimensions of a fundamental legal issue. In the 1960s and 1970s many Americans have refused to submit to the power of the state for ideological reasons. Some persons have refused to pay their taxes by withholding small sums due on the federal telephone tax as a symbolic protest against the war in Vietnam. Others deduct sums from their income taxes which represent the aliquot share spent on programs of which they disapprove. These acts are trifling inconveniences to the government.[5] They raise primarily academic questions of the right of civil disobedience. The law violators experience the thrill of pricking pins in the body politic. The issue of conscience versus the state is not resolved by such conduct.

Other forms of civil disobedience today are not always so civil. Nor are they met with tolerance or official disregard. Dissenters know that they may be imprisoned in brutal jails for long periods of time. They cannot expect relatives to pay nominal fines on their behalf. No latter-day Emerson can visit them in jail to discuss philosophy. Bail is high; fines are substantial. Prisons are rigorous and often brutal. Dissenters today will not spend a safe and secure period of isolation in jail writing memoirs. They will perform labor for ten or fifteen cents an hour. Their lives may be endangered by other inmates or guards. The issue is no longer one for philosophers but for policemen and judges.

The number of people who do not consent to the enforcement of law by the duly constituted public authorities is growing. It is found in every stratum of society. Yet the viability of a free state depends upon the voluntary consent of the citizen. As Professor Thomas C. Cochran explained, "To function adequately, bureaucratic hierarchies have to be supported by shared values." [6] Even prison officials know that they maintain a precarious control dependent upon the voluntary compliance of the inmates. There are always more prisoners than guards, just as there are always more civilians than police and soldiers. Today many prisoners no longer consent to the imposition of the rules and laws which they deem unfair. The consequences of their dissent are frequently bloody and fatal.[7] The soaring crime rate affords dramatic proof of the fact that even the harshest law enforcement is ineffective when large numbers of people do not voluntarily consent to the legal system.

This raises a problem qualitatively and quantitatively different from the control of a so-called criminal element by the police. Such traditional criminals recognize the validity of the legal system. Their concern is simply not to get caught. When they are apprehended, they utilize every available legal remedy to stay out of jail. If imprisoned, they may attempt to break out of jail. But in all of these illegal and criminal acts, they are not challenging the system and the right of the state to enact laws and to prosecute and to punish law violators. Such criminals are often cruel, vicious and dangerous people, but they do not threaten the system.

Those who do explicitly declare their right to break unjust laws pose a far more difficult problem. Such ideologies are no longer confined to scholarly "revolutionaries." They are found in all strata of society. Curtis Brown, Nathaniel Ragsdale and Richard DeLeon, described as leaders of the uprising by the untried prisoners in New

York's Tombs, asserted as their defense a section of the penal code which justifies violation of law when "such conduct is necessary as an emergency measure to avoid imminent public or private injury which is about to occur by reason of a situation occasioned or developed through no fault of the action and which is of such gravity that, according to ordinary standards of intelligence and morality, the desirability and urgency of avoiding such injury clearly outweigh inaction." They contended that conditions in the Tombs and the certainty of prolonged incarceration before trial justified their action. Their behavior may be likened to the uprising of Spartacus and the slaves. The force and brutality with which they were subdued is also similar.

Deliberate violation of laws asserted to be unjust also occurs among peaceful middle-class citizens. Twelve New Jersey school teachers publicly declared that they broke an injust law and were proudly demonstrating a belief in conscience to their pupils as they defied a court order prohibiting public employees from striking. They were promptly jailed.

Draft resisters and deserters, peace demonstrators, and other dissidents openly defy the law as a matter of principle. Having been in jail is no longer a disgrace but a badge of honor. As of January, 1972, there were more than 500 draft resisters in federal jails and 3,900 under indictment. At least 70,000 Americans were living abroad to avoid the draft, which they considered an unjust law in aid of an illegal and unjust war. All of these people saw their actions as challenges to the legal system. Although they constitute only a small fraction of the population, they are a sizable percentage of the draft-eligible population, and many of them are the intellectual and spiritual leaders of the young. Their influence on public attitudes toward obedience to law far exceeds their numbers. Anyone concerned with the viability of the rule of law in the United States cannot dismiss these dissidents as a small extremist fringe of society. Their claims must be examined in the context in which they are asserted, that is, as questions of Constitutional law.

The arguments which favor individual conscience over the state and those which favor submission of conscience to law deserve a

careful analysis in the light of contemporary conditions and beliefs. Heretofore the problem has usually been posed as one involving either philosophy or the claims of rival theories of jurisprudence. The historical quarrel between natural law advocates
and proponents of positive law is of more than antiquarian interest. Both theories are carefully developed, logical and rational.
Natural law acknowledges the problem of the unjust law. Legal
positivism attempts to avoid it. Neither provides a satisfactory
answer for contemporary American law.

Natural law is based upon moral and eternal values. Formerly
such values were found principally in religious teachings. St.
Augustine declared: "That which is not just seems to be no law at
all." But who is to determine what is just? How is the state to deal
with those who disobey those laws which the individual concludes
are unjust? One looks in vain for answers from the proponents of
natural law. They believed that there are eternal and immutable
truths which are revealed and have no need of proof.

The transitory quality of such eternal laws of nature is strikingly
exposed in the writings of Von Haller. In arguing for natural law as
a basis of jurisprudence, he cites as a law of nature that the
husband rules over the wife, the father over the child. Professor
Alfred Ross sums up natural law doctrine by saying, "Like a
harlot, natural law is at the disposal of everyone." In each generation and in each Western nation, the proponents of natural law
have found in it justification for their most cherished beliefs.

The proponents of legal positivism ignore the entire question of
justice and morality. Perhaps the clearest definition of this theory
was presented by John Austin who stated: "Every positive law is a
direct or circuitous command of a monarch or sovereign to a
person or persons in a state of subjection to its author." Even
Thomas Aquinas adopted this "practical" view of law. "Whatsoever pleaseth the sovereign has the force of law," he declared.
While today one might accept this as a description of law under
Louis XIV, the tsars, Stalin or Chairman Mao, few Americans
would be willing to concede that they are in a state of subjection
to elected or appointed officials or that government in its unfet-

tered discretion may issue edicts to the citizen which must be obeyed regardless of humanity, decency and fairness. The trials of Calley, Eichmann and other war criminals are too much a part of our lives and beliefs to permit a public view of law that requires blind obedience to law and authority without consideration of morality and fairness. The American citizen has been taught that he is not an automaton who, like the members of the Light Brigade, must not reason why but do and die.

It is part of the American ethos that the citizens are sovereign. All of the government—elected and appointed, from the President to the local legislators—owe their positions and their authority to the electors. This is the lesson of high school civics. Between elections, however, the citizenry has little control over government. With increasing force and dismay, the average citizen feels that the electoral process does not express his wishes. Neither governmental executive actions nor legislation are of his making or responsive to his demands and desires. Yet he is bound by them. He looks in vain to the law for a means to control his government and to protect his rights.

How did the great Oliver Wendell Holmes answer these questions? He sloughed them off by declaring that law is nothing more pretentious than "the prophecies of what the courts will do in fact." This view of law based on "brute fact," as Professor Philip Selznick described it, cannot satisfy a free people. The public is more inclined to agree with Blackstone, who declared that "No human laws should be suffered to contradict the laws of God." But the difficulties with such a definition, as with the definition of natural law, are legion. What are the laws of God? To whom are they revealed? If the laws of man are alleged to contradict the laws of God, who is to determine the fact and resolve the dilemma of the individual facing jail or his conscience? What must the individual render unto Caesar? And who is to make the decision? In a secular state such claims involve jurisdictional difficulties. Even in devoutly Catholic France, Joan of Arc, who had probably never heard of either natural law or positive law, had to make the choice. George Bernard Shaw expressed the quandary of the modern person of conscience when he has Joan say: "My lords and bishops, what other judgment can I judge by but my own?"

Many Americans might find Joan's answer appealing. But a moment's reflection causes one to reject this view. It is obvious that the unfettered freedom of each of the more than 200 million Americans to choose which laws to obey and which laws to disregard would result in anarchy. One must unfortunately return to Judge Botein's harsh alternatives: order versus freedom.

These questions, of course, are not new. They have been discussed since long before the Periclean age. But in other societies a small elite group of philosophers or theologians could treat these issues as intellectual problems, like the paradox of Zeno (theoretically one progressing from A to B by going half the way each step will never arrive at B). It is a nice, neat problem. But even Zeno knew that by moving out of his intellectual framework, as a practical matter, he could reach point B.

Today we can no longer treat the problem of obedience to an unjust law as an intellectual exercise. It is a critical question imperiling the functioning of the entire legal system. One must note that mass disobedience of a single unpopular law, such as prohibition or the use of marijuana, does not pose this problem. The United States survived the lawless gangsterism of the prohibition era with the legal system intact. The countless people who bought illegal bootleg liquor were simply defying a single unpopular exercise of governmental power; they did not challenge the right of government to exercise its authority. As John Austin noted in the nineteenth century, "The *bulk* of a given society are in a *habit* of obedience or submission." Today that is no longer true. The habit of obedience has been lost or destroyed. Today the exercise of authority requires moral and legal justification.

Those sympathetic to the views of the individual law violator will often concede that he has the "right" to break the law if he is willing to pay the penalty. Former Supreme Court Justice Abe Fortas, in a book entitled *Concerning Dissent and Civil Disobedience*,[8] expresses the conventional wisdom clearly. He approves civil disobedience only when engaged in by Martin Luther

King and anti-Nazis. Others who refuse to obey unjust laws may do so only for the narrow legalistic purpose of litigating a Constitutional challenge to the law. If the challenge fails, even by a five to four vote of the Supreme Court, the individual is supposed to suppress his conscience. Fortas declares that once he has been "properly arrested, charged and convicted, he should be punished by fine or imprisonment, or both, in accordance with the provisions of law, unless the law is invalid in general or as applied. . . . He may, indeed, be right in the eyes of history or morality or philosophy. These are not controlling."

Most people's consciences cannot be so neatly controlled. If it is wrong to kill before a Supreme Court pronouncement, does it suddenly become right thereafter? The person of conscience who violates a law is, under the Fortas view, in the same category as a murderer and all other law violators. The murderer kills and goes to jail. The corporate violator of antipollution laws simply pays a fine, which he treats as a cheap license to continue polluting rather than going to the trouble and expense of complying with the intent of the law. The person who refuses to obey an unjust law is considered no different. However, he will not pay a nominal fine and go free. Judging by past experience, the civilly disobedient person of conscience will be given a stiff jail sentence. Although a Jimmy Hoffa and many killers will be pardoned long before serving their minimum sentences, the civilly disobedient person is most unlikely to receive executive clemency. Simon Roth, for example, who was convicted of violating federal law by publishing "obscene" books, served a full five-year sentence. Many of the books he published are now recognized as classics: *Ulysses*, by James Joyce, *Lady Chatterly's Lover*, by D. H. Lawrence, etc. Obviously this scholar-poet-publisher constituted no danger to society other than asserting his First Amendment rights. But he served a far longer sentence than many street criminals, tax evaders and perpetrators of fraud.

In the past, the civilly disobedient person—one who refused to be an informer, who refused to go to war, or who claimed the right of free speech—did comply with the procedural provisions of the law. He submitted to arrest and he was given a "fair trial." The facts were admitted. Few questioned the ritualistic nature of such a trial. The legal system condemned him after according him the procedural formula contained in the rubric "due process of law." The frontiersman who caught a cattle rustler expressed this view succinctly: "We'll give him a fair trial and then hang him." The man of conscience having had his "fair trial" then meekly went to jail.

Neither the justice system nor the authority of the state was seriously challenged by such individuals. As recently as the 1950s, scores of people who refused to cooperate with the questionable tactics of Senator Joseph McCarthy, after exhausting their legal remedies, unresistingly went to jail. Like medieval believers that doomsday was inevitable, they sold their worldly goods, took leave of friends and family and unresistingly entered the prison gates.[9] The habit of obedience was still too strong for rational consideration of alternatives.

Kurt Waldheim, Secretary General of the United Nations, exemplifies that point of view. He served in the German army under Hitler. "We had to serve, whether we wanted to or not," he explained in an interview with the press. "There was no choice —either you were able to get out of the country, or be persecuted, or serve."

Less than a generation later, Father Daniel Berrigan refused to submit voluntarily to prison. Scores of young men have also chosen exile rather than submission to a law that they deemed unjust or to the penalties for violating that law. Many of those who chose jail rather than freedom have regretted their choice. They find little comfort in Thoreau's statement: "I might have resisted more forcibly with more or less effect, might have run 'amok' against society; but I preferred that society should run 'amok' against me." [10]

Today when society runs "amok" against the civilly disobedient the results are painful and disillusioning. A young conscientious objector in jail, interviewed by psychiatrist Willard Gaylin,[11] stated ironically, "I'm just getting a wee bit dubious as to whether I selected the best way of doing things. Because all it means is that all the talent you have is being locked up. If I were advising someone right now ... I would tell them to avoid this whole court process. . . ." Dr. Gaylin quotes another young conscientious objector whom he interviewed in prison. This man explained: ". . . we were operating within the rule of law on which this society is based, and I accepted this. Now I don't believe this. I don't believe we're operating under the rule of law. I have very little regard for this rule. This for sure has changed since I came in [to jail]. My basic feeling about the law is that it's merely an abstraction which has no reality outside of the way it's enforced. Law, per se, is nothing."

Neither the Waldheim nor the Berrigan position is satisfactory. The person of conscience finds it difficult to submit to the force of law when that law is unjust and inhumane. Nor can such a person find exile or being a fugitive from the law a tenable status. One looks in vain for a factual and theoretical posture that recognizes both the rights of the individual and the viability of the state. For the civilly disobedient person is not a conscious revolutionary seeking the overthrow of the government.

How does one, safely living his life outside of jail, answer them? Mr. Justice Fortas and Chief Justice Burger have rejected St. Augustine and principles of justice and morality. The law is the law is the law, and it must be obeyed though the heavens fall. Is it mere brute force that makes the law valid and binding? Or can every unjust act be justified by the abstraction, "the rule of law"?

One of the more appealing justifications for obedience to law irrespective of conscience is the "social contract" theory. A contract under law involves an agreement freely entered into by two parties. There is a mutuality of obligation between them, a quid pro quo. This accords better with notions of citizenship and individual rights than a concept of law as the imperial fiat of the sovereign commanding those in subjection or the quasi-religious doctrine of natural law. The contract theory comes with unimpeachable authority from Plato. How many generations of students have read with awed admiration the "Crito"! Bravery in the face of death is an old heroic theme. *Dulcis et propria* may be a bit romantic for the late twentieth century, which has seen death in gas chambers and rice paddies, death by nuclear explosion and napalm, death of astronauts trapped in spaceships, and death of infants exploded, mutilated and starved. There is nothing sweet or fitting about any of this dying.

But Socrates' death was different. He comes to us across more than two millennia as a singularly modern man. In a democratic society he was condemned by the authorities under an unjust law. We can relate to that. His crime was preaching unpopular ideas. And that, too, is familiar. Socrates sits in jail. His friends come to visit him. The amenities of the prison scene do not jar most readers of the classics who have little familiarity with penal institutions. His friends urge Socrates to flee. They have collected money for him; they will bribe the jailers. How human and contemporary these ancient Greeks seem; anything can be accomplished with a little money. No risk is involved. It is very simple. Socrates can walk out of the jail, go to Thessaly and peacefully live out his remaining years. He stoutly maintains that his teachings were wise and sound. He does not doubt the injustice of the law. But he bravely and willingly drinks the hemlock. Why?

His answer has bedeviled Western thought for more than two millennia. It still confuses many wise and intellectual people. But increasingly there are those who do not find it satisfactory. Socrates replied to his friends:

> For, having brought you into the world and nurtured and educated you and given you and every other citizen a share in every good which we (the State) had to give, we further proclaim to any Athenian by the liberty which we allow him, that if he does not like us when he has become of age and has seen the ways of the city and made our acquaintance, he may go where he pleases and take his goods with him. None of our laws will forbid him or interfere with him. Anyone who does not like us and the city and who wants to emigrate to a colony or any other city may go where he likes, retaining his property. But he who has experience of the manner in which we order justice and administer the state and still remains has entered into an implied contract that he will do as we command him. And he

who disobeys us is, as we maintain, thrice wrong; first, because in disobeying us he is disobeying his parents; secondly, because we are the authors of his education; thirdly, because he has made an agreement with us that he will duly obey our commands.[12]

It is a clever argument and proceeds logically point by point. Without disputing the truth of Socrates' premises for the citizens of Athens, one must see if they are valid in the United States today. Socrates' first point is that any citizen who is dissatisfied with the life and liberty in Athens may leave and go where he pleases taking his goods with him. In an age in which passports and visas are required and few nations permit aliens to receive work permits, not many Americans can freely and openly leave this country, whether they like its laws or not. Socrates could go to Thessaly or a dozen or more other states without legal documents. He would have had no language problem and no difficulty in obtaining employment. There were no restrictions on taking money or goods out of Athens. The plight of an expatriot today, if he does not have a Swiss bank account, is precarious. It is dismaying to note that 30 percent of college students questioned in an opinion poll stated that they would prefer to leave the United States if they could. A Gallup poll in 1974 reveals that 14 million Americans over the age of seventeen would leave the country if they could afford it. Even assuming that the dissatisfied American can immigrate to Canada, Sweden or Australia and fails to do so, has he entered into a binding contract with the state that requires him to obey all its laws and edicts, even unjust and immoral laws?

The notion of a social contract in Western law is relatively recent, an idea of the French enlightenment. Under the English common law the subject received his status at birth. It was not dependent upon consent or agreement. In the United States, citizenship is also a birthright for the native born and a grant of right for the naturalized citizen. Contract, express or implied, has no part in citizenship. But even assuming that by failing to renounce citizenship, there is an implied contract to support, defend and obey the Constitution, does this prohibit disobedience to an unjust law or an unjust system of law?

Philosopher John Rawls [13] posits a more abstract and sophisticated contractarian theory. He declares that the primary subject of justice is the basic structure of society. He then asks, What structures would a rational person choose when acting under a "veil of ignorance," i.e., being unaware of his own status, social, economic, racial, sex, age and any other conditions leading to a special point of view? Such a representative person, in order to secure his liberty, Rawls believes, would enter into a contract establishing priorities and principles determining the moral facts. This hypothetical, reasonable, educated person would voluntarily accept an arrangement which would provide a fair share in society for everyone regardless of status. In his words, "This principle holds that a person is required to do his part as defined by the rules of an institution when two conditions are met: first, the institution is just (or fair), that is, it satisfies the two principles of justice; and second, one has voluntarily accepted the benefits of the arrangement or taken advantage of the opportunities it offers to further one's interests."

In passing, Professor Rawls notes that "By the principle of fairness it is not possible to be bound to unjust institutions, or at least to institutions which exceed the limits of tolerable injustice (so far undefined)." [Emphasis supplied.] Countless Americans today find that the legal system has exceeded the limits of tolerable injustice. Unfortunately, there are few philosophers who have developed a dialectic defining the limits of tolerable injustice and a coherent rational and peaceful method of responding to such conditions.

In the absence of such philosophical doctrine, a lawyer can only analyze the contractarian theory from a legal viewpoint. Here there is no dearth of precedent or theory. Legal relations, rights and obligations between individuals, between institutions, and between individuals and institutions are governed by the law of contract. The rigidities and inequities of earlier law have been modified through the centuries, by statute and by judicial decision.

Today neither a notarized signature nor a seal makes a contract absolutely binding, although as late as the nineteenth century a seal was binding. Courts will examine the provisions of the contract and the relative positions of the parties. Without the convoluted explication of "justice as fairness" of Professor Rawls, the law approaches this essentially decent goal. The law of contract as developed in the United States permits rescission of a contract if it was entered into by reason of fraud, accident, mistake or duress.

A sound legal argument could be developed under contract law that the conscientious objector is not bound by the acts of the United States Government. First, that the government by fraud embarked on an undeclared war. Second, that because the government concealed material facts, the Congress passed the Gulf of Tonkin resolution under a mistake of fact. Third, that the citizens have been subjected to duress by the CIA, the FBI and other agencies engaged in wiretapping, data collection and dissemination, and that through explicit or implicit threats of loss of job, status or reputation the government has chilled the citizen's exercise of his First Amendment rights. Surely this is classical duress. All of these acts should constitute grounds for rescission of the "social contract."

At a minimum, the obligation of a government should be to deal with its citizens openly and honestly and without coercion or duress. Physical torture offends the contemporary American. So does psychological coercion, or "brain washing." Deceit, fear of loss of employment or social status are simply more subtle and refined forms of duress. If the government acts deceitfully or coercively, what is the legitimate legal response of the citizen? Certainly, under such circumstances, the obligation to obey an unjust law or to accept the penalty of disobedience cannot be justified by the pat phrase "social contract." For by enacting or attempting to enforce an unjust law, the state itself has breached a fundamental term of the contract. Under general principles of law the contract is rescinded. The citizen is no longer bound.

More and more average citizens are viewing their relationships with all of the institutions affecting their lives as rescindable contracts. Milton Machlin, a weary commuter, harassed by the delays of his railroad, its dirt, heat and intolerable conditions refused to pay the fare. He was ejected, arrested and tried. His defense: the railroad breached the contract with him by failing to provide proper service. A jury unanimously acquitted him.

Similarly, many disgusted tenants, installment purchasers of appliances and purchasers of homes feel that they are not bound by their contracts of lease or purchase. Therefore, they refuse to make the payments due under the terms of those contracts. Many people believe that regardless of the fact that one has signed an agreement or contract requiring payment, if there are defects in the goods or property, they are not bound to comply with that contract. If the agreement is unjust, they believe, they are or should be relieved of their obligations. While some courts have found implied warranties of merchantability or habitability in contracts and leases justifying rescission or refusal to pay, neither the railroads nor the United States Government recognizes principles of mutuality and rescission. The railroad demands its fares no matter how unsatisfactory the service. The United States treats the violator of an unjust law, the person of conscience, the same as a common criminal. He is imprisoned with rapists, arsonists and murderers. He is subjected to the same dehumanizing and brutal conditions. He is imprisoned not because it will protect society or benefit him but because he must be punished. He has broken the law, often, as Mr. Justice Fortas concedes, an unjust and unwise law. Therefore, he must be punished. Is this conclusion ineluctable?

Usually the penalties meted out to the person of conscience are harsher than those imposed upon the common criminal, tax evader, manufacturer of unsafe products and the faithless public official. All of these miscreants violate the law, often to the great detriment of the public at large. But no philosophical question is raised by their routine crimes anymore than by the prosecution and sentencing of a burglar or rapist. The person who claims obedience to a higher or different law than that of the state, however, threatens the legitimacy of governmental action and is dealt with more harshly. In fact, the law reserves its extremely severe penalties for him. There are exceptions well recognized in the law for one who kills another human being. The man who slays in a fit of passion is not guilty of murder. But there are no legal exceptions for the man who refuses to kill by reason of conscience. Nor does the law recognize mitigating circumstances for one who disobeys a statute or even the command of a policeman for reasons of conscience.

The appeal to the executive for relief from an unjust law is very limited. The President can pardon persons convicted of violation of federal law. The governors of the several states have a similar power to reduce sentences and to grant pardons. The legislature may also pass a private bill granting an individual some privilege or right which the law has denied him. This is a costly remedy and not available to the average citizen. It is unrealistic, to say the least, to expect the executive who has directly or indirectly ordered the enforcement of an unjust or unconscionable law to grant clemency to the conscientious violator of that law. As has been noted, the sentences of conscientious objectors and others who for reasons of principle violate laws are rarely commuted.

The traditional language of social contract rings very hollow to one who faces the threat of imprisonment. It is a facile and obsolete response to a moral and practical problem. Before the trial of Daniel Ellsberg, Rebecca West declared, "I do not believe that Daniel Ellsberg had a right to breach his contract with the state." Apparently she did not consider the state had breached its contract with Ellsberg and with many other Americans by acts of fraud, deception and burglary.

Increasing numbers of thoughtful people no longer subscribe to the social contract theory as the basis for obedience to the law. They no longer consent to the exercise of power by the state when they consider such power to be exercised unjustly. This startling change in the attitude of the citizen toward his government is unprecedented. Rebellions, revolutions, uprisings and coups d'état are traditional methods of overthrowing a government. The citizen of conscience who knowingly and intentionally disobeys an unjust law often does not wish to engage in revolution. He does not seek the downfall of the state. But he no longer sees himself as the creature of the state, who must unthinkingly obey all of its commandments, the unjust as well as the just.

The Supreme Court has held that when a statute interferes with the freedom or privacy of the citizen there is a heavy burden upon the government to prove an overriding interest in the state which will suffice to subordinate the citizen to the power of the state. For at least half a century American legal doctrine has slowly been developing toward this end, under the doctrine of the "right of privacy." It has been a matter of slow accretion, of bits and pieces accumulated in varied circumstances and unrelated cases. Doubtless the jurisprudentialists who contributed to the growth of this theory of the relation of citizen to government did not foresee its far-reaching effects. In the Connecticut birth control case,[14] the United States Supreme Court described rather fully the limitations on the power of the state to interfere with the private rights of citizens under the exercise of the police power. Significantly, the case arose out of a knowing, deliberate and willful violation of a duly enacted statute. The law violators, the executive director of Planned Parenthood League of Connecticut and a licensed physician who served as medical director, provided contraceptive materials to married couples in violation of a Connecticut statute. They acted out of conscience, a belief that the law was unjust, unwise and unconstitutional. They were prosecuted, convicted and fined. Ultimately their appeal reached the Supreme Court, which held the statute unconstitutional.

Not all challenges to unjust laws have a fortunate outcome. Frequently the challenger cannot afford to carry his defense to the Supreme Court. The Court may not have an already developed doctrine—like the right to privacy—to enable it to strike down the unjust law. Public opinion may lag behind or oppose the challenger. Such individuals are then faced with voluntary submission to the power of the state, which usually means a jail sentence, or evasion through flight or subterfuge.

The Ninth Amendment to the Constitution provides that rights enumerated in the Constitution shall not be construed to deny or disparage others retained by the people. Professor Patterson [15] described the Ninth Amendment as the "Forgotten Amendment," but it has been discovered by lawyers and citizens concerned with the excessive and unfair exercise of governmental powers. A generation educated to believe in the legitimacy of the claims of conscience cannot easily dichotomize between the duty of Eichmann to disobey the commands of the Third Reich ordering him to torture and kill the inmates of a concentration camp and the duty of an American to obey the commands of the United States Government to take up arms against an unknown people on the opposite side of the globe and kill them with modern weapons of unprecedented power and to lay waste their lands by all of the modern means of destruction. Even in lesser matters which do not directly involve the individual in acts of slaughter and violence, the citizen can no longer be expected to subordinate his sense of morality and his claims of conscience to the abstract concept of law.[16] Many of these people, even though they may be ignorant of Constitutional law, believe that the rights of conscience and liberty are reserved to the individual and cannot be commanded by the state.

Blacks, chicanos and women see that the law which claims to guarantee equal justice to all does not treat them equally or justly. Poor people find that the legal system operates to the benefit of the rich. Working people, black and white, see that the wealthy evade taxes while they struggle with an increasingly heavy burden and receive fewer and fewer benefits. The promise of upward mobility, of equal access to housing, education and employment has not been fulfilled for black or for white working men and women. Older citizens find their plight degrading and unfair. The promise of golden years is tarnished. The young are equally bitter. All feel betrayed not simply by society but specifically by the law which had promised them equality, security, and liberty.

Although very few of these millions of Americans crystallize their discontent in philosophical or legal terms, their actions as well as their words indicate that they refuse to submit unquestioningly to a legal system which permits and legitimates the obvious injustices to which they are subjected. The belief in the sanctity of law—the hagiocracy of the social contract—has been destroyed. Like Humpty Dumpty, all the government's soldiers, policemen and national guards cannot put it back together again.

This widespread loss of faith in the justice of the law presents philosophical and practical problems with which our legal institutions are wholly unprepared to deal. Evidence of increasing dissatisfaction with government and law has been apparent for some time, but few of the intellectual and jurisprudential leaders recognize the depth and seriousness of this widespread disaffection. Even so aware and knowledgeable an organization as The Hudson Institute, in its exemplary futuristic study, *"The Year 2000,"* [17] which was published in 1967, ignored this trend. In fact, they predicted the contrary. The authors suggest thirteen basic long-term trends in society and social attitudes. The second trend is called "Bourgeois, bureaucratic, 'meritocratic,' democratic (and nationalistic?) elites." This is a worldwide prediction applicable to all forms of government. It is described in part as follows: "Bourgeois democracy tends to rest on some form of 'social contract' concept of the relationship between the people and their government. The people hire and fire their government, and no group has theocratic (Ideational) or aristocratic (Integrated) claims on the government. Democratic government clearly is also an expression of democratic 'ideology'—it is sustained by the idea of the 'consent' of the governed. The idea is contractual; the factors of sacredness, occultism, or charisma are restricted."

We see that in 1974, long before the year 2000, this belief in the social contract is dead. The governed no longer consent. Until a new ideological basis is developed under which the bulk of the population gives a new and informed consent to the exercise of legal authority, the search for law and order will be delusory. Such new ideology cannot spring full grown, like Minerva, from the brow of a social critic. Like other ideas, it will require a tentative promulgation, discussion and revision before it imperceptibly becomes a part of the national ethos. One can suggest, although the outlines of such new philosophy have not yet been limned, that it will be more limited and less grandiose. Late-twentieth-century man no longer sees himself a colossus bestride the universe, dominating nature, indomitable. We know that all human beings are frail, that despite the extraordinary intellectual feats in the area of physical sciences and technology there are dark places in the soul that we do not understand. We know that the tenancy of human beings on this planet is insecure and that all life is fragile and threatened. We recognize the imperative for self-restraint and humility. Our much vaunted intelligence has given us only a glimpse into the extraordinary complexity and enigma of our universe.

We should recognize that we cannot fulfill promises of equality, freedom, security and happiness to every man, woman and child as a guaranteed right enforceable by legal process. We should know that we cannot entrust the regulation of society to a special class or profession through whom the populace must act to assert its rights. We should not seek to compress the richness and variety of human experience in a single mold—the law—for the creation and maintenance of an ordered society of free individuals. We shall obtain the willing assent of the American people only when the social and economic structure and the legal system in its daily operations meet the needs and aspirations of some 200 million men, women and children.

*Justice, sir, is the greatest interest
of man on earth. It is the ligament
which holds civilized beings and
civilized nations together.*
Daniel Webster

*One command, one joy, one desire
One curse, one weight, one measure
One King, one God, one law.*
William Blake

12: Law as Justice

The various elements of the legal system, the different classes of participants in the system, the public and its expectations and attitudes have been examined. Each of these groups of people and parts of the system has contributed to the failure of the law to function satisfactorily and thus each has been directly or indirectly responsible for the death of the law in the United States and the transformation of the citizenry into a nation of scofflaws. Now we come to one of the largest factors in the death of the law: the law itself.

Much dissatisfaction is directly traceable to substantive legal doctrines which lead to unjust results. Merely to point out several rules of law that are obsolete and contrary to the needs of the time is insufficient. With not too much effort those specifics could be remedied by legislation or by litigation designed to obtain landmark decisions changing the law. It is the implicit

293

beliefs and theories upon which so many of our legal doctrines are premised that inevitably lead to conclusions which contemporary Americans find unacceptable. Therefore, it is appropriate to examine the philosophical bases of law in the United States to learn whether the aims, purposes and premises of the law are compatible with the needs of the nation today. A brief backward glance is helpful in explaining how we have arrived at our present unsatisfactory status.

For three-quarters of a century Americans have been, consciously or unconsciously, bemused by the pervasive philosophy of legal realism. In the late nineteenth century Friedrich Nietzsche proclaimed that "God is dead." At almost the same time, Oliver Wendell Holmes announced that law is not "a brooding omnipresence in the sky" [1] but only a prediction of what judges will decide. This philosophy of legal realism provided the intellectual and jurisprudential cachet to the belief that law is not a fundamental code of principles governing human conduct but a fluctuating series of answers to discrete problems and that the answers depend in large measure upon the vagaries of the decision-makers. A bolder legal theorist might have used Nietzsche's phrase and declared that "Law is dead." Certainly the belief that conduct is governed by eternal principles of law and positive legislative enactments no longer prevails. The legal profession, however, has not recognized this fact nor does it know how to deal with this new situation.

Some theologians are now grappling with the problem of the death of God. Harvey Cox asks: "How do we speak of God in the secular city?" [2] He sees our contemporary society—urban and technological—as a universe from which God has been banished. The removal of God raises for him not only problems of nomenclature but also religious, sociological and political issues. The problems of a lawless society, however, extend beyond that to all intellectual disciplines and all areas of life. The implications are profoundly disturbing. But few leaders of the bench and bar are willing to face these problems, to ask searching questions and to seek useful answers.

When law no longer commands the obedience of a free people, what is the substitute? The alternatives are bleak: anarchy or repression. In fact, an all-consuming dictatorship, perhaps disguised as a benign, omnipotent presidency or an interim committee, is the only possibility. Anarchy could be at most a temporary condition. Our highly technical interdependent society requires organization and direction for physical survival. Without transportation to deliver food to the cities, without public utilities to provide water and power, without municipal services to provide garbage collection, police, and maintain hospitals, without a continuous flow of money so that necessities can be purchased, few of us could function for long. Even remote rural communes growing natural foods are not self-sufficient. Of necessity, dictatorship of some sort would quickly arise to prevent widespread suffering, disease and death, to say nothing of loss and destruction of property.

To date, hesitant, piecemeal tinkering with the legal system has not cured the law of its mortal ills. Conferences, think tanks, retreats and seminars abound. Bar associations, government leaders and judges meet to discuss specific small problems and small remedies. They ignore the totality of the challenge of maintaining a democratic government when law is ineffective. Henry Kissinger has noted "the inability of the 'establishment' to come to grips with a fundamental challenge." The legal establishment has not come to grips with the fundamental challenge of a nation of scofflaws. Although Kissinger was not discussing the crisis of law, his observations are pertinent. "A long period of stability creates the illusion that change must necessarily take the form of a modification of the existing framework and cannot involve its overthrow." The United States has had two centuries of relative stability, quiescence and obedience to law. I do not believe that the Constitutional structure of legislature, executive and judiciary must be overthrown. But I am convinced that the law and the framework of legal institutions must be drastically altered and simplified. The aims of the law must be not simply restated but reformulated, or the system will be overthrown.

Essential to the revitalization of the law is the recognition that the business and purpose of law is justice. It is assumed by most lawyers and judges that conformity with the technical requirements known as "due process" will provide justice and equal treatment for all. Consequently much time and effort has been devoted to the minutiae, the procedures by which government, policemen and courts act. But little attention has been paid to the question of what is justice.

Most contemporary jurisprudence ignores the meaning of justice altogether. Law is treated as a science. Until the mid-sixties science had assumed the arcane authority once reserved to oracles and priests. Anything deemed to be scientific had an aura of infallibility, significance, power and importance. The mystique of man conquering nature through science pervaded the attitude of the public and the intellectuals. From outer space to the inner secrets of the atom, science was men's tool for problem-solving. By calling law a science, jurisprudentialists ascribed to it the dignity and respect which society accorded to the physical and natural sciences. Max Radin, for example, in describing law as science, wrote that law is "the organized examination of all the data that affect social conduct which will enable us to predict what evaluation in the sense of 'ought' or 'may' a judge will make of some conduct. . . ." Law was and is often seen as a strict application of logic or of mathematical principles. Today many treatises on law are written in mathematical symbols rather than words. This is highly significant because mathematical symbols are value-free postulates. They have little to do with human emotions or ideals of justice. As Ortega y Gasset observed, "Scientific truth is characterized by its exactness and the certainty of its predictions. But these admirable qualities are contrived by science at the cost of remaining on a plane of secondary problems, leaving intact the ultimate and decisive questions."

Law must deal with the ultimate questions of fair treatment of human beings and the limits on government intervention in the individual's life. Justice is one of the ultimate questions which science avoids and which the scientific method cannot solve.

If the tacit aim of contemporary jurisprudence is to make legal decisions value-free, derived from the application of rigorous logic or scientific method, it is not astonishing to find Lord Justice Devlin suggesting that one cannot *"altogether"* divorce the law's commands from the accepted standards of moral behavior. Erwin Griswold, former Dean of the Harvard Law School and former Solicitor General of the United States, asked rhetorically, "Are decisions [of the United States Supreme Court] more 'result-oriented' than is ideal?" The implicit answer was affirmative. Griswold declared that the ideal judge should be guided "by an outside frame of reference, called for convenience 'the law,' in arriving at his conclusion. . . ." I submit that this apotheosized disinterest in result, what Professor Herbert Wechsler calls "principled neutrality," severs the necessary link between law and justice.

The emphasis on scientific method and value-free decisions has encouraged courts to apply rules mechanically, to be concerned with niceties of techniques rather than the effects of a decision upon individuals and society. It has also narrowed the role of the legal scholar. Rather than considering human, social or economic values affected by judicial decisions, the scholar, in appraising the work of the courts, notes that a rule of evidence was transgressed, that there was an error in the charge of the court, or that a statute is susceptible of an overbroad interpretation. An appellate court can with a disinterested respect for rules set aside a trial court's decision and remand a case to be retried without considering whether the result achieved was fair despite the error, and whether fairness to the individuals involved requires a new trial at which other errors may occur. Nor do the courts consider, the rules having been properly applied, whether the result is just and proper. This is neutrality; but is it principled? It is computerized and scientific; it is not humanistic.

Lawyers who represent human clients and judges who must decide questions affecting the lives of human beings see law as both more and less than Dean Griswold's "frame of reference." It is often a straitjacket requiring an essentially unjust result. It is often also an exercise in futility requiring actions which are too difficult or too costly and so will be ignored. Nonetheless, courts order workers not to strike, knowing that they will strike. A hostile husband is ordered to make payments to his wife, with the knowledge that the order is often disobeyed. An illiterate, hostile young defendant is sentenced to prison after a trial in which he was represented by a lawyer whom he did not choose and did not see until the day of trial. No witnesses were called for his defense. No one really knows whether he was guilty or innocent. He will be released in several years just as illiterate and hostile and unable to earn a living. But the forms of due process, a hearing, taking testimony and entering an order are observed. The parties involved will only add to the number of overt scofflaws. It is easy to be cynical when observing the system grinding out orders which have little relationship to or effect upon the realities of the lives involved. But law cannot be dismissed as a meaningless rite of a dead faith, a time-honored ritual celebrating a moribund democratic government, for without a base of law, accepted by the vast majority of the population, there can be no organized society of people living in relative security and freedom.

The purpose of law is to be a mechanism for resolving disputes fairly as well as providing a structure for a just organization of society. The method of law is the application of general principles, generally accepted, to specific problems. Although Holmes declared, "General propositions do not decide concrete cases," law cannot abandon the quest to apply the same rule equally and to all who are similarly situated. This is the essence of the rule of law. To treat each problem as if it were beyond the reach of an underlying principle and subject only to the personal predilection of the judge deciding the case and the peculiarities of the litigants would not only be arbitrary and unjust, it would constitute judicial anarchy. No one would be able to rely upon existing rules of conduct in personal life, government or industry.

The method of science is the antithesis of law. Science requires the examination of data and the derivation of principles from recurring patterns among large numbers of similar objects, persons or actions. Science proceeds by statistics and hypotheses. Its purpose is the discovery of truth. Justice and equality as value judgments have no place in the scientific method. The concept of justice has no role in logic. But law, to be a viable force in the community, must be humanistic. Dr. Howard Shevrin, a psychoanalyst at the Menninger Foundation, has pointed out that "there cannot be a science of being human." He sees the reliance upon the findings of science as the justification for legal decisions as "attacking inadvertently the independent, objective basis of law itself." This use of science and scientific conclusions to shore up the bases of law and to give an added imprimatur to statutes and legal decisions has been a conspicuous characteristic of American jurisprudence during the last three decades. The results have weakened the law and diverted the attention of the legal profession from the quest for justice to the search for scientific data.

In the early twentieth century, we have noted, legal activists rightly pointed out that the Constitution did not embody the economic principles of Herbert Spencer. No more should it today embody the sociological beliefs of Dr. Kenneth Clark, the educational theories of Professor Christopher Jencks, or any political or intellectual notions in vogue at any time.

Here are a few examples of the United States Supreme Court confusing transient contemporary scientific theory with principles of law, decisions which were lauded at the time they were rendered but are now revealed to be grossly unjust and violative of the Constitutional rights of the individual:

§The Supreme Court of the United States in 1927, in *Buck* v. *Bell*,[3] held that the state could require the involuntary sterilization of so-called mental defectives. "Three generations of imbeciles are enough," the Court declared with Olympian certitude, to the plaudits of the public. The scientific notions of eugenics upon which this conclusion was based were found to be unjustified and, if you will, unscientific, within a scant three decades. The fundamental legal right of the individual to procreate was reinstated by the Supreme Court in *Skinner* v. *Oklahoma* in 1942.[4] (However, involuntary sterilization of poor, illiterate and possibly mentally defective people continues to this day.) The Court was diverted from the basic problem of the rights of the individual human being and the limitations on governmental intervention by so-called scientific truths which justified a popular result.

§The treatment of alleged pornography by the courts also illustrates the quicksands of uncertainty and arbitrariness in which the law founders when courts base their decisions on the findings of social disciplines rather than legal principles. The First Amendment to the Constitution unequivocally states: "Congress shall make *no* laws . . . abridging the freedom of speech or of the press. . . ." Under the due process clause of the Fourteenth Amendment this prohibition extends to the states. If anything would appear to be clear it is that government may not interfere with the spoken or written word. Nonetheless, censorship of books, motion pictures and plays has been a common practice in most states for decades. When the United States Supreme Court turned its attention to this question, it appeared that the Court, by striking down censorship laws, was protecting the freedom of ideas. However, by engrafting upon the Constitution the notion that literature must have "redeeming social importance," the Court performed another sleight-of-hand trick. The "experts" were to provide data upon which the Court could support its finding of redeeming social importance. In the celebrated Roth case,[5] the court enunciated this new doctrine, for which there was really no precedent. The books were saved for the moment, but the freedom was lost and the law badly eroded. There is no need to protect what society deems important or valuable; freedom of the press is necessary only for that which the majority deems to be without value or truth. Sociologists and psychiatrist have offered abundant and differing opinions as to the harmful or harmless effects of movies, books and other material upon individuals. Depending upon the views of such witnesses, the majority of the Court tergiversates in its holdings as to what materials a free people may legally read and see. This unnecessary obfuscation of a clear legal principle has relied upon fluctuating data of psychiatry, sociology and penology.

§School desegregation has also foundered on the slippery shoals of sociology rather than resting on firm principles of law. It is obvious that classification of citizens on the basis of race for access to public facilities is an improper and impermissible governmental function. The Court spoke of equal access to educational facilities in a series of cases from 1938 to 1954. Then in *Brown* v. *Board of Education* [6] the Court justified its ruling on sociological findings that segregated education was harmful to children. Since 1954, much "scientific" data has been adduced tending to show that *integrated* schools in the midst of racial tension and hostility are psychically harmful to children and even physically dangerous. Whether educational tests show a rise or a fall in achievement as a result of the abolition of segregated schools is not a legal justification for segregation or for integration. It is irrelevant to the legal issue of classification by race for access to public facilities.

Having embarked on the notion that integration is a socially desirable goal to which the forces of law must be committed, the courts have become mired in the very impermissible conduct of classification by race and the reinstitution of the numerous classes anathematized for generations. If the genetic theories of Jensen (that there are intellectual inequalities based upon race) were to become accepted in the United States, would the courts sustain the classification of individuals by race for schooling, employment and a variety of other purposes? Under the equal protection clause, there would appear to be a right of all citizens to have equal sums expended on public facilities, such as schools, in all parts of the state. Some courts have so held. Recent data tend to show that the expenditure of money has little relationship to the effectiveness of the learning process. Would this justify wide disparity between the amounts spent on the education of black slum children and the education of white affluent suburban children? Goals deemed to be socially beneficent and scientific findings are too evanescent, too subject to temporary passion and prejudice, too dependent upon popular tastemakers to constitute a valid basis for legal doctrine.

§The exclusion of evidence in criminal cases affords another example of the dangers of abandoning legal principles for ends deemed socially desirable. Evidence in both civil and criminal cases is excluded from a trial when the circumstances under which it was obtained cast doubt upon its reliability. A coerced confession is of dubious reliability because under physical or mental duress most people will give the answer sought by the authorities in order to stop the torture. History presents a melancholy parade of both ordinary citizens and great thinkers who confessed, after incarceration, threats and sometimes physical torture, to being enemies of the state or to holding heretical or unpatriotic opinions. Galileo confessed that he was wrong in doubting Ptolemaic astronomy and then in the final moment as he lay dying, a broken and discredited man, he whispered, "It [the sun] still moves." Many people accused of crime, in the terrifying atmosphere of a prison cell or an interrogation tank, have confessed to crimes of which they are innocent. Consequently a legal system concerned with justice excludes statements obtained under these circumstances. It also excludes the testimony of incompetents because that, too, is unreliable.

The right of privacy—the right to be secure in one's home or office from intrusion by electronic devices or by brute force—is also a hallmark of a civilized society. Such privacy is specifically protected by law. It is rare, however, that police officers or detectives are tried, fired or even demoted for participating in activities that deprive citizens of this right. Evidence obtained by these illegal means may, however, reveal the truth clearly and reliably.

The courts have seized upon the power to exclude evidence from trial to accomplish by indirection what they have not done directly, namely, halt illegal police practices and invasion of privacy. Judicial frustration at observing a continuing pattern of government violation of law is understandable. Use of judicial power to induce the police to behave in a more acceptable fashion raises not only serious questions of overreaching by the courts themselves but also problems of just and equal treatment of individual defendants. The rationale of the courts has been clearly articulated in many cases. The Supreme Court has ruled that evidence, otherwise reliable, must be excluded from the trial if it was illegally obtained, in order to provide "an effective sanction to assure that law enforcement authorities will respect the accused's constitutional right(s). . . ." [7] The effect of this exceptional means to a socially desirable end has been a denial of equal treatment and justice. A murder weapon bearing the fingerprints of the accused is excluded from evidence not because fingerprints are unreliable evidence. They are probably the soundest, least suspect evidence available. They are excluded because the evidence was illegally obtained.

Is it a proper function of the courts to police the police in this fashion? Should not the offending police officer be given a proper, due process trial and be dismissed if he has broken the law? Is it just for a guilty person to be acquitted because the evidence of his guilt was illegally obtained by a third party, a police officer? Does the acquittal of this defendant deny equal treatment to another equally guilty person from whom similar evidence was legally obtained, who was convicted on the basis of such evidence? In both cases the evidence was intrinsically reliable. In both cases the evidence disclosed guilt beyond a reasonable doubt. But one defendant was convicted and the other acquitted because the court was more concerned with policing the police than with the guilt or innocence of the accused.

§The substitution of psychiatric findings for legal conclusions has also led to an impairment of basic law. Under the rubrics of "helping," or "therapy," the law deprives many individuals of basic human rights, often irreparably. If a court deprives a person of his liberty because a psychiatrist has decided that the individual needs treatment, then it follows that the court must see that he gets treatment, whether he wants it or not. The courts are now embroiled in medical decision-making, setting standards of care and treatment. The proper judicial function, however, is to determine whether an individual by his actions has forfeited his basic Constitutional right to liberty. This is a totally different question from whether he "needs" treatment and whether his medical treatment is adequate and proper. The incarceration of troublesome persons who have not been convicted of any crime under the guise of mental illness has had a sorry history in the Soviet Union. In the United States, the imprisonment of Ezra Pound in an insane asylum is a striking but not singular example of the uses by the law of psychiatry to get rid of difficult people in a polite and "scientific" fashion. Even ignoring the validity of the scientific opinion, one cannot avoid the conclusion that law has been misused and betrayed for purposes which at the time seemed humane, politic, and popular.

The use of the legal system to attain goals deemed to be socially desirable at the expense of legal principles is all too prevalent. This confusion of ends and means is frequently found today in the disposition or sentencing of persons convicted of crime. The function of imposing sentence is a difficult one at best. If the judge attempts to make the punishment fit the crime, he at least has guidelines. People who have done similar acts can be similarly treated. There is, at a minimum, the attempt to treat people equally under the law. By relegating the function of fixing penalties in many cases to psychiatrists or prison wardens, the task has become one of making the punishment fit the criminal, not the crime. The basic concept of equal treatment as an integral part of justice has been lost. A study by United States Attorney Whitney North Seymour, Jr., documents the disparities in sentencing in the United States Court for the Southern District of New York. Similar inconsistencies are found in every jurisdiction. A Republican judge convicted of fraud committed while he was a lawyer was pardoned by the President and returned to the bench. Similar fraud by a Democratic politician-lawyer resulted in a five-year prison sentence; there has been no Presidential pardon. Neither man constituted a danger to public safety, but both should have been disbarred to prevent future misconduct in their capacity as lawyers and given heavy fines at least to deprive them of the fruits of their misconduct. Here political considerations provided grossly unequal treatment for similarly situated individuals.

Darryl B., a poor black child who played hookey from school because he was hyperkinetic and could not sit still, was imprisoned in a juvenile detention center for several years. A middle-class white boy, similarly afflicted, was sent to a special school for emotionally disturbed children by the same court. A wealthy industrialist accused of committing sodomy on a young girl was given a suspended sentence. The judge found he had been sufficiently "punished" by the disgrace. A poor, obscure man who paid boys to engage in sodomy with him was given a long jail sentence after a psychiatric report indicated that his prognosis was poor. Significantly, the latest word from the psychiatric profession is that homosexuality is not an illness. Here, as in most cases, wealth and social status constitute major factors in sentencing. People who commit similar crimes are treated in very different ways. Mr. Seymour states, "The irrational disparities referred to are not abstract numbers but real flesh-and-blood problems involving the sense of justice and fair play of individual human beings. . . . Fairness in sentencing is absolutely basic to any system of justice."

Certainly it is unfair and unjust to treat people who have committed the same crime, both first offenders or both multiple offenders, differently. Psychiatry looks at the convict and what he is believed to need from an individualized, therapeutic point of view. The sentence recommended for A is not compared with that recommended for B. The psychiatrist sees one as a sociopath and another as a paranoid and recommends different sentences although the objective facts are the same.

In prison furlough and prerelease programs, the use of psychiatric criteria instead of rules, properly promulgated and equally enforced, causes many unnecessary problems. Prisoner A, who has served only six months of a three-year sentence, is given a weekend furlough because the psychiatrist believes the change will be therapeutic for him. Prisoner B, who has also served six months of a three-year sentence, does not receive a furlough because his adjustment is better and the psychiatrist does not believe he requires such "therapy." Both prisoners view the furlough as a bonus for good behavior. Hostility and rage at the patent discrimination is inevitable.

The substitution of therapy or rehabilitation for law inevitably leads to disparities in sentencing and a debasement of the principle of equal justice under law. It may even be that a recognition of fair treatment is in itself therapeutic. Certainly unequal treatment provokes hostility, rage and a pervasive contempt for the legal system.

The socially desirable goal of rehabilitating the convict has been confused with the legal function of making a finding of guilt or innocence and the imposition of a sentence established by the legislature. There can be little question that many of the jails and prisons in the United States for both children and adults are brutal, barbarous and medieval institutions and that they promote criminality rather than rehabilitation. Understandably, no judge with any sensitivity or regard for the well-being of the convict is eager to commit a child or adult to such an institution unless the crime is so heinous or the defendant so dangerous that he must be locked up. The criminal courts are, therefore, engaged in the unending recycling of law violators. They pursue the futile task of trying and convicting accused persons and then releasing them on probation for therapeutic purposes. The "scientific" basis of such therapy is dubious, to say the least. The attention of the legal profession has been diverted from the pursuit of justice to the pursuit of therapy. The basic question of whether it is *just* to jail an indigent thief who cannot make restitution and to release the more affluent thief who embezzles stock instead of burglarizing stores is all but overlooked in the futile and nonlegal quest for "rehabilitation."

Political and pragmatic considerations often have militated against the application of established legal principles to the great detriment of the law. A conspicuous example of unequal treatment of similarly situated persons arises in the retroactive application of judicial decisions. A court cannot ignore practicalities of government administration. But it is startling to read an opinion of the United States Supreme Court which acknowledges the unequal results of its own decision and justifies such inequality on the grounds of expediency. This is what happened in the "line-up"

cases. For generations it was the custom of law-enforcement personnel to bring witnesses in to the police station or jail to view a
suspect in order to identify him. The victims of crime or eyewitnesses to a crime were shown a person behind bars and then asked,
"Is this the man?" Obviously, the power of suggestion was great.
The police had found someone they believed was the criminal,
and the perplexed and uncertain citizen usually replied, "It looks
like him." The next time the witness saw the accused was at a
hearing. The identification of this person as the criminal was
repeated. By the time of trial, the witness making the identification for the third or fourth time had convinced himself that in fact
and without doubt the accused was the guilty person.

The Supreme Court, after denying repeated petitions raising
this question, suddenly turned its attention to the problem. The
solution was, as it always had been, obvious. A proper and reliable
identification can be made only if the witness is shown a group of
persons with similar physical characteristics in a line-up and asked
to identify the guilty one. The power of suggestion is removed by
this simple procedure. As a concomitant to ensuring that a line-up
is properly conducted, the Court specified that the accused had
the right to have counsel present.

Having so decided, the Court drew back from this application
of fundamental principle and declared that even though it was
unjust, no one convicted as a result of such improper identification
was entitled to a new trial except the particular individuals whose
cases it had chosen to hear. This was a rule for the future. The
Court stated: "We recognize that Wade and Gilbert are, therefore, the only victims of pretrial confrontations in the absence of
their counsel to have the benefit of the rules established in their
cases. . . . Inequity arguably results from according the benefit of a
new rule to the parties in the case in which it is announced but not
to other litigants similarly situated in the trial or appellate process
who have raised the same issue." [8] Expediency in the face of
difficult problems is a political solution, not a legal one.

The law has often been utilized to give a patina of propriety to a
decision that is wholly outside the legal system. The decision to

remove Americans of Japanese ancestry from the West Coast of the United States after the attack on Pearl Harbor was based on military considerations in wartime. It was done without leave of court. But within two years the Supreme Court sanctioned the classification of citizens by racial ancestry without any proof or even any allegation of individual misconduct, dereliction or clear and present danger to national survival. The Supreme Court sustained the conviction of a native-born American of Japanese ancestry who had not moved from the West Coast. No question was raised as to Korematsu's loyalty. Ignoring established principles requiring proof of individual misconduct and evidence of a factual situation of clear and present danger, the Court took judicial notice that there was "reasonable ground for believing that the threat [of espionage and sabotage by citizens of Japanese ancestry] . . . is real." [9] Time has shown that the "real" threat was as imaginary and unreliable as the scientific principles of eugenics, psychiatry and literary criticism on which the court had relied in the decisions previously discussed.

The most conspicuous uses of legal sanction for political purposes were the Nuremberg and Japanese war crime trials. These were conducted largely by American lawyers and American judges applying principles of Anglo-American common law to defendants who did not subscribe to this law and who were not under the jurisdiction of these courts when the alleged crimes were committed. Most significantly, there was no recognized crime against humanity in the conduct of war until after the defeat of the Axis powers. It was an ex post facto law. The concept of creating crimes after the event is repugnant to the common law. It is prohibited by the Constitution.

The political problem of dealing with a defeated enemy required a high moral tone. After Auschwitz, Bergen-Belsen, the Bataan Death March and scores of other acts of cruelty and inhumanity, the time-honored practice of lining defeated enemies against a wall and shooting them seemed to be both too brutal and too humane. It was necessary to expose the wickedness of the foe and *then* kill him. Very few members of the legal profession questioned the legality or propriety of using the judicial process for such political purposes. On the contrary, the war trials were lauded as an advance in civilized jurisprudence. General Yamashita, it was admitted, had no knowledge of the slaughter in the Philippines. He was found guilty,[10] although it is a fundamental tenet of the American law that there must be mens rea, a criminal intent, before one can be convicted. In time, the moral fervor and indignation of the victims waned. The public lost interest. In the end the legal process was used to acquit German generals who had directed and actively participated in the slaying of hundreds and thousands of innocent civilians.

Americans confronted with the evidence of wanton murder at My Lai, Bach Mai and many other villages and cities in Indochina are caught in the moral dilemma of the "good" and not-so-good Germans. Americans are torn between the ties of duty to obey the commands of the United States Government and revulsion against senseless killing. Telford Taylor, professor of law and former *chief prosecutor at the Nuremberg war crimes trials,* went to Hanoi to make a personal observation. He reported, "The results of our bombing undeniably are horrible, but Hanoi is not the only city that has undergone such horror. Immoral and senseless this bombing may well be, *but where is the law* under which to call it criminal? . . . Confronted with the appalling consequences, a legal approach to these events is bound to provoke impatience." [11]

It is ironical that the prosecutor at Nuremberg apparently had no difficulty then in finding a law, albeit ex post facto, that the defeated enemy had violated. Twenty-five years later, he looks in vain for a law which Americans violate when they slaughter civilians in Indochina. Significantly, there is the precedent of Nuremberg, which eliminates the ex post facto argument. Americans were put on notice at Nuremberg that there is a concept of crimes against humanity, that a soldier has a legal duty to disobey an order that requires him to commit a crime against humanity.

These are only a handful of examples of the uses of the law and legal trials to achieve social, political or military ends. The results are unequal treatment of persons by race or national origin, unequal treatment of equally guilty criminals, unequal treatment of one's countrymen and foreign enemies, unequal treatment of citizens and violations of the Constitution. Such clearly unjust decisions are inevitable when the legal process is wrenched from the context of the Constitution, when the limits upon the jurisdiction of courts and lawmakers are ignored in order to accomplish extralegal purposes.

The arguments of science, internal social problems and foreign policy, which seemed so compelling at the time, in retrospect appear to be little more than political expedience, sicklied o'er with the pale cast of law. Lawyers and judges debase the legal process when they presume to act as scientists, sociologists and statesmen.

Role-playing may be a useful experimentation device. In encounter sessions, husbands and wives assume each other's parts. Children act as parents and parents as children. Prisoners act as judges and judges as prisoners. The participants may gain understanding of the other party; they may even experience empathy. Everyone, of course, knows that this is just an experiment, a game of limited duration. When it is over, each person will resume his real-life status and functions. It is hoped that he will have a wider and deeper understanding, but it is not contemplated that children shall become their parents or that parents shall actually live as children.

The American legal system is now engaging in a dangerous form of role-playing, not as an experimental device for learning purposes but as an unauthorized transference of functions. Many lawyers and judges are aware of the limitations of their knowledge and their capacity to understand and treat wisely the people whose problems are entrusted to them. They assume that other disciplines are better able to deal with these difficult problems. Often this is true.

Neither lawyers nor judges are therapists. They cannot treat emotionally disturbed or mentally ill persons, chronic alcoholics or drug addicts. This is obvious. But it does not logically follow that a psychiatrist or other therapist can or should assume legal functions with respect to people who have such problems. The determination of guilt or innocence is a legal question. The decision to impose a penalty on a law violator is also a legal decision. It cannot be delegated to a psychiatrist. The therapist's proper function in the context of the legal system is to *offer* treatment to those who have violated the law if the therapist in his professional judgment believes that such treatment is needed and may be helpful. It is not his role to recommend to the judge incarceration *for the purpose* of treating problem people.

The decision to prosecute an alleged law violator is also a legal one. It should be made by the duly elected or appointed public prosecutor on the basis of legally admissible evidence that the suspect has committed a violation of law. The prosecutor is not a social worker. He cannot make an informed and valid decision that a child needs "help" or that unhappy spouses need "counseling." All too often, however, a child or parent is petitioned into court by a social worker in order to compel the child or his family to accept guidance and counseling. The sanctions of the law are utilized to compel treatment. This is a common practice in the United States.

Law is frequently perverted, then, by legal authorities for purposes deemed to be therapeutic, scientific or socially desirable. Correlatively, prosecutors, defenders, legislators, and judges abdicate their powers and their exercise of judgment to professionals from other disciplines whose methods and purposes are at variance with the role and function of law. The prosecution of people for the purpose of therapy, of helping, of changing their life-styles is not a legitimate function of law. Those who are financially able and emotionally secure resist such prosecutions. Usually they are successful in invoking the protections of the law. People who are poor, ignorant, helpless or simply outside the mainstream of socially approved philosophy or manners are seldom able to defend themselves against the forces of law which are being utilized against them for illegal purposes. The result again is unequal treatment under the rubric of due process, and public acceptance of the rule of law is further weakened.

It is apparent that the jurisprudential effort to make law scientific or value-free has had the opposite result. Scientific theories, social beliefs and political expedience have strongly affected the entire legal system in all its aspects, from the enactment of laws to the imposition of sentences and the management of prisons. The quest for equal justice has all but been ignored in the search for other values.

Equal treatment of similarly situated people is a sine qua non of justice. Professor Rawls proposes learnedly that justice is fairness. But such circular argument begs the question. Fairness and equal treatment under law are very different in concept and in actuality. We must recognize that all persons are not created equal. Some are healthy. Barring accidents they will live without physical pain for eighty or ninety years. Others are ill. They will suffer and die at an early age. Intelligence—however it is defined or measured—is not equally apportioned. Talent—musical, artistic, athletic, even the talent for making money—is capriciously and unequally allotted. Physical attractiveness, sexual allure, the capacity for joy, sensitivity to beauty—all attributes which make life enjoyable and the lack of which makes life miserable—are unevenly distributed among the population. Good luck and mischance do not even follow the law of probabilities. Some people have a disproportionate share of tragedy, hardship and sorrows. Others, who may be selfish, greedy, cruel or worthless, are nonetheless spared sorrow, pain and privation. Airplanes crash, automobiles collide, buildings burn. Purely by chance some individuals are victims and others are spared. Bombs fall on the just and unjust alike. Thornton Wilder's little tale of "The Bridge of San Luis Rey," told the life stories of the people who perished in the collapse of the bridge. The author found a purpose for the death of each of these seemingly innocent victims of an accident. This is charming fiction. Reality is random and reasonless. Life itself is unfair.

The quest to make law yield "fairness" is called "affirmative action" or "compensatory treatment." In essence, it proposes the unequal treatment under law of similarly situated persons for a presumed greater social good. The stated ideal of communism— "To each according to his needs; from each according to his abilities"—establishes such a goal of fairness. Under this slogan, the poor, the ignorant, the defective, the ill and the untalented should receive more from the state than the healthy, intelligent, gifted and able citizens. More should be required of the latter than from the former. The fact that no communist government has remotely attempted to effectuate this goal of fairness is irrelevant to this discussion. One must recognize that this ideal of fairness differs fundamentally from the American ideal of equal justice under law. The graduated income tax and the proposed negative income tax are small and peripheral measures to mitigate the economic unfairnesses of life. But even within the complicated structure of the graduated income tax, with its allowances for dependents and deductions for expenses and charities, the law purports to treat people with equal incomes equally.

The goal of fairness is appealing. We speak of each person having a right to his fair share of the good things in life. Does this mean that the less intelligent should have a better education than the more intelligent? Or does it mean the obverse? Should the dull, monotonous, back-breaking, dirty jobs be compensated more highly than interesting, challenging, intellectually and emotionally satisfying employment? The questions are endless. The answers elusive.

Are these so-called rights a social goal or legally enforceable entitlements? This is a basic juridical issue frequently overlooked in programs for a great society, a war on poverty and the abortive federal-state partnership.

In posing this question, I do not suggest that the gross and growing disparities between rich and poor, between the impoverished nonwhite inner-city residents and the white affluent dwellers in suburbia and exurbia are ineradicable or that government should not take bold and meaningful steps to lessen or eliminate these inequities. There are many ways in which the burdens and benefits of life could be more evenly distributed by changes in the economy, education and public services. But the function of law under the Constitution is to secure equal treatment of all individuals. In confusing these two goals, in attempting to utilize law to restructure society, the family, the economy and the diverse individuals and groups in the United States, not only have we failed to promote fairness we have also undermined the basic principle of equal justice. To cite a simple, common example: Under civil service laws and other public employment regulations, jobs are required to be filled on a merit basis. If the tests are properly designed to test fitness for the work to be done and are not racially or culturally biased and do not demand irrelevant attainments, should the best-qualified person be hired? Or should the job be filled on the basis of racial or sex quotas, or economic need, or moral or sexual standards? Similar questions are being asked with respect to admissions to institutions of learning, faculty employment, membership on boards of corporations, foundations and public and quasi-public bodies. In the past, job preference in the private sector was given to white male Anglo-Saxon Protestants. All others were often absolutely debarred or hired only when there was a shortage of preferred applicants. Catholics, Jews, blacks, women (especially married women) and homosexuals were second- or third-class citizens. Some were "invisible" or nonpersons. It has taken decades of education, legislation and litigation to obtain legal recognition of the right of the individual to public and private employment and access to education on a merit basis. The public also has an interest in obtaining the services of able employees, competent teachers, doctors, lawyers and scientists.

This legal principle of equal treatment is now being jeopardized by confusing legal rights with the socially desirable goal of encouraging the advancement of those previously subjected to discrimination. Illegal preference is, of necessity, also illegal discrimination. Unequal treatment, that is, treatment based not on merit but upon race, sex, economic or marital status or sexual behavior patterns is illegal no matter how benign the intentions or socially popular the ends sought to be achieved.[12]

"Fairness" is no more a substitute for justice than mercy or might. Both compassion and power often masquerade as law. The legal system is often perverted to serve the interests of the powerful, and only occasionally used to mitigate the hardships of the unfortunate. Appeals for mercy, compassion and qualities other than justice are commonly heard in courts of law. Often a lawyer will argue that despite proof beyond a reasonable doubt that his client is guilty, the court should acquit the defendant because he is poor and will lose his job, or because he is a prominent citizen and should not be disgraced, or because she is a mother, or because he is old. The poor person's need for a job or the mother's need to care for her children should appropriately be given consideration in imposing the penalty, but these matters are irrelevant to the issue of guilt or innocence. It is not necessary to incarcerate a harmless old man, a mother of young children, or the hardworking provider for his family. Often a kindly judge will dismiss charges with the offhand remark, "Today is senior citizen's day," or, "In the circumstances of this defendant I can find a reasonable doubt." The intentions of all concerned are benevolent. In the cases of wealthy and powerful clients, the pleas are seldom made openly. But courts will find doubt where none exists. Neither corruption *nor* softness is compatible with justice.

The conceptual bases of the law have for too long been ignored, while the legal profession has been concerned with a wide variety of specific problems. The answers have been sought in the sciences with little regard for the distortion and destruction of the law which ensued. A nation of scofflaws must find in its legal institutions and in the operation of the law, ideals, beliefs and principles more enduring and compelling than the transient intellectual chic. Law is not a problem-solving tool. Unlike science, it cannot adopt and discard hypotheses to conform to the latest data derived from the laboratory or the computer. The challenge to the legal profession and to the concerned citizen is to reformulate a definition of justice upon the basis of which the legal system can operate with equal treatment for all.

I do not know whether such a reformulation of justice is possible or whether it would achieve acceptance by the legal bureaucracy and the public. However, ignoring this fundamental question of the nature of justice will not cause the problem to disappear. The ostrich solution can only result in the spreading and acceleration of scofflawism with all its perils.

As we have seen, the drafting of one comprehensive statute in a narrow field, such as the Uniform Commercial Code, required years of work by eminent authorities and adequate financing. The drafting of a code is a work of technical craftsmanship. Of course, understanding of social, political and economic factors as well as principles of law is essential to achieve good results. How much more difficult will be the conceptualization and reduction to legal forms and language of the elusive notion of justice. We no longer have philosopher kings to assume such a monumental task. The problem today would doubtless daunt a Hammurabi. Can the government summon a great Sanhedrin to determine the meaning of justice? Great documents and enduring ideas have come from such ad hoc groups as King James council to translate the Bible, the American Constitutional Convention, and the French ency-clopedists. Surely it is worth trying.

New ideas and concepts which have altered global thinking usually have not been the work of committees but of private individuals such as Thoreau, Locke and Aristotle. Neither the people nor their governments can command originality or genius to order. But the climate in which new ideas and ideals will flourish can be promoted. Institutionally and popularly we must have a hospitality to the idea of justice and a concern for its formulation. Other times and places have succeeded in creating a hospitable climate for various forms of human endeavor. The populace of renaissance Florence was sufficiently concerned and aware that the people voted intelligently to select the winning design for the doors of the Baptistry. Elizabethan England saw an efflorescence of literature, ideas, geographic exploration and the growth of the human spirit. Americans are no less intelligent, inventive or creative. But are we as a nation sufficiently concerned and aware to undertake this great and fundamental search for justice? Never before has there been the technological means for a national discussion of issues and ideas which now exist in the United States. I believe that if the need is recognized, the legal profession, the media of communication and the academicians can cooperate in such an undertaking. The possibilities of realizing a new consensus as to law and justice may not appear to be promising. But the alternative is indeed bleak.

I would rather hear the first
philosopher of limits
sing his small song in the dust.
        Loren Eiseley, *The Boundary Keepers*

13: The Limits of Law

The philosophy of the possible does not excite anyone. It offers no instant panacea, no quest for a grail of justice, no cause to which the idealistic can devote themselves and no dream by which the power-hungry can manipulate the masses. A generation ago philosopher Morris Raphael Cohen asked, "What can or may the law achieve, and what is beyond its power or proper domain?" This question has been ignored by the legal profession and the public. Instead, we delude ourselves by thinking that the answers to all the complex and seemingly intractable problems of individual behavior, group conduct, national organization and international peace are to be found in law. Columnist James Reston writes: "The unity of the nation, the problems of Watergate, impeachment, inflation, jobs, unemployment, and particularly trust in the American system of government are probably not going to be settled by the struggling and confused men in the White House,

319

the Congress and the press but in the end by the courts." This is typical of the misplaced faith in law. The struggling and confused men and women on the bench cannot decide the routine criminal and civil cases with promptness and justice, let alone right the wrongs of the entire social order. It is too easy for the rest of the community to absolve themselves of responsibility by putting the onus on the law and the courts. The ancient Greeks might see in the shocking shambles of American government and ethics and our national lawlessness the inevitable penalty for this sin of hubris, pride in our vaunted rule of law.

The United States has embraced a faith in the omnipotence and omniscience of law at its peril. This belief may be stated succinctly as Forer's formula: "Outlaw the problem and avoid the solution."

While this may sound facetious, the belief in the power of law to abolish problems has, in fact, dominated much of our domestic and foreign policy during the twentieth century. The naïveté of this faith in the power of law is more readily visible in the sphere of foreign relations. Despite the manifest failure of all international organizations to prevent war or to impose peace, belief in world peace through world law persists. Perhaps the most fatuous example of the strength of this belief was the award of the Nobel Peace Prize in 1926 to M. Briand, who had devised a pact for "outlawing" war. It was followed by World War II and the numerous declared and undeclared wars waged by the signatories ever since. John Foster Dulles, a lawyer, devoted much of his time as a most energetic secretary of state to drafting and executing pacts and treaties. He applied to the delicate and complex problems of foreign relations the common law principle of contracts: an agreement signed and sealed by consenting parties is valid, binding and enforceable. It was apparently his belief that these international contracts, once signed by officials of the nations involved, would compel those countries to conduct their affairs in accordance with the treaties or pacts. The fact that the consideration for the agreement was inadequate—some nations gave up or promised more than others—that in many cases it was coerced by the implicit threat of military might and that there was no court or other body with judicial or actual power to enforce the contract did not deter him. The Kaiser's remark prior to World War I that a treaty is only a "scrap of paper" was forgotten. The truth of Santayana's famous aphorism that those who do not learn the lessons of history are doomed to repeat them has been affirmed in blood and suffering too many times.

When one turns to domestic problems, the belief in the power of law is virtually unchallenged. The endemic scofflawism and the failure of the legal system to meet the expectations placed upon it have already been documented here. Now it is appropriate to ask what lessons can be learned from the passing of the rule of law in the United States.

§The most obvious lesson is that the American propensity for passing laws to outlaw popular and popularly accepted behavior has not succeeded in changing public manners or mores. It is not merely futile to attempt to use the power of law to enforce standards of morals and behavior; it is also destructive to the legal system and the viability of law. The history of prohibition, with its continuing aftermath of a well-organized, wealthy and powerful underworld, should have taught us that laws prohibiting the use of drugs would be no more successful than laws prohibiting the ingestion of alcoholic beverages. Nonetheless, on both federal and state levels, Americans continue to pass laws prohibiting not merely the sale of drugs but the use of drugs. The creation of "drug courts" by the state of New York at enormous public expense will not materially curb the use of drugs. The drug users will continue to be scofflaws. The judges placed in the unhappy and preposterous position of imposing mandated severe and harsh penalties will "bend" the law to avoid enforcing it. Ultimately, it is the credibility of law and the viability of the legal system that is harmed by such legislation and the use of the legal system to enforce unenforceable laws.

Dr. Norman E. Zinberg, who has studied the problem of drug addiction, concluded that law is not the answer to this problem.

"We must think more about social control than legal control," he urged—in vain. It is evident that drug use by large numbers of nonaddicted persons will continue so long as it is socially acceptable behavior.

§The second lesson is that nonvolitional behavior cannot be controlled by law. Law is based on the behavior of rational people who can make a volitional choice between obedience to law and violation of law, assuming that they will calculate the cost/benefits of violation and conclude that crime does not pay. If the individual makes the wrong choice, he will be punished. But when people are unable to control their behavior the proscriptions and penalties of law are meaningless. Despite the knowledge that certain conduct is illegal, that it may be followed by arrest, trial and punishment, some individuals still cannot restrain their own behavior. For them law is also a futility and a meaningless expense for society. It is obvious that a drug addict cannot be "cured" by prosecution, conviction of crime and incarceration. Many drug addicts who appear in court tell me, "Prison is just like the street, Your Honor. Nothin' but talk of drugs. Drugs are just as easy to get on the inside as on the outside." The judge, sworn to uphold the law, must impose penalties that are not beneficial either to society or the defendant.

Chronic alcoholism too is a crime. Approximately one-third of all persons convicted of crime are convicted of some form of drunkenness. They are no more able than the drug addicts to stop this habit. Law, with its sanctions and penalties, is meaningless to the alcoholic. Similarly, problems of sexual deviancy are not susceptible to legal remedies. Many homosexuals began their practice while in prison. So long as they are deprived of heterosexual contacts, they will inevitably continue their homosexual behavior. Once released from confinement, they may or may not continue these practices.

If cigarette smoking were made a crime, it would not materially reduce smoking. Such a law would, however, create a flourishing illegal tobacco business. Once legislation outlawing any behavior has been enacted, the entire machinery of the legal system—police, lawyers, courts, prisons, probation and parole —becomes involved in the effort to apprehend, try, convict, incarcerate and "rehabilitate" people who will, despite all penalties, persist in such behavior. The only conclusion that can be logically drawn is that behavior which the individual cannot control society cannot feasibly control by the simplistic method of "outlawing" it. The diversion of the time and financial resources of the legal system to this futile task simply overloads the system and makes it less able to function in other matters, such as murder, rape, embezzlement and corporate crime, which are its proper and essential function. The credibility and viability of the legal system are drastically eroded by this misapplication of a rational process to irrational and uncontrollable behavior.

§The third lesson is that legal intervention in the lives of noncriminals creates criminality. For more than three-quarters of a century the juvenile courts have been using the law and the legal structure to impose certain standards of behavior on children who persistently resist these efforts. Juvenile courts have not reduced truancy, the number of runaways or misbehavior on the part of young people. If anything, incarceration and other legal punishments have enforced antisocial behavior. This "intervention" in the lives of children by law and the institutions of law admittedly has failed. Tens of thousands of children incarcerated "for their own good" have been started on a life of crime by the legal system. Nonetheless, juvenile courts continue to jail children who have not committed crimes.

Similar efforts to establish compulsory regulation of adults under the aegis of law are growing in popularity. It is an undeniable fact that divorce is extremely popular, indeed, commonplace, regardless of religious or moral teachings or personal and legal obligations to spouse and children. The answer of many states is to enact laws establishing compulsory conciliation before permitting divorce. Legislators operate under the naïve faith that the power of law will enable social workers and marriage counselors successfully to patch up broken marriages and keep hostile spouses living together and maintaining a home for their children despite all evidence to the contrary. The causes of broken marriages are many: psychological, economic, sexual, sociological and even philosophical. The brute force of law, even when disguised as benign helping administered by social workers, cannot solve or even ameliorate these problems. When the causes of disruption are not legal, the force of law is unlikely to solve the difficulties.

§The fourth lesson is that conduct that is not considered deviant by the participants and a sizable segment of society cannot be controlled by the process of criminalizing that conduct. The causes of much illegal behavior are to be found in specific environments in which such actions are not deemed to be deviant or antisocial. Gang membership by slum youths is a way of life, not too dissimilar in many aspects from fraternity or club membership in other strata of society. Crimes committed by gang members should and must be prosecuted under law. The police must seek to apprehend the mugger, robber or slayer whether or not he is a gang member. Government attorneys must prosecute the suspects, and the courts must try the cases and convict those found guilty of the crimes charged. The judges who try many of these cases, as well as the lawyers who prosecute and defend them, all know that conviction and incarceration of one youth will not deter other similarly situated youths from joining gangs and being drawn into crime. Yet hundreds of millions of dollars are spent each year on "gang control," which usually consists of police surveillance of gang members. Gang membership has not dropped, nor has crime. The futility of such legal controls, however, has not been admitted. The programs continue, co-existing with the gang society, neither affecting the other. Gang "rumbles" will continue despite the tragedy of senseless killing and maiming so long as it is approved in the subculture in which the gang members live.

Other crimes in other social milieux are socially acceptable. Cheating on one's income tax, selling worthless or harmful pharmaceuticals, and manufacturing substandard products are considered socially acceptable behavior in many strata of society. Bribing public officials, accepting kickbacks, cheating the public, are all considered part of the political process by large numbers of people. Among other groups, "ripping off" is approved conduct.

We must accept the fact that the controls which law can exercise over any conduct are specific and limited. The law acts only *after* the fact and only on named individuals charged with specific violations of statutes and ordinances. It does not operate directly on other individuals or groups. Law does not and cannot directly change attitudes, motives, or the social ambience in which such crimes and antisocial acts occur. It has little preventive power. To reduce crime and the prevailing scofflawism of Americans, it is necessary to look to means and methods beyond and apart from the law. Professor B. F. Skinner's suggestion of social controls to encourage and reward desirable conduct and to make socially undesirable conduct unattractive cannot be cavalierly dismissed as totalitarian or antihumanistic. Brainwashing, coercion, economic privation, incarceration in prisons and mental institutions, and social isolation are some of the methods of social control employed by totalitarian governments. Abhorrence of such methods, however, should not foreclose considerations of other social controls which are consonant with freedom and dignity.

Americans are now subjected to many forms of influence which are not antihumanistic or violative of individual liberty and Constitutional rights, although the results may be the enrichment of a few at the expense of many. Americans are induced by advertisers to spend voluntarily billions of dollars for products they believe will make them slim, youthful-looking, attractive, and sexually alluring. Tens of thousands of young Americans who have little academic interest or talent have been induced to spend thousands of dollars and years of their lives in pursuit of college degrees which they believe will increase their earning capacity and raise their social status. Dedicated people with minimal amounts of money have awakened the nation to ecological dangers. We have been taught to abhor fat, wrinkles, dingy wash and forest fires. We have been induced to believe that an automobile is a necessity, and perhaps a sexual symbol. A counter movement toward bicycling and jogging is now growing in popularity. This change in taste and habits was produced with very little expenditure of money.

Our present ignorance of how public sentiment changes should not preclude the investigation of the methods and means by which such changes are induced. If the public as a whole can be persuaded to shun violence, chicanery and lying, the law will be better able to function. Society will be more secure and stable and the values of equal justice and the rule of law will be less endangered.

The Beatles in less than a decade changed popular taste in music. Bluejeans, the working clothes of the poor, suddenly became the favorite attire of the jet set, college students and even the young people behind the Iron Curtain. Why? How? These questions cannot be answered now. But this nongovernmental, noncoercive power to change public attitudes is a potent force which should not be ignored in our efforts to control crime and antisocial behavior.

If one examines popular forms of entertainment today, it is evident that violence is glorified in many of the art forms, especially literature, drama, cinema. It is the violence of the gun, the smashing fist, and the brutal sexual encounter which is seen on the movie screen and television and described graphically in bestsellers and books lauded by critics, for example, Kubrick's film "A Clockwork Orange," depicting brutal violence; and Mailer's novel "An American Dream," in which the hero murders his wife and gets away with it. The irony of the title seems to have escaped many critics. Americans have a continuing preoccupation with violence—whether it be the Old West, organized crime, or the new black violence. This is reflected in literature, movies and TV shows such as *Wyatt Earp, The Godfather* and *Shaft*.

It should not surprise us, then, that muggings and forcible rape have risen more rapidly than other crimes. Even fashions in violence change. In Elizabethan England bear-baiting and public hanging were popular forms of mass entertainment. Such exhibitions would be considered barbaric today. Although illicit sex has existed throughout history, usually in secret, forcible rape of total strangers seems to be peculiarly a characteristic of the present time. Is there a relationship between the prevalence of this crime and popular literature and drama? These are questions not solely for psychiatrists like Dr. Bruno Bettelheim but for the citizen and those involved in the legal system. I am not suggesting censorship, which is practically unsuccessful and ideologically incompatible with a free society. I am, however, proposing to use popular taste for constructive rather than destructive purposes without the ineffective coercive power of law.

The reaction of the establishment in the United States to changes in taste appears to follow a pattern: aesthetic disapproval, then moral denunciation, and finally legislation and futile efforts at law enforcement. Ultimately, after years of vain efforts to enforce unpopular laws, tastes change and the laws are permitted to become dead letters.

If there is sufficient opposition, the laws may be repealed. Disapproval of the Southeast Asia war followed this pattern: violation of draft laws, repeated arrests, and prosecutions of antiwar demonstrators; as the mood of the nation changed, the judges imposed progressively lighter sentences and juries refused to convict; ultimately compulsory military conscription was repealed. The same pattern prevailed with respect to the use of marijuana. First, it was denounced. Medical opinions given with certainty ranged from "scientific findings" that marijuana was physically and mentally harmful and led to addiction to hard drugs to the equally certain and scientific opinion that it was harmless. Nonetheless all the machinery of the law was invoked in a vain effort to halt marijuana smoking. Sentences were so severe that large segments of the public became outraged. Again, some courts and juries refused to convict despite clear evidence of guilt. Finally the prosecutors ignored violations and the legislatures of some states reduced the penalties. The machinery of the courts was invoked to undo the most severe and shocking, though legal, penalties which had been imposed.

If one examines so frivolous and peripheral a matter as hair styles, this same pattern becomes clearly evident. Male and female hair styles have been subject to change from prehistoric times. Decorations on shards of pottery, walls of ruined palaces, ancient carvings and statues reveal boundless human ingenuity in arranging the hair and clothing or decorating the body. What tribal elders or the governing caste of early societies thought of these changes in fashion we do not know. But the reactions of upper-class Stuart England to a dramatic change in male hair dress is a matter of record. Long, flowing locks, elaborately curled, and huge wigs were the appropriate male hirsute adornment. The sudden appearance of men with short-cropped hair, the "round heads," was greeted with scorn, disapproval, moral outrage and even violence. As with almost all fashions, the old styles ultimately gave way to the new. But it is interesting to note that England did not enact laws forbidding men to cut their hair and compelling them to wear long, curly locks. Nor did the British courts clutter their dockets with cases involving the right to wear short hair. In the past decade in the United States, the reverse change in fashions occurred. Long hair, instead of short, became popular among the young. It spread to the middle-aged and the wealthy. Nonetheless, public schools expelled boys who wore their hair long. The courts became involved in the litigation of this earth-shaking issue. Constitutional rights of the youths and the school systems were invoked. Policemen, firemen and other public employees were fired from their jobs for wearing long hair and moustaches. Government agencies issued regulations as to the legal length of sideburns, head hair and facial hair. Moral issues were raised. Again the law was invoked and battles over freedom of expression, pension rights, union rights and countless other questions were brought to court. Inevitably styles, in their mysterious manner, changed, and hair became shorter for the moment. But the law was bruised if not shorn by this use of the power of the state and the machinery of the legal system in an attempt to compel conformity to outmoded fashions.

A hypothetical rational visitor from another planet would be struck by the absurdity of debasing the power and sanctity of the law and utilizing the courts to resolve such unimportant questions. This apparently trivial example illustrates the fatal overuse of the law to control behavior and the relative inability of the law, even when backed with the powers of police, courts, prisons and the militia, to prevail against popular taste.

Since social controls are exercised in our society most effectively through public entertainment, the mass media, and paid advertisements, is there any reason why such methods, completely compatible with Constitutional rights, should not be used to change the prevailing climate from one which promotes violence to one which abhors it? The Russian child who drops a piece of paper on the street or subway is scolded by any adults who happen to be present. The child is not beaten or taken to juvenile court. He feels the hostility and disapproval of the people on the street. In the United States severe laws and the most energetic efforts of the police and courts have failed to curb the spray-can graffiti that deface American buildings and the litter which accumulates in streets, parks and walkways. Increasing the penalties for such acts and hiring more and more policemen will not curb this behavior. The user of the spray can does not calculate his chances of being caught; he does not weigh the cost of the penalty if caught against the psychic benefit of defacing property. He unthinkingly adopts a pastime which is in vogue among his peers and for which he feels no social pressure of scorn or obloquy. Such irrational, popular activities are not controlled by law but by popular taste.

The limits of the legal sanction in determining or changing public appetites, manners and amusements should be recognized and acknowledged. We have experimented with the shocking remedy of psychosurgical control of antisocial or criminal behavior, but on the whole we rely on the belief that contempt for law will automatically be eliminated by prosecution, conviction and punishment. Between such an uncritical reliance on law alone and drastic surgery there is a vast uncharted area to explore. What social controls are consonant with individual liberty and humanity? What controls promise a likelihood of effecting social change, not merely isolating, sterilizing or "restructuring" individuals? If the problem is, as I believe it to be, that American society breeds a contempt for law, then the solution is to change the attitudinal values of the society. The thrust of this book has been to make it clear that imposition of more and harsher laws will only increase the contempt. Government must look to the tastemakers, not the courts, to make respect for law popular and contempt for law unfashionable, passé—in other words, unacceptable to the vast majority of the people.

Reformers in many areas of activity are beginning to recognize the limits of law and litigation as tools of social engineering. They realize that enactment of laws and abrasive litigation have not solved their problems. Many seemingly significant battles were won in the courtroom, but the wars against poverty, discrimination and misuse of national resources have been lost. The problems were outlawed but no solutions were found. Recognizing that the basis of many of these problems, which recur in courtroom confrontation, lies in economic conditions rather than law, perceptive reformers are looking to economic tools rather than the law as a means of bringing about change. The Sierra Club, which has for decades utilized litigation as one of the principal methods of carrying on its fight to curb pollution and to conserve natural resources, is now looking to other means of action. Michael McCloskey and Julia Hillis of the Sierra Club report: ". . . conservationists have looked to legal solutions to curb this conduct [industrial pollution]. When private legal remedies such as the nuisance action failed to cope with the onslaught of pollution, they then looked to government to use its police power to devise regulatory schemes to abate excessive pollution, with prosecution authorized and penalties provided. The schemes that have been developed, which first looked to setting air and water quality standards and now look to specific discharge standards, continue to make disappointing progress. Despite years of work and continuing revision of the laws, the overall problems seem to be getting worse." [1] McCloskey and Hillis suggest economic deterrents and incentives instead of legal sanctions and litigation.

The economic carrot might prove to be more effective than the legal club. Obviously the primary motivation of industry is profit. Pollution and waste of resources could be made unprofitable through taxation. Antipollutive measures and conservation, if given economic incentives through tax write-offs, capital funding and similar measures, could be made profitable. The solution to what are essentially business practices can be found by society through government incentives compatible with business practices and motivations. Ineffective legal sanctions are not society's only means of dealing with these urgent problems.

Many other problems now being litigated as great Constitutional issues also have their roots in economic conditions. For example, de facto segregation of public schools in the Northern states is primarily an economic problem. The nonwhite poor are trapped in the decaying slums of the inner city. The middle class, including blue-collar workers, have moved to the all-white suburbs, purchasing homes with the assistance of the Federal Housing Administration. Without the FHA mortgage and down payments of as little as $500, most of these families could never have left the cities. The "slurbs"—suburban slums—the blighting of the landscape by housing developments, and the wasteful use of land for single-family dwellings are the unintended results of an economic policy that encouraged the middle-class mass exodus to the suburbs. Economic policy favored the building of either slum-clearance housing or extremely expensive housing in the cities, unsuitable for the average middle-class family with children and economically beyond its reach. Within a generation these economic policies have created a white noose around the cities. They have compelled the middle-class workingman—and workingwoman—to spend as much as two to three hours a day commuting. They have created an artificial suburban life of segregated women and children. Courts faced with a city public school population often more than two-thirds nonwhite have vainly devised legal schemes to meet Constitutional mandates. But the courts cannot overcome economic reality through the power of law, even when backed by military force.

I do not suggest that white racism was not a motivating factor in the minds of many who moved from the cities to the suburbs. White rioters who vandalized the home which a black family had bought in Levittown, Pennsylvania, and engaged in a concerted campaign of harassment to drive out all blacks, stated their feelings explicitly. The Commonwealth of Pennsylvania sued the rioters and obtained a court order enjoining their actions of destruction and harassment. At the court hearing, many of these white residents testified. Most of them were young couples with several children. There are few older people, childless couples or single people in the white suburban ghettos. Most of them had made only a nominal down payment on their homes. They were financially strapped, unable to keep up the mortgage payments, or pay for the second car, which was a necessity, or keep their children occupied in an area without boys' clubs, libraries, recreation centers and the services and amenities of the city to which they were accustomed. Many of these families could not afford to belong to the swimming pools which were a part of the Levittown development. "We were told," they testified, "that this would be an all-white neighborhood." Many of the homes were barely furnished. The children and wives were bored. The husbands exhausted. All felt cheated and were hostile. The lawsuit designed to enforce the rights of all persons, regardless of race, color or creed, to live wherever they wish and to purchase housing freely on the open market was a nominal success. The overt acts of violence by the white residents were halted by order of the court enforced by platoons of state troopers. The power of law could not prevail over the facts, however. Inevitably, the black family gave up the struggle. This scenario of legal rights enforced by law being eroded by economic and social realities has been replayed again and again.

The solutions to the national problem of the predominantly nonwhite low-achieving inner-city schools and the white suburban schools are not legal orders but economic policies designed to foster communities containing a healthy mix of people of all races, all economic levels and all age groups. Educational policies and programs must be devised by educators, not courts, to close the widening chasm of academic achievement between slum children and suburban children. Again these are not problems susceptible to solution by the fiat of law. We cannot outlaw the problem. We must find the solution by changing the social and economic conditions of life.

Labor disputes furnish another trenchant example of the futility of outlawing the problem and ignoring the solution. For many years the struggle to unionize was the cutting edge of hostility between the rich and the working poor. In countless lawsuits, judges have ruled upon the right to strike, regulated the number of pickets, the conduct of elections and all the elaborate machinery established by legislation to attempt to equalize the bargaining power of the workingman and the owners or managers of industry. When strikes by public employees became a threat to social stability, the answer again was to outlaw the problem. The Taylor law forbidding strikes by public employees was enacted in many states. The strikes continued nonetheless. Union leaders of public employees such as school teachers and sanitation workers have been jailed for actions protected by the courts when engaged in by auto workers and construction workers. Equal treatment under law has yielded to economic reality.

The problems between employees and management are essentially economic. Some employees and unions, recognizing this obvious fact, had loaned money to employers to keep the businesses operating. In other situations, there have been bloody battles in the street over the hiring of nonunion labor. The usefulness of the law and the legal system in resolving these differences is questionable. Laws prohibiting strikes are violated. Court orders compelling good-faith bargaining cannot compel either good faith or good results. Legal recognition of the right to strike was, of course, a milestone in according the economically oppressed a voice in their own destiny. But once principles are established in the law and accepted by the public, the necessary adjustment of differences involving essentially economic problems are better resolved in a more knowledgable forum without the threat of legal sanctions. The widespread use of voluntary arbitration procedures has been notably more successful in producing equitable results accepted by all the parties than court orders enforced by armed power or imprisonment. Some labor leaders have recently urged the abandonment of the strike as a tactic or weapon of organized labor. Legislators, lawyers and judges have not yet acknowledged the futility of legal sanctions to solve economic problems.

Certainly the operations of railroads, manufacturing companies, school systems and police departments, hospitals and prisons should not become the province of the courts. The problems of these institutions are not legal; the machinery of the law may prohibit certain conduct and exact penalties, but it will not provide solutions.

The long series of trials dating from the era of Senator Joseph McCarthy and continuing to the present time have essentially involved governmental invocation of the legal system for political purposes. Whether the accused defendants were convicted or acquitted provides neither a justification nor a defense of this practice. Lawyers who recognized that the prosecutions were political rather than legal and, therefore, conducted the defense of their clients as a political campaign rather than a lawsuit have been criticized and censured. The misuse of the law for political ends by both prosecution and defense has unfortunately contributed to scofflawism and public contempt for law and the legal process. These trials revealed clearly that the purpose of the prosecution was not to ascertain facts and to compel enforcement of recognized principles of law but to punish political dissidents and to enhance the political power of the officeholders. The electoral process, with all its flaws and corruptions, not the courts, is the appropriate forum for the public airing of such public issues.

These are but a few of the many problems which Americans attempt to outlaw. The overuse of law and legal methods has failed to solve the problems. Instead it has resulted in an endemic contempt for all law. Our urgent need today is to find new and appropriate means of solving our critical economic and social ills. But fear and hatred of new ideas prevents a rational consideration of other approaches and disciplines. We cling with devout fanaticism to "the law" as the only means of resolving problems and conflicts.

In other nations and societies law has never been the sole or principal agency of social control enabling people to live together with a modicum of physical safety and emotional security. Tradition, caste, economics, religion and military force have been far stronger in binding peoples together than the threat and execution of legal process. Until World War II, despite the frontier tradition of violence, racial enmities and brutal economic practices, the American people were subject to the pressures of family, community, religion, economic exigency and shared aspirations of upward mobility. These factors held in precarious balance the diverse and often hostile segments of the American people. Today these ties and restraints have been so weakened by changing conditions, values and geographic mobility as to exercise only minimal controls. The only identifiable power remaining in the community with authority to compel obedience to a code or standard is the law. *Law alone is insufficient to replace all of the other institutions and shared beliefs upon which society has relied for stability.*

Family, church, class, education and the national goal of upward mobility are obsolete. Nonetheless, there is among many Americans a yearning for a sense of community, a fear of loneliness and anomie. The faddist search for cults, for faith rather than reason, and for new life-styles indicates an awareness of the need for new substitutes for the old social controls. In this time of flux and scofflawism, the legal profession must recognize the limitations of the law. Instead of urging the public to seek simplistic answers from the legislature and the courts,° lawyers and judges should instead call upon the other disciplines to find meaningful and workable

---

° Note the appeal by Whitney North Seymour, Jr., to the public in *Why Justice Fails* (William Morrow & Co., New York, 1973) to improve the administration of justice by being "concerned." These difficult problems will not be resolved merely by good will and concern. Intelligence, research, technical skills and a willingness to recognize the present crisis and to make far-reaching changes are required.

solutions to economic, racial, ecological, educational, family and emotional problems. The legal profession can save the law only by drastically reducing its claims, limiting its functions, and finding more effective substitutes to control undesirable individual, corporate and government conduct.

Equal justice under law is, I believe, a goal worth pursuing. It can be achieved only if the legal structure is simplified and made accessible to all people, if the courts are limited to the resolution of conflicts and disputes within their capacity to decide, and if the aim of justice to treat similarly situated individuals equally is adhered to. The law should abandon its efforts to restructure the economic and social order and modify behavior of individuals. The limited aim of securing equal justice is a difficult and taxing goal to attain. It is a task sufficient for any single institution of society, but the legal system is only one institution among many. Equal justice cannot be even dimly approximated if law is utilized in an effort to provide all or a major part of the correctives, changes and controls required by our complex and diverse society.

Literature is replete with jeremiad denunciations of human inequities and injustices. This book does not decry evil but blindness and stupidity in refusing to recognize obvious facts.

In the past, governments have risen and fallen, societies have grown and then vanished into the dust upon which later societies were built. Great civilizations flourished and died in the Andean highlands, the steamy islands of Indonesia, the deserts of Africa and Arabia and the more hospitable climates of Europe and Asia, each relatively independent of the rest of the world. The death of one culture did not imperil the future of humanity. Nor, with some notable exceptions, did these vanished kingdoms have an ideological base upon which the future of civilization depended. In each, there was a small, ruling priestly class and a large populace on whose labor and military strength the principality, kingdom or empire depended.

Today the world is totally different. The threat of global annihilation binds all nations in a tenuous and fragile web. While the vast majority of people still labor for a meager existence, unaware of ideological struggles, nuclear dangers and dreams of human fulfillment, those of us who know the dangers and visualize the terrifying curve of finite space must speak and act. The dream of human freedom still animates many people around the globe. They look to the United States as the exemplar of a society in which the individual is no longer shackled to the whims of capricious nature for daily food and the fiats of an all-powerful ruler to escape the dungeon and the forced labor gang.

This brief two-hundred-year American interlude in the human struggle is in a critical, if not terminal, state. We have apotheosized law as our national deity, we have relied on law as our problem-solving mechanism, we have built upon law as the philosophical and ideological basis of the structure of our individual lives and our government, we have invoked the concept of law to control the furies of individuals and the cataclysmic powers of nations. But in the day-to-day conduct of life and government we have permitted the misuse of the law and the death of the law by attrition, erosion and the growing disparity between law and justice. Several million Americans devote their lives to the pursuit and enforcement of law as police officers, jailers, legislators, lawyers, judges, students and professors. More people are involved in the legal system in the United States than in any other country. But we have lost our central faith in the law as we are enmeshed in a bureaucracy of growing complexity that wreaks injustice rather than justice upon more and more individuals. The consequences to Americans and to all people of the death of the law in the United States require immediate awareness of the facts and intelligent, concerted action if liberty and order are to be saved.

Notes

INTRODUCTION

1. Romain Gary, *White Dog* (New York, World Pub. Co., 1970).
2. M.B.E. Smith, "Is There a Prima Facie Obligation to Obey the Law?" 82 Yale L. J. 950 (1973).
3. Botein and Garden, *The Trial of the Future* (New York, Simon & Schuster, 1963).
4. *New York Times*, 10/8/72 E, p. 8.
5. Charles A. Reich, *The Greening of America* (New York, Random House, 1970).
6. Joseph S. Clark, *Congress: The Sapless Branch* (New York, Harper & Row, 1964).
7. Fred P. Graham, *The Self-Inflicted Wound* (New York, Macmillan, 1970).
8. Eugene Victor Rostow, *Is Law Dead?* (New York, Simon & Schuster, 1971).
9. William James, *The Varieties of Religious Experience* (New York, Random House, 1902).

CHAPTER 1: THE BANALITY OF LAWLESSNESS

1. David Halberstam, *The Best and the Brightest* (New York, Random House, 1969).
2. Recent studies bear out this unwelcome conclusion. Participants in an experiment were told to press a button which would activate increasingly longer and more dangerous electric current to shock other participants in the experiment when they gave incorrect answers to questions. No one refused to press the button, although several persons expressed concern that they might be hurting, injuring or even killing the other party. Another study of role playing had to be discontinued when the college students who were acting as jailers behaved with excessive brutality toward their classmates who were acting as prisoners.
3. Clive Staples Lewis, *God in the Dock, The Theory of Humanitarian Punishment*, (Erdman's Pub. Co., 1970).
4. The same thought is expressed in the popular song "We Can All Be Together" by Jefferson Airplane.

We are all outlaws in the eyes of America
In order to survive we steal, cheat, lie
    forge—and deal
We are obscene, lawless, hideous, dangerous,
All your private property is
Target for your enemy
And your enemy is
We-e-e.

Words and music by Paul Kantner, © *1969 by Icebag Corp. All rights reserved.*

Chapter 2: The Unredeemed Promise

1. *Harper v. Virginia State Bd. of Elections*, 383 U. S. 663 (1966).
2. Letter to the author.

Chapter 3: The System

1. *Philadelphia Magazine*, May 1974, p. 44.
2. Schuck and Wellford, *Democracy and The Good Life in a Company Town*, Harper, Vol. 244, p. 56 (May 1972).
3. Calabresi and Melamed, *Liability Rules and Inalienability: One View of the Cathedral*, 85 Harv. L. Rev. 1089 (1972).
4. See *Two Guys from Harrison–Allentown, Inc. v. McGinley*, 366 U. S. 582 (1961) and *Gallagher v. Crown Kosher Super Market of Mass., Inc.*, 366 U. S. 617 (1961).

Chapter 5: The Manufacture of Criminals

1. Stephen, *History of the Criminal Law of England* (London, Macmillan, 1883), p. 144.
2. Address before the National Conference of Christians and Jews, Philadelphia, Pa., November 16, 1972.
3. At this writing the death penalty is in abeyance. But the move to restore it steadily gains momentum despite irrefutable evidence that it has never constituted an effective deterrent to crime.
4. 372 U.S. 335 (1963).
5. See Menninger, *The Crime of Punishment* (New York, Viking Press, 1968).
6. See, *e.g.*, Goldfarb and Singer, *After Conviction* (New York, Simon & Schuster, 1973).
7. See Richie Thompson, *The Ultimate Tragedy Between One Decent Man and the Son He Loved* (New York, Saturday Review Press, 1973).

Chapter 6: The Nature of Litigational Process

1. See, *e.g.*, the classic statement by Mr. Justice Cordozo, *The Nature of the Judicial Process* (New Haven, Yale University Press, 1921).

2. Prentice-Hall, New York, 1965.
3. Joseph C. Goulden, *The Superlawyers* (New York, Weybright and Talley, 1972).
4. *Brady v. Maryland*, 373 U. S. 83, 91 (1963).
5. *U. S. v. Kras*, 409 U. S. 434 (1973).
6. *Legal Services and Landlord-Tenant Litigation: A Critical Analysis*, 82 Yale L. J. 1495 (1973).

CHAPTER 7: ULTIMATE ERROR

1. Compare *Danner Estate*, 439 Pa. 82 (1944) involving a dispute over the will of a testator who had died twenty-seven years before the court rendered its decision. Countless hearings and appeals had occupied the time of lawyers and judges during these years.
2. 704 U. S. 514 (1972).
3. *Turner v. Pa.*, 338 U. S. 621 (1949).
4. At this writing, the United States Supreme Court has limited the scope of the Miranda rules in *Michigan v. Tucker*, 42 U.S.L.W. 4857 (U.S. June 10, 1974).
5. *McPhee v. Reichel*, 461 F.2d 947 (3rd Cir. 1972).
6. *Malinsky v. New York*, 324 U. S. 401, 414 (1945).
7. 359 U. S. 693 (1958); 388 U.S. 426 (1967). Compare *Wyoming v. Colorado*, 310 U. S. 656 (1940) in which suit was instituted in 1917 and final decision rendered in 1940.
8. 401 F. 2d 833 (2d Cir. 1968), cert. den. 404 U. S. 1005 (1971).
9. On the fourth trial, "The Harlem Four" who had been arrested in 1964 and held in custody were finally acquitted in 1971. *New York Times*, 11/30/71, p. 50.
10. *Liberty Mutual Insurance Co. v. S.G.S. Co., et al.*, Pa. Superior Court, 3/27/73.
11. *Fuentes v. Shevin*, 407 U. S. 67 (1972).
12. See dissenting opinion in *Martin v. Creasy*, 360 U. S. 219, 228 (1959).
13. 447 Pa. 389 (1972).
14. 451 Pa. 241 (1973).
15. As early as 1955, Judge Simon Sobeloff urged appellate review of sentencing in order to permit correction of outrageous sentences imposed by a trial judge without requiring a finding of error in the trial and remanding the case for a new trial. See 41 A.B.A.J. 13. This sensible proposal has not been adopted and the complaints about unequal sentences continue to multiply.
16. *Burstyn v. Wilson*, 343 U. S. 495 (1951).
17. See, *e.g.*, *Sierra Club v. Morton*, 405 U. S. 727 (1972) holding that the plaintiffs had no standing to sue to protect the environment, and *DeFunis v. Odegaard*, 42 U.S.L.W. 4578 (U.S. April 23, 1974) in which the Supreme Court refused to decided whether affirmative action giving preferential treatment in admission to law schools to blacks violates the equal protection clause of the Constitution.

CHAPTER 8: COPS AND COURTS

1. Working Papers, p. 119.
2. *McAuliffe v. Mayor and Board of Aldermen of New Bedford*, 155 Mass. 216, 220 (1892).
3. The Nixon Court has already retreated from the decisions in this area rendered by the Warren Court. See, *e.g.*, *Michigan v. Tucker*, decided 6/10/74 limiting the scope of the Miranda decision.
4. All statistics are taken from FBI reports.
5. Soule, *Police Power and Individual Freedom* (Aldine Publishing Company, 1962), p. 25.
6. *New York Times*, 8/1/73, p. 33.
7. *New York Times*, 11/11/73, p. 1.
8. Report of Pennsylvania Attorney General issued 8/18/72.
9. *Miller v. Pate*, 386 U.S.1 (1967).
10. See *Com. v. Burgess*, 446 Pa. 383 (1972) referring to a police crime laboratory technician who lied about her qualifications. On the basis of her testimony scores of people had been convicted.

CHAPTER 9: THE HATED HESSIANS

1. *Philadelphia Magazine*, August 1973, p. 1.
2. This figure is an estimate. There are no adequate statistics on the income of lawyers engaged in the practice of law.
3. 120 U. of P. L. Rev., 851, 869 (1972).
4. Becker, "The Decline of Private Practice," *The Legal Intelligencer*, 7/25/72, p. 1.
5. 36 U. of Chicago Law Review, 455, 599 (1969).
6. See *New York Times*, 2/21/71, p. 27.
7. A writ which permits a person, usually an alleged parole violator, to be confined not more than 24 hours without a court hearing to determine the validity of the charge. Unless a hearing is held, the individual must be released at the expiration of 24 hours.
8. Packer and Ehrlich, *New Directions in Legal Education* (New York, McGraw-Hill, 1972). Sponsored by the Carnegie Commission on Higher Education.
9. 56 Harvard L. Rec. 245 (1942).
10. Harvard L. Rec., 1/26/73, p. 1.
11. Letter to the author.
12. Arnold, *Fair Fights and Foul* (New York, Harcourt, Brace & Jovanovich, 1965). p. 263.
13. *New York Times*, 7/29/71, p. 33.

CHAPTER 10: THE DYING PRIESTHOOD

1. *Marbury v. Madison*, 1 Cranch 138, 5 L. Ed. 137 (1803).
2. The decision of the United States Supreme Court in *Furman v. Georgia*, 408 U. S. 238 (1972), has not completely abolished the death penalty. The

clamor for its return is loud and persistent. The power of death may again be placed in the hands of judges.

3. The Supreme Court has ruled that no one may be compelled to salute the flag. Nonetheless, local school districts and other agencies of government attempt to compel flag salute and prosecute those who do not comply with such unconstitutional orders. Similarly, the Supreme Court has ruled that prayers may not be required in public schools but innumerable school districts persist in compelling public prayers in the public schools.

4. Justices of the United States Supreme Court have three law clerks and the Chief Justice has four.

5. *New York Sunday News*, 3/25/73, p. 38.

6. Note that some judges who have been convicted of crimes remain on the bench.

7. *Pollack v. The Farmers' Loan and Trust Co.*, 157 U. S. 429; reh. 158 U. S. 601. Graduated income tax held unconstitutional (1895).

8. U. S. Constitutional Amendment XVI permitting tax.

9. *Kelley v. Kalodner*, 320 Pa. 180 (1935). See also *Saulsbury v. Bethlehem Steel Co.*, 413 Pa. 316 (1964); *Amidon v. Kane*, 444 Pa. 38 (1971).

10. *Scott v. Sanford*, 19 How. 393 (1857).

11. *West Coast Hotel v. Parrish*, 300 U. S. 379 (1937).

12. *Lindsey v. Normet*, 405 U. S. 56, 31 L. Ed. 2d 36, 92 S. Ct. 862 (1972) at 74.

13. Center Magazine V, No. 3, May/June 1972, p. 59.

14. *New York Times*, 8/26/73, p. 1.

15. Smithsonian Magazine, Nov. 1972, p. 6.

CHAPTER 11: WE DO NOT CONSENT

1. Hannah Arendt, *Crisis of the Republic* (New York, Harcourt, Brace & Jovanovich, 1972).

2. *Minersville School District v. Gobitis*, 310 U. S. 586 (1940).

3. *West Virginia State Board of Education v. Barnette*, 319 U. S. 624 (1943).

4. *Welsh v. U. S.*, 398 U. S. 333 (1970). See also *U.S. v. Sisson*, 399 U.S. 267 (1970).

5. Nonetheless, the United States is suing Rev. David Gracie, an Episcopalian minister, for the telephone tax which he refused to pay because tax revenues were used to support the war in Vietnam which he considered both immoral and illegal.

6. Address to the American Historical Society at Philadelphia, Pa., 12/25/72.

7. The uprising at Attica, N. Y., is only one of many prison revolts in which the inmates, many of whom had not yet been tried, were unwilling to endure the brutal conditions of an imprisonment which they considered illegal and immoral.

8. Signet Press, N. Y. (1968), p. 32.

9. The Hollywood Ten, screenwriters and actors who refused to inform on their friends in hearings before the House Un-American Activities Committee, tested their position in court. They were held in contempt of Congress and went to jail. Probably all of them could easily have left the

country or gone underground and avoided imprisonment. None of them chose this course of action.

10. Thoreau, *Walden* (New York, Holt, Rinehart & Winston, 1948), p. 143.
11. Gaylin, *In the Service of Their Country* (New York, Viking, 1970), pp. 314, 77.
12. Plato, *The Crito.*
13. Rawls, *A Theory of Justice* (Cambridge, Harvard University Press, 1972).
14. *Griswold v. Connecticut*, 381 U. S. 479 (1965).
15. Patterson, *The Forgotten Ninth Amendment* (Indianapolis, Bobbs-Merrill, 1955).
16. A common criminal complaint of resisting arrest arises out of the refusal of black slum dwellers to move when ordered to do so by the police. The arrestee believes that as an American he has a right to stand on the corner, to congregate on the streets, to lounge on the steps of bars and taprooms. He will not move on even when ordered to do so by a fully armed policeman who is attempting to disperse a crowd which he fears may erupt into disorder. The citizen refuses to accept the lawfulness of an order of a properly authorized law-enforcement officer when he feels that such an order infringes upon his rights.
17. Herman Kahn and A. J. Wiener (New York, Macmillan, 1967).

Chapter 12: Law as Justice

1. J. Oliver Wendell Holmes, *The Common Law* (ed. Mark D. Howe) (Boston, Little Brown & Co., 1881).
2. Cox, *The Secular City* (New York, Macmillan, 1966).
3. *Buck v. Bell*, 274 U.S. 200 (1927).
4. *Skinner v. Oklahoma*, 316 U.S. 535 (1942).
5. *Roth v. United States*, 354 U.S. 476 (1957).
6. *Brown v. Board of Education*, 347 U. S. 483 (1954).
7. *U. S. v. Wade*, 388 U. S. 218 (1967).
8. *Stovall v. Denno*, 388 U. S. 293, 301 (1967).
9. *Korematsu v. United States*, 323 U. S. 214 (1944).
10. In re: Yamashita, 327 U. S. 1 (1946).
11. *New York Times*, 1/11/73 E, p. 39. Compare views of Leonard E. Boudin, Esq., 84 Harvard L. Rev. 1940 (1971).
12. At this writing the United States Supreme Court has avoided ruling upon this issue of affirmative action and preferential treatment, although it affects admissions to almost all institutions of learning, faculty employment, public employment and private employment on public contracts. It is an issue which festers and exacerbates tensions and hostilities. See *DeFunis v. Odegaard*, 42 U. S. L. W. 4578 (U. S. April 23, 1974).

Chapter 13: The Limits of Law

1. Sierra Club Bulletin, Oct/Nov. 1971, p. 9.

Index

About the Author

LOIS G. FORER has served as a Judge of the Court of Common Pleas in Philadelphia since 1970; in 1973 she was elected to a ten-year term. (The Court of Common Pleas is a trial court which hears all types of criminal cases, including murder, and all civil suits involving more than ten thousand dollars.)

Before going on the bench Judge Forer practiced law for thirty-two years. She has practiced before the United States Supreme Court and all levels of federal and state courts. For more than eight years she was Deputy Attorney General for Pennsylvania, and represented the state in many landmark cases, including the opening of the Barnes Art Foundation to the public, desegregating Girard College and integrating Levittown, Pennsylvania, as well as prosecuting many other criminal and civil cases. As an attorney in private practice she has had extensive experience in both criminal and civil litigation.

In 1966 she established, under the federal anti-poverty program, the only law office for juveniles in the United States. From this experience she wrote her first book, *No One Will Lissen: How Our Legal System Brutalizes the Youthful Poor*, which is now used as a textbook in many law schools and universities.

Judge Forer has served on the Lawyers Committee for Civil Rights at the request of President Kennedy; she has acted as a consultant to the United States Commission on Civil Disorders and to the 1970 White House Conference on Children and Youth; and she is a member of the Regional Counsel of the Law Enforcement Assistance Administration.